MW01250990

Shy Love Smiles and Acid Drops

Born in 1954, Jane Sinclair grew up surrounded by art and artists. Her parents, Jean Langley and John Sinclair, were part of the early modern art scene in Melbourne and were particularly close to John and Sunday Reed.

Jane was a painter for many years before starting to write and discovering that writing was her new obsession. This is her first book but another is already well on its way.

Shy Love Smiles AND Acid Drops

Letters from a difficult marriage

JANE SINCLAIR

HYBRID
PUBLISHERS

Published by Hybrid Publishers

Melbourne Victoria Australia

© Jane Sinclair 2021

This publication is copyright. Apart from any use
as permitted under the Copyright Act 1968, no part may be reproduced
by any process without prior written permission from the publisher.
Requests and inquiries concerning reproduction should be addressed to
the Publisher, Hybrid Publishers,
PO Box 52, Ormond, Victoria, Australia 3204.

www.hybridpublishers.com.au

First published 2021

 A catalogue record for this
book is available from the
National Library of Australia

ISBN: 9781925736588 (p)
9781925736595 (e)

Cover design: Gittus Graphics
Typeset in Minion Pro
Printed in Australia by McPherson's Printing Group

Front cover: detail from an oil painting by Jane Sinclair.
All photos come from the family collection.

"Few of us can live with the whole truth, but it seems to me
to be the only way. It is just easier for me."
– Jean Langley, author's mother

"Our children and their children are all we are leaving behind. How
well will they know us? Does it matter? Perhaps not, but let us not
pretend we were saints. Let them know we had heat in our blood
and made fools of ourselves sometimes."
– Jean Langley

Contents

Introduction

After our mother's death in 2017, my sister and I spent many months sorting through her possessions. As it turned out, she'd left quite a lot behind. She kept everything, every scrap of paper on which she'd scribbled some momentary thought, every newspaper clipping she thought was of interest, and much besides. So it's not surprising that she kept all of her correspondence.

My father had died more than twenty-five years before my mother and it was only after his death we discovered that he had kept most of her letters as well. It makes me a little sad now to contemplate why he did so. Maybe it was because his sense of connection to her never really waned, or maybe it was in the hope that one day my sister and I might read them and soften the image we had of him as the lying, cheating husband who made our mother's life hell. Possibly it was a little of both. My mother gave me all these letters several years before she died. She thought I'd be interested, and she was right.

Her journals and her correspondence with Sunday Reed were already housed in the State Library of Victoria.

For most of my adult life my parents lived apart. In my early teenage years my parents fought with each other a lot and I, in turn, fought with them. That changed after I left home at the age of seventeen. Living apart from them, and them living apart from each other, helped me get on reasonably well with both. I had an open and honest relationship with my mother, which made reading these letters while she was still alive quite difficult for me. At the same time that old age and a touch of dementia was causing her to become more defensive, bitter and unreasonable, I was starting to seriously question the version of herself as the aggrieved, wronged wife that she had cultivated, and genuinely believed to be true. I also felt a mix of guilt, regret and sorrow for my own part in never allowing my father to tell his side of the story. If he ever tried to explain something regarding a fight with my mother, I would forcefully tell him I'd had enough involvement in childhood and didn't want to hear any more. I clearly remember one such time, and the look of weary resignation that crossed his face as he gently told me that he understood. It haunts me a little.

Originally my intention was to not edit these letters at all but, as both parents wrote very long and often repetitive letters, I realised I couldn't expect everyone to be as interested as I was in reading every word. Sometimes quite large sections of letters have been removed but I was always aware of the need to be sure nothing was cut that altered the intended meaning. Some spelling mistakes have been corrected and occasionally punctuation was added for the sake of clarity.

Chapter 1

In the Beginning ...

My parents had a lot in common. They shared a passion for classical music, had similar taste in art and furniture and both lacked the will or ability to end their volatile and destructive relationship. For eight years I was the only child caught up in this tumultuous marriage. The source of conflict wasn't differing opinions on politics, philosophy or child rearing – it was always deeply personal. My parents were pacifists who encouraged imagination and creativity in their child and believed that heavy-handed discipline was detrimental to psychological wellbeing. Smacking a child was frowned upon but when their own bitterness and disappointment escalated to fury, they hit each other. They both loved me but forgot me too easily when the arguments started.

I was a nervous child who believed in ghosts and fairies. I believed in fairies because I wanted to, and ghosts because the darkness of night allows only the imagination to see. I didn't believe in Santa Claus or God, as my parents thought it unnecessary to fill a child's head with nonsense created by adults. Yet my mother knew how to create magic. On Christmas Eve she didn't need a belief in baby Jesus to transform half the living room overnight into a wonderland for me to wake to on Christmas morning. The tree was usually a branch cut from a big she-oak in our garden. Entwined in its delicate olive-grey foliage would be glittering Christmas decorations and many strands of silver tinsel. Long strings of colourful Chinese paper lanterns were hung from wall to wall across corners of the room. And underneath the drooping fronds of this unusual Christmas tree would be enticing presents wrapped in pastel-coloured tissue paper tied with fine silver thread.

My mother could create sparkle and shine in the very best of taste; she understood a little girl's dreams of fairyland and gossamer wings, beautiful princesses and handsome princes. She understood, because she also wanted the world to be a beautiful place of happy endings and in her mind she tried to make it so. But reality is hard to avoid. Sometimes it creeps in like a clever thief, other times it crashes through dreams like an out-of-control truck. Either way, whenever harsh and unpleasant reality invaded my mother's romantic world, it made her angry, very angry.

⸙

Not long before the start of the Second World War when my mother, Jean Langley, was still a teenager, my father, John Sinclair, was a promising young art student at the Gallery School in Melbourne. It was there he met Australian artist Sidney Nolan. The friendship that developed turned his view of painting upside down and changed his life. He and Nolan were sharing a dingy flat in the city when my father became seriously ill with bronchitis. As his condition deteriorated, Nolan asked his friends John and Sunday Reed for help. Nolan and Sunday were romantically involved, a situation accepted with grace and civility by John Reed, and the three of them spent a lot of time together at Heide, a large rural property owned by the Reeds on the outskirts of Heidelberg. Upon hearing of my father's plight, Sunday and John immediately drove to the city to pick him up. He was brought back to Heide where Sunday nursed him back to health.

So began a lifelong friendship between my father and the Reeds. But his friendship with Nolan ended badly when Sid broke Sunday's heart by leaving Heide to marry John Reed's sister, Cynthia. Despite the hurt caused by his abrupt departure, neither the Reeds nor my father doubted the importance of Nolan's work to the future direction of Australian art. As a consequence, my father rejected his

Gallery School training in favour of attempting to paint in the free, expressionistic style of Nolan.

Unhappy with the results, he gave up painting altogether and, in need of a new direction, approached Keith Murdoch for a job at *The Herald*. Despite his lack of qualifications, he was given a job as *The Herald*'s music critic. It was through this job he met Dorian Le Gallienne, a fellow music critic and composer. This was another important friendship for my father, which lasted until Dorian's death in 1963.

By the time he met my mother in 1947, who was eleven years younger, my father was well established in his career. Jean had also attended the Gallery School and was working as a window dresser for Georges department store in Collins Street when they were introduced by a mutual friend in 1947.

Their relationship was intense and difficult from the start. Towards the end of 1949 my mother had a brief but passionate affair with the artist Clifton Pugh. It seems my father took this relatively well. In a letter to my mother, Cliff described my father's initial reaction:

> Not slinging mud at John but he said what so called
> intellectuals would say   you behaved like a couple of animals
> – all right we did, we behaved as is natural, as is meant.

In the same letter Cliff offered my mother his undying love and friendship, absolute freedom to be herself, and a home of her own if she so wished, but he begs her to be courageous, to face up to the situation and choose between himself and my father. He also told her he wanted to be the father of her children – a commitment my father was so far reluctant to make. Cliff ends his letter with:

> You must decide darling, it can't go on with this uncertainty.
> I can't take it anyway. I'm sure John can't either. In fact I don't
> think you can either if you are really serious with yourself –
> be natural, be simple, be just you, and decide. Love is the
> strongest emotion in the world, the most beautiful and
> sincere. I love you.

According to my mother, she decided when she caught Cliff in bed with another woman.

Later she worked for the Boyd family at their Murrumbeena pottery. Nearby was the sprawling, busy home of Merric and Doris Boyd as well as several of their adult children with their spouses and babies. My mother quickly became one of the gang, enjoying their company at pubs and parties as well as at work. She adored Doris, the gentle matriarch, and Mary Boyd was to become one of her closest friends. She developed a lifelong affection for John Perceval, who was married to Mary at the time, and she was very fond of Arthur Boyd. She thought him gentle and sweet but had no idea then that she would fall passionately in love with him several years later.

Another important life-long relationship for my mother started when my father introduced her to the Reeds, and a special bond developed with Sunday in particular. Despite a twenty-year age gap, both women recognised in the other an intensity of emotion that was to be the bedrock of their friendship. Sunday's whole being was still reeling from the shock of Nolan's departure; she was in need of both a confidant and the distraction of listening to the troubles of her new young friend. My mother also shared with Sun her hopes and dreams. One of those dreams was to become a bride, and in 1952 that dream came true.

The Reeds, my maternal grandmother, and a couple of friends were the only guests at the registry office wedding, with a young, cherubic Sweeney Reed as flower child.* My parents spent the first couple of days of their honeymoon staying with Kate and Gordon Thompson. Gordon was a close friend of my father's, while Kate had been my father's girlfriend until she rejected him to marry Gordon. The Thompsons were a cultured, sophisticated couple about ten years older than my mother who was shy, insecure and easily intimidated.

It was not a good start to the marriage. In bed for the first time as

---

* Sweeney was the child of Joy Hester and Bert Tucker. At the age of five he was legally adopted by the Reeds. He had been under their care since 1947 when Joy was diagnosed with Hodgkin's disease.

husband and wife, my father turned his back on his new bride and for the next eight nights ignored her confused tears and distress.

I was a young adult when my father told me of this deliberate act of emotional cruelty. He didn't give me an explanation and I didn't ask, but there may be a clue in a letter my mother wrote to Sun not long before the wedding: *I fear now that I shall be married only because I cried so much last week.*

My father had no such dreams of a legal commitment but he knew when he was beaten. Unlike many marriages of the time, it was far from the first time my parents had shared a bed. Before the wedding they had been living together in an old loft in Parkville.

After the wedding they moved into Rose Cottage, a dilapidated old house surrounded by trees on a very long block of land in the beachside suburb of Mentone. Among the neat, suburban properties of Venice Street, Rose Cottage stood out like a bush oasis for those who liked that sort of thing, or a hairy mole on a pretty face for those who didn't. My mother loved it passionately.

I was born on 5 October 1954.

The wedding of my parents Jean Langley and John Sinclair,
with Sweeney Reed as 'flower child'.

Jean and Jane in Rose Cottage garden, 1954.

Photo from an article about my father as a music critic,
from *People* magazine, 5 December 1951.

Chapter 2

Rose Cottage

Despite the quaint sweetness of the name, Rose Cottage was never going to be a peaceful home while my parents lived there. My birth only seemed to intensify the emotional turbulence, and over the next five years they separated many times. Yet there remained an irresistible attraction that kept them returning to each other.

A note from my father John Sinclair:

28 October 1957

There is no more to this letter. It is an embrace
- a deep one - but no more than that. Darling
Jeannie, as I am still possessed by the touch of
your hand and the feeling of your body as we stood
together last night in the darkness, I cannot but
write - to say not much beyond the fact that your
presence is so tangible that if I close my eyes,
you are with me. The tired, screwed-up man of
yesterday no longer exists. How much I wanted to
take you to the beach last night, to stroke your
forehead and to banish the past. OK, I know life
is complex - but not so complex that I do not know
what I need - and what inexpressible joy it was ...
I'm sorry, I write this in haste - but with love -
and with a humble feeling that I owe you more than
I can tell. All I want to do is send you a kiss so
gentle that it will not hurt, but heal.

XXX John

Through my childish eyes, Rose Cottage was both an untamed

fairyland and a haven for ghosts and witches, depending on when dark shadows fell or sunlight illuminated. From the street the main house was dark and mysterious with only the steeply angled, slate-tiled roof and two vine-covered chimney stacks visible above the wild tangle of tea-tree and eucalypts. The second, much smaller house on the property was made up of two old tramcars placed parallel to the back fence, with a room built between. On one side of this little house a long line of tram windows looked out to the back garden. The windows of the other tram looked out through fruit trees to the back of the main house. Between the fruit trees in this middle garden grew daisy bushes, poppies and wild herbs. Small paths fit for fairy folk meandered through, allowing me access to harvest a variety of fragrant leaves for magic potions.

There was also an old laundry house where my mother sometimes stood pulling steaming wet sheets through a slow, hand-turned wringer on the side of an ancient copper boiler. Attached to one side of the laundry was a disused cattery made of chicken wire. In front of the cattery grew a thick patch of nasturtiums where dewdrops became clear, silvery pearls that shivered like quick-silver with every vibration of the large peppery leaves. If I was very careful I could pluck a large, round leaf without dislodging the little ball of shining water and roll it around the leaf held gently in my cupped hands.

From the nasturtium patch a path curved around to the back of the tramcar house where a rickety wooden ladder led to a small door high up near the roof. This door opened inwards to a dusty secret place, empty but for an enormous black-speckled hollow egg, some carved wooden snakes and a woven grass dilly bag. I dared go there only when long shafts of late-afternoon sunlight reached into the corners where the sloping roofline left a space so small that even a leprechaun would need to crouch. It was a forgotten place – forgotten by all but me.

When spring came to Rose Cottage I would take my favourite invalid doll into the front garden to enjoy the warmth of the sun. She was made of a floral-patterned material stuffed with sawdust. Her face of moulded plastic had cracked and much of it had fallen off, exposing the floral cloth underneath. Only one plastic eye was left to see the beauty around us. After sitting her up in her little pusher I would walk her around the circular garden bed in the middle of the lawn. When we got to the corner where the large, spreading apple tree stood with its four solid trunks leaning outwards, we would stop and look up to admire its snow-white blossoms against the blue of the sky. This apple tree had a mysterious mound of stone at its core and by some magic produced four different types of apples. I was worried by the thought that the strange stone within may have been a gravestone, but it didn't stop me eating the delicious apple pies my father made from the fruit of the tree that grew around it.

Rose Cottage itself had nine rooms. At the front was a sleep-out, a closed-in veranda with panels of small wooden-framed windows on two sides of the rectangular room. A glass-panelled door to the front garden was almost hidden by a wild climbing rose that grew over an archway outside. This sleep-out contained my mother's single bed, a large desk and a chair. It was the only room in the house that allowed in enough daylight for my mother to paint the delicate wildflowers she collected on bush trips. The desk was filled with her watercolour paints, fine brushes and many clean milk bottles each containing a native orchid or sprig of a bush flower.

The other small room at the front of the house was almost filled by my father's single bed. Both of these small front rooms led into big living rooms. The Brown Room and my father's room were on the dark side of the house. Tall trees and a high, wooden fence outside the window of the Brown Room kept much daylight from entering. But it was a very large room and at night with a light on and a warm fire in the grate it was perfect for my mother's life-drawing sessions. The Yellow Room had no window and four doors. One door accessed the sleep-out, another led to the Brown Room, the third was one end of a short hallway and the fourth was originally the front door of the house. It had a large clear glass panel that let in the eastern light.

Only strangers came to this door that was halfway up the long, dirt driveway. Most visitors continued to the driveway's end, turned right and came through a rickety wooden structure to the back door. Above the mantelpiece in the Yellow Room hung Nolan's "Kiata", its desert landscape blending with the colour of the room.

I have two strong memories of this room. One is of my mother hugging me as we sat on the floor with our backs against the wall. She was sobbing and saying she was sorry, over and over. My beautiful Japanese parasol lay nearby with its broken wooden struts sticking chaotically through the ripped waxed paper. It was broken when she whacked my father with it. I wasn't upset about the parasol – I just remember feeling a sort of stunned confusion. I hardly recall the fight or the breaking of the parasol; it was the intensity of my mother's remorse that shocked me into numbness. The second memory is of a surprise birthday present. Led into the room by my mother, I found a new dress draped across a chair opposite the fireplace. I don't know how well I hid my disappointment, but at my mother's insistence I picked it up and found, to my delight, a beautiful new doll underneath.

Next to the Yellow Room and halfway up the dark hallway was my bedroom, which my mother had decorated with delicate rose-buds around the skirting boards. The walls were painted a soft pink. Opposite my room a boarded-up door spoke of mystery. I knew what was on the other side of this door but it did little to calm my fear. On the other side, on the dark side of the house, was a dust-filled, junk-filled room that was rarely ventured into. At night the house creaked and groaned with the stories of past residents long since buried, and often I lay rigid in my bed, scared that my rapid breathing and fast-beating heart would alert ghosts to my presence.

In reality, Rose Cottage was just a big, old house on a large parcel of land. And after it was sold the bulldozers came. All the rooms, the sleep-outs, the Yellow Room, the Brown Room and my pink bedroom were bulldozed into a big pile of broken glass, splintered wood, broken roof tiles and chimney stack bricks. And the tramcar house with its signs of "Hold on while rounding curves" and "Gentlemen please stand for ladies", was bulldozed to the ground. Bulldozers came for the garden as well. Trees that gave peaches, nectarines, apples, figs and lemons lay uprooted and smashed. Gumtrees, wattles and tea-trees all destroyed as the massive machines prepared the earth for the laying of foundations for the many units that were to be built there. Ghosts, goblins and fairies were gone in a billowing cloud of dust and there would be no sweet nectar the following spring for the birds, bees and butterflies. But this destruction of Rose Cottage would come much, much later.

Rose Cottage.

Another photo from article about my father from *People* magazine.

The 'Yellow Room' at Rose Cottage, with Sidney Nolan's painting 'Kiata' above the fireplace.

Uncle Robert (Bob) sculpting in the tram-car cottage.

Chapter 3

The Feeling of Fate

My mother's affair with Arthur Boyd started in 1958 with secret visits to Rose Cottage. His wife Yvonne was slowly recovering from a breakdown after the birth of their third child, and life at their house in Beaumaris was quite stressful. It was a short and easy drive along Beach Road for Arthur to find some relief in the arms of his lover. If my father's old Citroen wasn't in the driveway, he would wait in the darkened front garden for my mother to let him in through the glass-panelled door of her little sleep-out. These visits went on for many months, but things were about to change.

Melbourne in the 1950s seemed narrow and parochial to the small group of free-thinking modernist painters and actors who were my mother's friends, and most had plans to travel overseas as soon as they could raise the fare. Arthur Boyd was no exception. So in November 1959, Arthur, Yvonne and their three children boarded a ship bound for England. My mother planned to follow as soon she could.

A couple of months later, she was missing him dreadfully when David and Hermia Boyd invited her to a party. At the time she was keeping a journal. Although it was never intended that Arthur read it, she often addresses him directly. Her journal entry of 29 January 1960 tells of meeting Stuart King. She describes the party as being raucous. Simmering sexual jealousies surfaced with the heavy drinking and a couple of fights broke out. My mother was disgusted by the behaviour of her friends and writes that she felt very alone. She then wrote:

I was rescued by a beautiful handsome man whom I had met that night after knowing him at the Gallery ten years ago. He was a student there and I didn't even know his name. He had seen my unhappiness and like a gallant knight rescued me with sensitive gentle eyes. I spent the party with him from that moment and when I danced with him I found his body as beautiful as his face and I floated in his arms. T'was too much for my poor tired heart. We sat together in a little dark corner and he was kind and charming. T'was the first kiss I'd wanted to give since you left me.

Oh My Darling, I am so lonely and I was too depressed and the sweet comfort of beautiful strong, yet gentle, arms. He was too like you I became confused in my loneliness. He touched me like you do and had a soft quiet muttering tender voice. Darling, I wanted to love him more and more. I didn't, I got frightened. My conflict was too great and so I came away leaving him, feeling sorry yet glad. Too confused for love. Besides I love you too dearly, I couldn't wash away my memories.

I was upset by myself being tempted and on Tuesday, after much thinking, I raced in and bought one and a half tickets to London. The boat sails on the 14th April via the Panama to Southampton, and my Darling you. Oh God I was shocked into it all. I cannot pay the price as yet but my deposit is down and I shall have to find the extra. I have let my half of the house as from next Thursday. It is sad to think of strangers sleeping in our dear little heart sleepout of love and joy and treasures of bodies and roses and hearts. The best of you and I.

Oh My Darling, I must come to you but I am frightened. My husband is furious, raving mad at me. He didn't really think I would ever manage to go. I will be on that boat my Darling. That was how I felt on Wednesday, until my beautiful man turned up to pursue me. I was flattered indeed and realised he too, really felt something. I was determined to go to London and so I could see no

*point in mucking around with new relationships. But we went for
a swim, and as I had Jane, Lucinda and Cassie* with me it seemed
jolly enough. He was charming and gentle and I enjoyed being with
him. He is a most handsome man and I am indeed flattered.*

*Whilst we were happily swimming in the lovely clear sea he
suddenly took my hand with such sensitive, tender and strong
command in his eyes, I felt myself melting. I do not know what is
happening to me, I am so tired that I find it hard to resist his arms.
Darling, I could love this man with my whole female body and
heart, yet my intellect could never be at peace because although he
is an artist it might as well mean something else. The strange thing
is that this glorious brown eyed handsome strong man is already
so deeply attached to me that he is declaring most serious and
sensitive feelings. He wants me to go away with him and live as his
wife. It is strange I could almost do it.*

*I am so worried about you and me and my future of loneliness,
as I know you would never leave your wife and I shall end my days
on my own as I feel you will all outlive me as already I feel too
tired in my heart. This good man after two meetings wants me for
life. God, why am I so tired. I am not that beautiful that men go
mad, and I feel tenderly and passionately towards this comparative
stranger. I am in conflict. I have not given any sort of love but I fear
myself if I am pressed further. We shall see.*

*This does not mean any change in my feelings for you, my
natural master, you are the master of my soul as well as my body,
but I feel frail and fear London and I fear very much your mad
wife. I fear she will turn her madness on me and I have a violent
loathing of the insane as I fear such lack of control. I fear that we
shall find it hard to love in London as there will not be my little
garden to hide our hearts in. I fear that I will be left broken-hearted
because your duty is always first to your family. I wish you would
write to me. I wish I knew what to do. I wouldn't enjoy London*

---

* My mother was minding Lucinda and Cassie Boyd while David and Hermia
worked.

unless I could enjoy you too. My Dearest I love you with so much of myself that I want to run away. I hope you love me enough. I am coming to London but I fear so much. My Dear if only you were here. If only you could help me to feel secure. I feel so child-like and lost and so bitterly lonely. This man could so easily persuade me to run away from what seems too big for me. Yet I look twice at your painting "The Hunter" I know that only you will ever really own my heart, so it will hardly be fair to lend it out. Goodnight. I trust all will be well.

Stuart King visited Rose Cottage again and invited my mother to come on a bushwalking holiday with him. They spent six days together at Wilsons Promontory before Stuart had to return to his job in Papua New Guinea. By then he had seriously fallen for her and wanted us to join him there as his new little family. The only problem was he already had one. His wife and their three young children were waiting for him to come home. He intended to go back, end the marriage and then arrange for my mother and me to join him in Port Moresby.

❧

Entry from my mother's journal (excerpt):

Dear little book, Dear little book. Dear Sweet Person who, for so long was the complete master of my heart. I have a story to tell. Strangely a love story. I seem gifted in evoking love in people and it is a happy thing that now I am able to enjoy the whole idea of life as do some other lucky people. My story is strange and completely unexpected and had anybody told me this story and said it was about me I would not have believed a word of it possible. I met my handsome hero, as you know, at a party. The first half of the night I was so aggressive and bitter, tired and despairing that I never even looked at a soul. All the people seemed so ghastly and I was so cross as I had just discovered that my fare to London and my lover, cost too much money. I was furious with life. I could have easily left the world that night. I met Stuart King whom I knew vaguely years

Stuart King, 1960.

and years ago when I was at the Gallery. It seems, we find out later, that he had cast a vague eye on me in those days. After all, I was very pretty then and lots of people admired me …

The rest of the long entry is of a similar fairytale quality.

❧

Sunday, 6 March 1960

Tonight I am off to bed with a tremendous sense of excitement. My fate is to be decided for me as I expect a letter in the post in the morning which will tell me what to do. I know not really what I think should happen, nor do I find it easy to know what I really want to happen! It will be in the post. I will do whatever Stuart bids me. That is how I like life. Once I love a man I like to follow. He will tell me. I love the feeling of fate. Fate, his fate, my fate. We do not really know but it will all happen whatever our fate is to be. I will know tomorrow whether or not I shall go to Papua. I want to, yes I want to, but I do not really know what it is, what awaits me in Port Moresby. I do not really know. If I am to go I will know in the morning. The force of the happenings are enough for me. Tonight I have been making myself a glamourous nightgown dreaming as I go, of a honeymoon. A real one without sneaking and creeping.

⁓

Wednesday, 16 March

Time is passing quickly now. Life seems directed from above. No wonder people love to believe in God. Ha, not me but I see the point. I am well and happy. I am off to London. My letter from Papua was indeed a brush off. Not really, but there was not the same fire, the same love. There came conflict and guilt and fear. I thought it was a rare man to be brave as to start life afresh and cast off a wife like a shoe. It couldn't have worked and although I suffered from the effect of the last letter and felt for some days as if my heart was full of razor blades and my head full of acid drops. But a little time and realisation soon put me back on the London road.

Chapter 4

London Bound

In April 1960 my mother and I boarded a ship bound for Southampton. It was during one of my parent's frequent separations, so at the time my father was living alone in South Melbourne in a house that belonged to family friends, Anne and Douglas Cairns. My mother's brother, Robert (Bob) Langley was living in the tramcar house at Rose Cottage which my father refers to in his letters as "the cottage". The ship's departure was delayed by many days due to bad weather and the storms were still raging when the ship finally sailed from Port Melbourne on the evening of the 22nd. My mother didn't want my father to come to the ship but he did, which caused a huge argument in our cabin before the ship sailed.

Sunday Reed wrote to my mother describing how she, John and Simmer (my father's nickname – thanks to young Sweeney's inability to pronounce Sinclair) watched our ship depart.

> We went to the end of the wharf and watched you getting
> further and further away. Simmer was kneeling in all the
> tempest looking through his telescope. He said he could still
> see you in the stern. When he stood up, he suddenly tore off
> his overcoat and waved it frantically in the air.

⧆

A note from my father (no date):

Monday night.

Dear Jeannie, This is not at all the sort of letter

I intended to write. But just a few minutes ago,
I discovered to my horror that I only had until
10am tomorrow, to get to you in Auckland. So I
scribble this, and take it to the GPO at midnight
to be sure. Needless to say I watched you through
the telescope until the Castel Felice dissolved in
the mist and only the stern light was showing - and
on that pale image were my two loves. Since then
you have never left my thoughts, and that night I
was wholly in spirit in your cabin. But of course
I was worried, was it very rough, were you sick,
and was Janie frightened? But I hope you will write
from Auckland - and I will write, rather better to
Papeete.

XX John

An entry from my mother's journal:

April 1960

On the Castel Felice fourth night out on the Tasman Sea.

*So it is true I am heading for London. Only disaster can stop me
now. I do not know as yet what exactly I think of it all. There has
been so much to think of and so much to do. So troubled about
money and organisation was I for so long that I scarcely thought of
my feelings. Now it is so. It is completely so. I am going to London.
It is not yet time to feel real or excited as I am as yet trying to get
used to this confounded movement of the ship in this heavy sea.
So this is the Tasman Sea. It is throwing the ship up and down, up
and down and having paid the price for the cheapest cabin for eight
people in the bow of the ship low down, I now pay the price of being
poor as I do not find it much fun. I love being on deck but down
here is Hell and my soul is suffering. London seems a long way off
as yet. I am not sea-sick, cross my fingers, but I feel most miserable
of spirits. A depression of mind and body. My legs feel weak and
my body cold and shivery. I will be glad when the sea is calm once
more.*

Next week I trust we will see the sun as we head North East towards Tahiti. I do not know what I want in London. I do not feel glad as yet. I think sometimes of my true love, hoping he is my true love. I think of my friends and Stuart and my mad husband John. All these people I have left, perhaps for good, who knows. I think of Jane. Taking her away from the land of sunshine to a land of my choice. I thought much of Stuart when we passed around Wilsons Promontory so closely that one could almost touch it. I could see the waterfalls on the mountains as the sun shone onto them. I thought of Stuart and I standing hand in hand beside that very waterfall, in that very mountain, loving each other so well. So much in love, so young, so true, so soon to be parted most likely forever. You are a beautiful man, My Dear Stuart. You did love me better than anyone I think.

All these thoughts. I am going to London to where the love that will always be is, I hope, waiting for me. But who knows what to find. I do not know what you want, My Darling. Are you glad I am coming? Here I am crossing two of the greatest oceans to be near you. Will I find you still warm? Will I find you the same? Do you still love me or have you learned it is more peaceful without this illicit loving? Do you cry Barley? Who knows? I sit in this miserable cabin rocking like a mad thing. It is so rough and I am irritable with it. Will you be jealous when I tell you about my Stuart? Did you think I would come? You asked me to. Did you get a surprise when you read my letter? All these things I wonder as I toss and toss. I do not like this tossing. I hope it will be worth it.

Poor you, I think of you. You must have hated it all. I cannot imagine you with shipboard life. You were so miserable before you left. You were frightened of crossing the oceans. Now you are there. It is already six months since I have seen you. Six months since you loved me so beautifully and bade me farewell. It will be seven months before we arrive and then I wonder how I shall cope with meeting up with you again. So much has happened to me. I wonder what has happened to you. Sometimes I think you may meet me off the boat and then I think you wouldn't dare.

Who knows, I must go to sleep now. Sleep is the answer to rough seas. Goodnight My Darling in London, Goodnight my lost one in Papua. We are all so far apart but I am slowly getting nearer to London. Farewell Papua, I so nearly went to thee instead. What determines our fate? Common sense perhaps. I wonder what the future will bring for us all. We are all so lonely and so ill-suited to our mates. Me and my dear ones. I am free. When I get to London I hope I will not be too sad if things aren't easy for us. The sea gets rougher, now I must go to sleep. I am nearly falling asleep as I sit here. Goodnight, how I wish I was not by myself.

(The sunlit waterfalls mentioned in this entry must have been a figment of my mother's vivid imagination. Our ship left Port Melbourne in very bad weather as darkness fell. By first light the following day we would have been far from the sight of land.)

❧

Wednesday 4th May 1960

Sitting up in my bunk as the ship gets nearer and nearer to Tahiti. When we wake in the morning we will be there. It is a great thrill and I look forward to the day spent ashore. I take with me tomorrow my sketch books and pens and hope I shall feel relaxed enough to use them. The sun is getting hotter every day and at last I am beginning to enjoy myself. I swim in the pool and play mermaids. I adore it. I let the sun caress my body and my soul floats on the water. The sea is glorious now and the world looks as a dream. We are really in the big ocean.

I hate the social life on the ship. People are ordinary and stupid. The only two men who interest me on board are a trouble rather than a pleasure. One is married to a sweet girl who I like immensely. I am tired of married men as the problems are too numerous. He is a handsome soul and I feel most attracted to him. Life is always out of the frying pan into the fire. My other shipboard romance is unbelievable. A young, fair-haired Italian man with a loutish hairdo and tasteless clothes who sits at my table. When I

22

first saw him I thought him a tough, unattractive lout. Time has passed on and we are all good friends at the table. There are ten of us every meal and we are all jolly. Jokes are the point of contact between Australians, English and Italians. This young man, about my own age, appears ordinary in every sense except that he has a delicious, boyish, humorous, charming smile that screws his whole face into human merriment. I enjoy seeing him and we exchange giggles. At first I cannot believe my eyes when one day I see him look at me as if surprised in his own being. There was pure love in his eyes. I cannot understand. This strange, tough, Italian with smiling eyes suddenly looks at me as if I was an angel. Me, so severely dressed, so precious, so ladylike, so proper, my hair pulled back tight, dressed in such tasteful but sexless clothes. How could this young man who flirts with tarts, look at me like that?

The days pass, the look is repeated, shyly, purely, lovingly. I am intrigued. More meals pass and I find he peeps at me like a child. Waiting in some shy sort of terror. He looks so utterly confused and almost blushes like a girl. What lies behind these loving moments? What can he think, I am so out of his world and he out of mine. I am married with a child and he knows nothing of my life. Yet it continues. Now I find him peeping quickly at me around the deck. I spoke to him one day at the swimming pool and like a startled animal, as if he had seen a ghost, he flustered his answer and blushed. Then yesterday I looked straight at his glance to find the answers to my questions. His eyes lingered on my question and they seemed to become hazy and the love shone through the haze. They are such sweet, tender eyes to go with such a great tough fair Italian He-man. My heart was smitten by his feelings and I felt my whole body and soul fall into his eyes. 'Tis a strange world for two people so different in taste and interests. The lady and the peasant. Such a sweet peasant. He is now somewhat overcome and peeps at me all day with a serious and bewildered face.

I am moved by him. He is handsome of body and today at the swimming pool he caught my glance and held me spellbound with the most melting, loving look. Why does he love me?

Today I asked him a question about how to pronounce "Ravenna". His English is fair and he told me with his words and loved me with his eyes. He is greatly frightened I think. Why is it so? What will be the end to this little romance? How could I have anything to do with this person who wouldn't know Mozart from cheese? Who would never have heard of Holbein. Who would never have read anything but thrillers and who spends his life as a working Jack of all trades. He migrated to Australia and is going home to see the games in Rome. Yet somewhere in my tired 34-year-old face, that is no longer beautiful, this man sees an angel. Now the angel turns into a woman and the young man radiates more than pure love in his boyish eyes. He is shy but I feel so drawn to him. Is it my loneliness that makes me wish I could fall into his great strong arms, so smooth and so handsome. His hands are large and ugly and make my fine bones look like Dresden. Now there is something normal between us that our bodies at the swimming pool recognised. But what was it that started him so strangely to love someone such as me long before he saw my beautiful body. What strange quality lies dormant to fall for an angel when he is used to common girls to flirt with.

⚬⚬

Friday, after a day in Papeete:

Now I have something in my mind to remember for many a day to come. Unbelievable Tahiti. Is it true? What a world to unfold in front of my eyes. A day in Tahiti. Just a day, but enough to give me a feeling of great satisfaction. I adored it. Woke up at six o'clock and went up on deck eager to cast an eye on the land of such reputation. My first vision caused my hair to stand on end and water flood my eyes. The island opposite Tahiti that we approached first. We had not reached Tahiti but there was this glorious sight. This island so heavenly in the early morning light. Great jagged, razor sharp mountains covered in strange dull green foliage. So big,

so high, so dramatic. Sweet pastel grey, soft, heavy clouds caressing
all the peaks. This extraordinary mountain, volcanic-looking set
of peaks pointing straight and sharp up to heaven, so brittle rising
out of the sweet, soft, loving sea, so calm with just a few gentle
murmurs as the ocean played over the outer reefs surrounding the
island. My heart was chocked with love and wonder as we sailed
gaily past. Most people were on deck and within an hour we were
outside Papeete in Tahiti itself. By eight A.M. the sun was too
hot for comfort but the heavenly world of Papeete was teeming
with hidden treasures and visible beauty. Tahiti was even more
gigantic and dramatic than the small island. No wonder the Tikis
and carvings of the natives have such a weird ugliness. There is
something so unsympathetic in these great war-like spear heads of
mountains, in some places the mountains point like a jagged spear-
head as if cursing God himself. But down the mountains the same
strange green foliage, which as it gets closer to the wharf, takes
shape in palms and bananas and mainly vivid flowers. Two sweet
little churches dominate the small town. Both painted red and
white and both very old and most charming to see.

There is a little photo of me that my mother had given to my
father. He refers to it in his first long letter to the ship as: "The photo
of that sad little girl you gave me". In the letter he recalls the days before our departure when I exhibited signs of anxiety and burst into
tears several times for no apparent reason. By then my mother and
I had left Rose Cottage and were staying with the Reeds at Heide.
My father had shown me the ship's route on a globe of the world and
I knew we were embarking on a big adventure, but along with the
excitement I was scared and confused. I thought my daddy didn't
want to come with us and I didn't know why.

Once on board I found the ship held pleasures beyond my
dreams. Outside our cramped cabin was a world of bright lights,
noise and people. I had other children to play with every day and
there was even a room dedicated to our amusement. To me it was
a magical world of glitz and glamour, so unlike the large, silent

rooms of Rose Cottage where I played alone with my dollies. There wasn't much time for missing my daddy but sometimes I still did, so I drew for him lots of drawings, including one of what to me was the most amazing and wonderful thing that happened on board. A waiter, resplendent in a freshly starched uniform, would appear in the children's playroom holding a silver tray overflowing with lollies. We would leap excitedly around him until he brought the tray down to our level allowing us to grab handfuls of the sugary treats.

⁂

Back in Melbourne, a couple of weeks into May, the weather was miserable with rain most days and bitterly cold winds. My father hadn't yet received my drawings, in fact he hadn't received anything at all from us. The postcard we sent him from New Zealand, along with five others to friends and family, hadn't arrived. He sometimes suffered from depression and our apparent silence was like a lead weight in his already heavy heart. His increasing worry and sadness permeated his letters until, much to his relief, he received a letter my mother sent from Tahiti.

Darling Jeannie, your letter came this morning. Would you ever believe how glad I was. I had not even hoped for one from Tahiti and it was the most wonderful surprise. I write tonight in great haste and only to be sure that this gets you at Panama because my last letter was mainly so gloomy. I have felt lousy to put it mildly but your letter was a great help. Not that all its contents were fine and dandy. Not a night goes by without me thinking about you and for a very large part of my time I live in imagination in that not very lovely cabin on the Castel Felice. But you are worried about money. Try not to be and I can only hope that you have enough to be able to buy yourself enough whisky to make the trip endurable. So long as you have enough money for your train fare and to book in at your club, there will be at least 25 pounds Sterling waiting for you at the bank, and a little more if I can make it, and that will have to last

you a fortnight. But I have just not had the time
to work out how I stand. I have 13 concerts in 14
days, and a lot to do in the office besides, and
am very nearly exhausted. But I will send you all
I can, and today I thought of how I could send you
a few quid to Panama, but could not see how this
could be done. But don't worry, the harder you find
yourself stuck, the more certain it is that I will
send you whatever you need.

I am, of course, very happy about Janie enjoying
herself, disappointed that she is not eating and
I hope she is not missing me. The drawings were
a tremendous joy ... as you know the globe that I
showed her so often, and with the somewhat erratic
course of the ship drawn in too. The remarkable
thing is the closer one looks the more one
recognises shapes, which she has remembered, shapes
of Africa, South America, Australia and even the
two islands of N.Z. All haywire, but there. But do
in future send me, if you can, a few explanatory
comments, the girls surrounding the waiter and
his tray of lollies, and that tantalising drawing
with the boat in it. Perhaps she has been looking
at maps on the boat every day, but if not I am
astonished, touched, and even a little saddened
to find how closely she observes and how well she
remembers.

But I must go now, it is 1.30 and I must take this
to the G.P.O. and then get some sleep before 7.30
in the morning. On reading through your letter
once again, it is all very cold and distant, but
never mind, I was glad to get it, and still am. Do
enjoy the rest of the trip as much as you can, at
least you are out of Melbourne where the weather
continues to be cruel.

Off now.

XX John

There were times when my mother took my father's expression
of sadness almost as a deliberate attempt to infect her with it, causing her to react with spontaneous and unreasonable fury. At port in

Balboa she received both my father's gloomy letter and his buoyant reply to her letter from Tahiti. But the friendliness of the second letter was ignored when she wrote back with waves of blinding anger washing over her. My mother was in such a fury she dispensed with the usual, "Dear John".

Darling Jeannie, Darling Jeannie, Darling Jeannie. What do you mean by that? You put me in a rage that I cannot endure. Why say that when you send me a letter fit to depress a Cheshire cat. What do you think? You are thoughtless and infuriating and I couldn't be more cross. Each person has their share of sadness, struggle and insecurity in this life and it is high time you coped a bit better with yours. You have made your own bed, you have driven away the only person who ever loved you and ruined your own life with your misery and self-pity. How could you dare to write such a letter to me.

Today I have had a happy day, we have been ashore at Balboa. I love being in port. All the agonies of the trip and insecurities and anxieties of travelling with a child on a ship riddled with nasty illnesses, suddenly are worth the beauty and magic of such ports as Tahiti and Panama. I am me, and full in my heart to feast my eyes on such wonderful worlds as these. I come back on board tired but glad and take my letters into the bar to read them, and what then.

What then? Your letter. Ever since I couldn't care what happens. All the magic is gone. Only the memories of you and your tiresome agonies. Have you no pride? Have you no guts? Are you the child begging so often of the mother? You, who have treated me so appallingly. You are older than me but your character gets more frail and you become more of a parasite emotionally as the years go on. I cannot sleep now. I am in my bunk. We are still in port. Everybody else is ashore still. It is after midnight and I cannot sleep. I am in a rage with you. I sit in this hot bunk, Jane sleeps soundly. She is happy and well but I have had some great worry as there is not a person on board who has not had this fearful dysentery and flu. Most of the children have been seriously ill but your daughter has a good mother and when the illness hit her first I pounced on the first symptom, put her to bed and off food and stayed in the cabin all day with her, even missing my meals and going mad with heat and boredom. The other mothers have been more stupid than I would have believed. But Jane recovered without getting a second symptom and is now fine and back on food.

You will not hear again from the ship as this will be posted at the last port (Curacao) of call. I will let you know how we cope in London. Nothing is easy but one has to take control of one's own life. You think you are lonely. My God if you had stared into as much ocean as I have in this last month. I am so lonely that my heart is cracking. But I am lonely because you have cheated me. Everybody else has a husband and a family, it is a natural way for people. But you with your heart full of hatred can only love with words out of a typewriter. It is dishonest, you do not love me and never have.

Friday. Today we came through the canal. It is worth one's whole life to see these things. Jungle beauty for twenty miles through the natural lake. Glorious, glorious lake looking like a paradise. I adored every moment in spite of an enormous thunder cloud that cast the last lap into blackness, then tropical rain in torrents. But rain or shine it was magnificent. The gates are extraordinary. It is a credit to mankind. We go through the ocean at sea level and through the lake at 85 feet above sea level. Exciting and tremendous. Janie was too young to comprehend. It is all so quick. Such engineering. I take my hat off. In fact I adored the whole day.

Now we are cheerfully sailing the Caribbean Sea. I am not in such a temper today but I was truly depressed by your letter and I cannot afford to be thus affected as I have a difficult time and need all my faith. You ask do I ever miss you. I have missed you since the night you came home from Tasmania many long years ago. You came in a raincoat and I was in bed at the loft waiting for you. I remember every moment but my heart is closed to you now. That night was the only night that you loved me as much as I loved you. Now go to blazes because I am fed up with you. You are a child emotionally and if I wasn't Janie's mother I would give you bigger fireworks than this. Leave me be. I owe you nothing. Start paying me back with kindness but leave me alone emotionally. Do what you like but don't talk about love to me. If you keep up that sort of talk I will pay you back.

Now, one last page. Next letter will be from London. We will be there in two weeks from now. That drawing of Jane's, of the world, I'm glad you understand. The child is remarkable. She has seen no other map. She is a most brilliant child and I ask you never to mention it as people would not understand. I think her drawings something to treasure and I have never thrown any away. She is a sensitive and intelligent child and you can thank your lucky stars that she exists. She is happy on board and certainly enjoys herself more than I do. Today they had a fancy dress party for children. Each child got a good present and they had a feast. The Italians do the festivities with real feeling. The crossing the line was elaborate and well done. Their feasts are really good but some days the food is poor. We are in the Caribbean Sea and it is very hot. Tomorrow Curacao and then Southampton.

There is some complication about tomorrow's post. I may not be able to post this. We shall see. I am sorry you have been upset but you did annoy me those last few days. You make things so difficult I cannot stand it. I had asked you not to come to the ship – you take no notice of anything. You are irritating and then you complain all the time about how you are treated. There is no reason in your head these days. I am tired of all this. Please respect my life in future if you want any friendliness from me. Janie is well and happy and too busy to think about the past. I post this with some hesitation. We are nearly here now. I'm sorry I'm so cross but what would you expect? Hope you cope better with things. I am only as cruel as you force me to be.

Jean

As it turned out she didn't post this letter until long after we had arrived in London. Posting it so long after the heat of her fury had dissipated seems a curious decision, but many letters had been exchanged by the time he finally got to read it, which might have helped take a little of the sting out of it.

A moment of terror as a child has a way of embedding itself in the memory like a short, looped bit of film. My mother talks of the Crossing the Line ceremony as being "elaborate and well done" and I'm sure through adult eyes it was all fun and slap-stick comedy. Through the eyes of a nervous five year-old Australian girl, it was confusing and frightening. Unlike film, my memory includes sensations as clearly felt as the image is seen. I was standing on the metal steps between decks, looking down on the strange and noisy activity happening around the swimming pool. A man with very long curly white hair and beard was giving orders to a couple of crew members who would then grab a bystander, pour spaghetti or some other sloppy food-stuff over their heads and throw them in the pool, amid peals of laughter and much shouting. The surface of the pool quickly became a disgusting mess of floating food slops. I watched with timid curiosity from my safe distance until a kindly crew member spotted me. Mistaking my wide-eyed apprehension for nothing more than shy reticence, he attempted to lift me into his arms to take me to join the fun. Instantly my nervousness turned to terror and I clung desperately to the rail with both hands until he realised his mistake and released me. Somehow I received my Crossing the Line Certificate without going anywhere near King Neptune. Did I really see him climb onto the deck from over the side of the ship? That would be a stunt impossible in these days of strict workplace Health and Safety regulations. Or did I just imagine it after being told he lives in the sea on the equator and climbs aboard every passing ship?

❧

Letter from my father, undated:

> Dear Jeannie, This is the most hasty of notes -
> scribbled out at midnight so that I can be sure

31

```
that it will be waiting for you at Southampton.
It seems a lifetime since you left - and yet you
do not get to England until the end of this week.
Needless to say I have been worried - and still am.
Have you enough money? And how will you manage to
drag poor Janie around London looking for a room.
The absence of any real news from you has made me
even more sad and tired than I would have been.
But this is not that sort of letter. It's main
and only purpose is to tell you that last Monday
May 23, I sent another 15 pounds sterling to your
account in London - and on Monday week - June 6 - I
will send another 15 pounds sterling, and the same
fortnightly thereafter. Should I get a desperate
letter from you during the week I will send money
sooner, or do whatever seems sensible. But I am
cruelly busy. Please date your letters. And please,
how is Jane? Did she have enteritis, is she eating,
did she wet the bed every night on the boat? I
got a card from the Mentone council about a polio
booster due now - you might ask someone if you can.

I would be happy if I could believe that when you
signed your letters to me, you felt something of
what I feel now.
    John
```

My father's "hasty note" would have been on its way to Southampton when my mother wrote a letter that started with:

Dear John, Just about to arrive in Curacao. You are lucky as I wrote you a great, angry letter of many, many pages but it would have cost me nearly a quid to post it so now you get a fresh letter of 1 page.

It's a truncated and less heated version of her long letter. My father's immediate response upon receiving this shorter, but still angry, letter was to sit writing a reply late into the night. He decided not to post it, choosing instead to write a short, calm letter in which he explained:

```
I feel that only more sadness can come from any
kind of argument. I was, of course, hurt by your
```

letter. I was pleased and excited when I found it in the office, but on reading it, it did the job that your long, unposted one was meant to do, with absolute efficiency.

❧

Excerpt from my mother's journal:

Tuesday 31st May

Sweet Darling, I am coming. I am nearly in your arms again. Three more days of ocean and then London. I can hardly believe it, after all this time I have to focus my thoughts towards you, as so many different places and faces have lived in my eyes and brain for the last seven months. I once thought, when you left me, I wouldn't be able to live life without you. I have managed. I have made new friends, travelled several oceans, thought millions of thoughts, happy and sad. I have even had my sweet affair with Dearest Stuart whom I sometimes pine for, as he surely loved me more than you do and thus it was that he gave me great comfort. Sometimes I think his shoulders more desirable than yours as I often am in need of the protection that his very masculine body and soul gave to me. He allowed me to be soft and frail, and loved to feel protective. Yet even so with you it is a hard, hard road, lonely and sad and I have to stand alone. But I am willing, once again, to be as strong as you think I am. I love you dearly, you alone in all the world are perfect in my eyes and even when I am in a fury with you, you are still perfect.

Here am I, so lonely on this ship, so lonely for people like us, for our friends and the way we live. I cannot stand this suburban type of all nations. The people on the ship drive me to distraction and I wonder how you coped with it on your ship. Here I am surrounded by glamourous Italian men and yet the only soul who has any contact with me is a charming Scottish boy with whom I have just been looking at the midnight sea. Young, sweet and intelligent, strong and handsome, rather like David. There is always someone! My little Italian boy went the way of all the Continentals. In the end I am looking into the eyes of yet another Scotsman. How strange, but dear I am safe with this one as he is younger than I by light years and I am so close now that I can wait for my kisses another week.

What will you say when I tell you about Stuart? Will you be jealous? I remember you saying that in front of your fireplace at your party. "I wonder would I be jealous?" you said. You haven't had to be jealous as yet. I wonder too. You said you had never felt jealousy. It is likely you are too strong. Yet I wonder. Does it mean you don't love me enough? I am jealous, even of your wife just because she shares your legal bed, even though I know you don't love her and she doesn't love you. I would be green with jealousy if I saw you look at another woman. I would be insane if I thought you had another affair. Yet I wonder, will you be jealous?

What would torture you my dear, would be that he was the most handsome man. That is your sort of jealousy. Poor, sweet Darling, you think yourself ugly, but it is not so. I think your face is that of an angel and I long for one more glance at it. I thirst for the sight of the most treasured and sweet smile, the most sensitive and beautiful blue eyes. Your face is for me, heaven. Yet you won't believe me. You are not handsome by ordinary standards. Your features are not regular and you stoop too much. Your hair is not soft and your nose too soft for a man. These things written down are true. You are not good looking, agreed. Yet put all those features together and the sweetness into your lips and the light of your soul into your eyes and the brown, masculine texture into your skin and the strange, passionate aura that hovers from cheekbone to cheekbone. Darling it is the most beautiful face in all the world. I do truly love you. I weep for you. I wouldn't change your face for anything, except that I would love you to be happy. I cry with love when you say you think yourself ugly. You say I can't love you because only beautiful things are loved. Your one bitterness. Your face. Dearest face, I wish I had it to gaze upon every moment of my life. I love it too dearly. I weep for your sensitivity. Sweetest face.

34

Excerpt from my mother's journal:

Wednesday 1st June

The first day of June. My English June. On Friday I will be there. In England. How strange. I cannot really digest it as fact. Yet here I am having repacked my bags, Arthur's painting is down in the hold. God help me, what will he say to that? Poor Darling, he did give it to me. "Never part with it." That's what you said. So here am I, and with me "The Hunter".* Is it real. Will I awake to reality? It is hard for me to believe that you are in London and now me too. I hope it is a good thing.

Jean on the Castel Felice, 1960.

---

*   Arthur had given my mother "The Hunter" but within a year of us arriving in London he asked to borrow it for an exhibition of his work in Australia. Before he took it he wrote on the back, "This painting belongs to Jean Langley". My mother never got the painting back.

Jane's drawing of the ship they sailed on to England.

In their flat underneath the Blackman's flat in Jackson's Lane,
London. Behind Jane, two Blackman paintings, including a
portrait of Jean in black ink. The landscape painting behind Jane
is probably by Arthur Boyd, done on Hampstead Heath and
mentioned in Jean's journal, as he left it for a while in Jean's flat.

Chapter 5

On English Soil

A couple of days after arriving on English soil, my mother and I visited Arthur and Yvonne. By all accounts Yvonne was not suspicious about the arrival of their old friend and was pleased to see a familiar Australian face.

Tuesday 7th June

My heart is at peace. Tonight I saw you my dear and I do not need to hear any words from you, your eyes have told me everything I want to know. How happy I am. How contented. You love me well. I love you very much. It was lovely to see you. Just a small touch of welcome, a sweet, nervous but warm grip of the hand. How well we both were. Who could have guessed by our behaviour that our hearts were leaping. How nice it would have been to have gone to bed with you tonight. But I am content. I felt more pleased than passionate.

My mother then wrote that she felt glad to see Yvonne too, suggesting there was "something sweet and yet sad" about her. In a rare concession, my mother also admitted to feeling a little guilty.

❧

Letter to my father:

London, Friday 10th

Dear John,

Here we are after a week in London. I have just tucked young

Jane into bed. She looks like an English rosebud and as I kissed
her goodnight I thought of you. I'm sorry, you must be missing her
terribly. If it's any consolation you can take it from me that she
is having the most marvellous time and is indeed sparkling with
health, love and vitality.

She has seen Buckingham Palace and the guards in their great
bear-skin hats practising [illegible]. They do their parading to the
fyfes (don't know how to spell it) band etc. Jane was enchanted.
Also the horse guards at Whitehall. Buckingham Palace always
looks so dull in photos but I was quite moved. It's an ugly building
but it's surrounded by the most beautiful parks and lakes, and has
trees and flowers and white statues with black and white glorious
London in the distance. The parks are a joy. I never dreamed they
would be so beautiful. So clean, so peaceful. I feel they are the
essence of the whole English way of life. People live in them with
love and dignity. They belong to the people. It is the most flower
loving, nature loving race of people. They are very friendly and
kindly. They love children, and complete strangers will always
stop and say hello to Jane. She talks to all the dogs. There are dogs
everywhere.

The cockney Londoners are great people. Sparkling and witty
and warm. It's a man's city. I think the English male is the peacock.
The town is lousy with pansies. The men's clothes are perfect and
the men of the town dress perfectly. The women are either frowsy
or tarts. Women's clothes are in bad taste and the women dress
without any feeling. There is little money spent on clothes. There is
little money spent at all. The attitude to money is vastly different
here. There is not the glamorous dressing or careless drinking. Yet
I would think the people much happier and contented. People are
grubby looking and parts of London smell foul. Buildings inside
are dark and unwholesome. London is large but delightfully so. It
is not too large for me to digest. It is not high as in Melbourne and
there is no shop like the large Melbourne stores. The shops are never

crowded, not even in lunchtime. Working people don't shop. Clothes are cheap but clothes come last.

Even at 5.30 the streets are never as crowded as Collins Street, as the city is so large with about 20 different tube stations and millions of buses. All the talk of London queues is mad because it's only a method. Buses every two moments and no standing allowed, so you are only in a queue as a method of entering the bus. It is excellent. People are most civilized in every way. No one ever pushes or is rude.

Children are not allowed in pubs. Took Jane to see Charlie Chaplin in some old film. She adored it. Full price in the theatre which nearly wrecked me. 5 shillings front stalls each. Jane has become a great comic. All the funny Cockney paper selling men talk to her and she has taken to clowning in return to their clowning. Even great dignified men in bowler hats have a mad, but cheerful method of clowning with children. Everybody is very sweet. Jane is a bit over the fence sometimes, and then sometimes she is absolutely shy.

We eat at night in a little arty café and Jane feels so much at home that she parades around and entertains everybody. She carts around this tiny doll she calls Thumbelina. It has no arms and no clothes and its hair is all in strands but she carries this doll wherever she goes and has everybody delighted. She is a sweet thing.

We are still at the Overseas Visitor's Club. Unfortunately I have to pay full fare for Jane so it is costing me 31 shillings a day, just for bed and breakfast. The flat come room situation is not good as London Landladies are not keen on kids. I am a little worried about this now as my inquiries have not been very successful. Looks as if I will have to pay more than I bargained for. This last week has cost me a lot of money for fares and treats and food. I will have to manage something smartly. You never see children in London. It is not a children's city … It is all so different but very wonderful.

Very, very beautiful. Some of the streets in London with little two story houses are like fairy-lands. Roses and trees and prettiness everywhere. The people aren't fussy about personal cleanliness but they keep their city clean of human ugliness. Australia is ruined with its crazy need of new things and brightness and vulgarity. There is no prettiness. It isn't that there is excellent taste everywhere, it is that there is no bad taste. I am more than pleased with the place even though I feel anxious about finding somewhere to live. Money is passing too quickly for comfort. However I hope to have a new address by this time next week.

Do not worry about Jane. She is eating quite well and drinking pints of milk. Milk is a great favourite here. They are funny people, the English. I think they are pretty happy on the whole. No. 10 Downing Street is a classic example of English madness. It's the funniest, shabbiest little dirty building. I would have been doubtful about renting a room in a house that looked like that. Love from sleeping Jane.

Jean

After reading my mother's description of the shabbiness of Number 10 Downing Street in her last letter, my father may well have had concerns about her ability to choose affordable lodgings. And with good reason. For those who know London, my mother's taste was more Hampstead than Knightsbridge. Unlike the obvious and ostentatious wealth of Knightsbridge, in 1960 Hampstead was like a slightly arty village, quietly tasteful and partially surrounded by the wildly beautiful woodlands of Hampstead Heath. But rental in such a salubrious environment was far from cheap.

Excerpts from my mother's journal:

Sunday 11th June

Well, my friend, here I am, sitting in my new flat. Thank God all my hunting is over. I was getting tired and depressed as all the

flats I looked at were gloomy and unsuitable for either Jane or you.
Now I have really let my hair down and moved into a flat at six
Guineas a week when my sole income is seven. Am I mad? Well we
will see. I shall have to work. I hadn't wanted to but that is that. I
don't mind really. It was so obvious on the telephone that you were
coming to my night life again regardless of where I lived or how
I lived. I couldn't stand the mess of you creeping around corners.
Sorry Darling, I am too old. I like my love in the light. Poor pet,
even now you will have to wait for your kisses as I must first settle
in and get the lay of the land. I shall see you tomorrow.

I am strangely disinterested in my body these last few days. I am
not entirely well and the anxiety has been a bit much for me so far.
Perhaps when I feel better, yet I am a little shy of you. It has been
so long and you are a wee bit insensitive or indelicate in your desire
to rush straight to my bed and love me regardless of where or how.
It has been so long. I feel strange somehow and tired and perhaps
even a little old.

One week in England. An enchanting week. Spending more
money than I can afford, no security. Trailing around like a lost
dog and finally having to take a flat without much idea of how I'm
going to pay for it for long. I wish so for a man to look after me.
Yet my heart is bound to yours, so I will always be a lost dog trying
to cope with life. But here I am living in Hampstead. Just adore
the Heath. Just adore everything about London. Thank God the
flat is elegant and peaceful. Will enjoy life here. It is a dear room
I'm sitting writing in. All blue. Charming blue wallpaper dotted
with little pink flowers. Not perfect but very charming. Nice large
windows overlooking trees and a dear sweet church. I will be happy
here. Peace at last.

I am a little frightened of you disturbing the peace with your
midnight passions. Is this me? I must be ill! Me, who thought
I would die without your beautiful loving. Me, who has come
thirteen thousand miles over the sea to be in your arms again
because I couldn't live without you. I am an odd fish. I feel nothing

but a desire for peace. Yet I love you too well. Where is my famous warmth that men love me for? Has it gone? Dearest, you will settle the matter. I can't even raise the desire for a kiss tonight. Tomorrow we shall meet in the city. At last a city where we can be together without anyone knowing us or our guilty loving. Yet I will have Jane with me. We shall have to sit in the park. I shall love to see you. Why am I heavy of heart? I cannot understand myself. My man, I want so much to live a peaceful life. I am so taken with the roses and flowers and parks of these dear English people. I just want to look at it all and draw and paint flowers. Gentle England has quietened my passionate, wild Australian body and soul. Now I want to dwell amongst the fairies. Perhaps the poet in me has won out. Let me feel your kisses and we shall see.

I love England after one hard and lonely week. I hope to settle here. I feel flat when I know you will go back and leave me here one day. I think I fear belonging to your body again. I fear all the mental tortures of wanting to live with you and wanting to have your body and wanting to own you. I should keep myself free of such tortures and stay in the world of roses. I would marry and love a new heart if I could find one. Dearest, my loyalty is poor tonight. I am unwell. The sea voyage has disturbed my balance. Fear not, I love you.

⌒⌒⌒

Arthur's planned secret meeting with my mother was disrupted by the news from Australia that Arthur's beloved mother, Doris, had died suddenly.

Excerpt from my mother's journal:

Monday 12th June

Today was to have been our first meeting alone. I imagined so much. I thought we would spend the day in the park, smiling shy love smiles at each other, touching hands, loving gently. My dearest friend. How can we ever recover from this dreadful day of woe? Will there ever be smiles again? Will I ever be able to look into

your eyes again? Will life continue now? Great tragedy of tragedies.
Terrible day of sadness, not only for you my dear, I too loved her.
I loved her as a daughter. If only you knew how dearly I loved her.
To me, you and your mother were the treasures of my life. Sweet
Darling frail little pet, I weep so in my heart. I cannot bear to think,
to realise, I do not want it to be, I need to be convinced in my deep
heart, it cannot be, yet I have been told it is so, I cannot bear it,
how will you be, my dearest, my treasure, my dear, dear love, if
only I could be with you, if only I could hold you in my arms, if
only your tears could fall on my shoulders. I cannot bear to think of
your terrible sadness.

The long entry continues in a similar fashion, ending with:

Darling, I cannot bear it. Let your heart sleep. Think of me and
fall asleep dreaming that you are comforted by my warm breast.

❧

Letter to my father:

42 BELLSIZE SQUARE HAMPSTEAD, 13th June

Dear John, As you can see we have an address now. It is good
in some ways but very expensive. Last week was very difficult
as London is not a place for children. I became very depressed
at the situation of rooms and flats. Landladies are dead against
children and generally refuse to even meet you if you have a
child. Flats are expensive. Rooms about 4 gns in any sort of happy
district. Districts vary in price very much. The cheap districts are
unbearable and certainly no place. I saw a room like a cupboard
for 3 gns and then a flat like a slum for 5 gns. I couldn't face letting
Janey live in some districts and depressing furniture and pokey
stoves and gas rings. So when I phoned about this flat and the
woman said she loved children, I nearly collapsed in the phone box.
So I took it, in my anxiety, for several reasons. It is costing some six
guineas a week. I will go to work just as soon as I can. Part-time
work is easy to get and jobs plentiful. Anyhow it is for the best, as
life is pleasant in London if one lives in a charming area. Here we

are in a marvellous position between Regents Park and Hampstead Heath.

The Heath is unbelievable. The most beautiful place. Hundreds of acres of the most sweet and wild parklands just so close to London. Lakes and ponds, ducks and birds as tame as possible. Jane just adores it. Never seen anything like it. I am sure that these marvellous parks are the essence of the whole English way of life. I find the English most charming and friendly – they all adore Jane. Every adult speaks to her wherever she is. The landlord and landlady are Welsh and have never had any family, and they make a great fuss of the little one. We have a charming bed sitting room with large windows looking out over trees and a sweet little old church. Then we have a nice new kitchen with everything clean and nice. The whole flat is decorated in charming wallpaper, and although it is not in perfect taste at least nothing jars. However I never imagined paying that much money, but I am too old to cope with slumming and being a mother at the same time. I think Jane needs a cheerful atmosphere. We have a tiny little balcony and Jane sits out there in the sun. We get all the sun, and between this and our numerous walks in the park, we are having an outdoor time. The working class districts are terribly sooty and depressing. I couldn't have lived with a child like Jane in such a part. Also, the whole of London is so closely woven that we are within easy walking distance of five underground stations and two of the biggest parks, so you can imagine that the traffic on the main roads is fantastic, and all the streets are narrow and curling, so that it is dangerous for children. This is a quiet street in a quiet little area.

We were very cheerful when we took this little room. We tramped around half of London and I just couldn't take it anymore. Jane is well and happy. Her latest craze is donkey rides at 1 shilling a pop. She loves it. It's just like a story-book to see a funny bloke in a cap leading three or four donkeys with kids on them. Jane insisted on having rides. She could make a good horsewoman as she is absolutely confident with all animals. London is lousy with dogs, and well fed cats. We have seen three Siamese so far. They are all very friendly. Animals aren't afraid of people in England. The ducks are so tame that they come swimming over and walk right up. Wild ducks, of course. The little birds will just about sit on your lap. We saw one squirrel which was greatly exciting and makes one want to choke Walt Disney.

Meat is very dear, but like everything else here, is good quality. I have never tasted such delicious bananas. Peas are beautiful, lettuces are green, and carrots, wee little things, very nice. Cucumbers are quite different from ours but very nice. There are hundreds of cake shops. The English must live on cakes. People on the whole look pretty untidy and carelessly dressed. No one bothers about clothes except the toffs, and they do it very well. They are all crazy flower lovers. It is a pleasant, peaceful and civilized race as far as I can see. There seems to be a little bit of a poet in everybody.

The main cry against London seems to be that you're a nobody in London. Well it's not the place if you want to be a somebody but it's a jolly good place if you just want to like your fellow beings. Jane is a wee bit nervous. Kids on the boat introduced her to ghosts, and the invisible thing is hard to argue about. I think she will forget it soon. We had our first home-cooked meal tonight and at last I am able to live without café food. Cream and milk and butter here is excellent. Australian goods on the whole are laughed at. This is my second night here and I feel it was the only move I could have made. Am very distressed about Doris Boyd as I loved her very dearly, and over the last year I spent a lot of time with her. It was a great shock.

Hope you are well.

Jean

❧

Excerpt from my mother's journal:

Sat. 17th June

My Dear, I am resolved tonight to live without you. I suppose somehow this will come about. I do not know why but I suddenly feel so happy about London, so in love with the people, the balmy night breeze, the whole life as I find it in England. I want to stay happy. I want to live in peace. It is many years since I have felt this sort of optimism. I just want to begin a new world. I love you very, very dearly and would gladly give everything to you that I am capable of giving. But I feel if I make a break now before we take up our love again, I can do it. If I never feel your love again I can be strong and save myself a lot of suffering.

Now is a new world for me. I love so much this land of peaceful, civilised people. I want to stay and live out a new existence. You shall go home without me. You shall miss me I know but I am not strong enough to ever lose you again. I couldn't bear another parting. You, who left me. Yet I love you so much. I wonder whether you love me the same way. I am in a doubting mood. It is your wife who has done this thing to me, just because the girl is as mad as a march hare. I felt like telling her. I would if it wasn't that I am so frightened of you. I could leave you but I could never bear to make you cross with me. I want peace so badly and I feel it now. I feel so very unpassionate for the first time in my life. I feel as if I just want to feed the birds and look at the roses. How strange for me to say this. My warm body that you love so dearly is still and quiet. Let it stay that way if it will give me some peace. My more pure love for you will continue for the rest of my life as I am dedicated to your very existence. But touch me not now as I do not want to feel the flow of your most passionate blood. I do not want to love you as well as I do. I found parting with you last year the most terrible experience in my life. It would always be the same. I am sorry. I love you so, so very beautiful you are. I weep because your life is a mess and I do not want to be part of it as it can only end in tragedy for me. Now I have a chance of peace.

Chapter 6

Rekindling and Disappointment

Excerpt from my mother's journal:

Sunday

My Dear Sweet, forgive me for what I have been thinking, I half believe myself, still yet I look out into the balmy soft English night. Ah I would so love you to be with me. I would so love to be in your arms tonight.

⤔⤔

Excerpt:

Tuesday 27th June

Since you left me I have been as one in a dream. I have cooked a dinner for Jane and I, eaten it, sat out on our balcony with Jane, put her to bed and then sat some more by myself. All this as one in a dream. I am a woman again, after all these long months. The world comes to one the whole of life, the love, the beautiful love comes to one so seldomly, when it comes it is beautiful, it is radiant, it is a glow from within, from without, from you to me, from me to you, it makes all other treasures fade, it fills the soul with beautiful spongy happiness, happiness that seems to have a substance as it floods into one's heart and soul. I am full to the brim, I am spellbound, my own love is out on the leaves and flowers now, it has left me sweet and balmy, like a beautiful butterfly I feel at peace, I have given all my love, I have released my female heart, I have created love. I feel so full and rich and beautiful. Did ever any woman feel more satisfied with love, you are perfect.

⁂

Wednesday

Tonight I think not of love. Finance has stolen my thoughts. Yours is bad enough, God knows. If you had any idea just how low mine was you would do a mental somersault. I've got enough money to eat only three pounds worth of food between two of us for one month, after that I shall have only enough for my stupid, enormous rent. Looks as if I shall have to stop playing Ladies and get a dreary working class room with a gas ring. Heaven knows I depend on my environment so for cheerfulness. My outlook is black, I must do some of my lovely drawings, the Londoners seem partial to drawings, maybe there is a place in the world for me. But I must work. At least I have my treasure out of my system for a day or two. Besides I think it is time I found a husband all of my very own. The English men like me and I like them with their fine handsome features and long hands. I will always love you my dear never fear, but a girl must live.

⁂

One of the things my mother and I had in common later in life was an interest in human behaviour and we often indulged in armchair psychology. Over endless cups of tea we pondered the tendency of people with inflated but unstable egos to protect themselves by pushing aside self-doubt, blaming others to avoid accepting any fault on their part, and reacting very badly to criticism. But my mother's interest in psychology was always outward-looking. Her inability to turn her gaze inward meant she barely acknowledged that her own ego was sometimes both inflated and fragile. So when her beautiful child threw an ugly tantrum at the age of five she needed someone else to blame and I was, after all, my father's daughter.

Monday

Tonight, My Dear, I am like lead in my heart. I do not know where

48

my spirits have gone. I have so little money and my life with Jane
seems suddenly most complex and I feel inadequate. I am not
really suited anymore to being a mother. Time has caused me to
become preoccupied and unable to tolerate the idiotic noises and
complaints of the child, who is after all only a child. Yet in spite
of my feeling some great understanding of Jane's problems, I find
myself irritable and exhausted. Yet you, My Dear Arthur, never
realise that I find life hard indeed. How well I would like a man
to share my burden, how well I would like tonight to fall into
your arms and forget all the difficulties. My London enthusiasm
is darkened by the great insecurities. I actually cope better when
I am disciplined by loneliness, and hard and brittle with longing.
Now you have left me, soft and feminine, awakened and true of
heart. All my gentleness flowed for you and my heart was as soft
as love itself. Once aroused and in full bloom, you cut yourself off
to return to your own cold existence and here you leave me frail
and so lonely for you, so very lonely for the man of my life. I love
you bitterly tonight as I feel so sad, so desperately unable to stand
the strain, the awful strain of this girl child, so rapidly growing up,
so different in temperament to myself, I find myself appalled at the
temper of the child and feel hatred for all Sinclairs and their filthy
tempers, God spare me, I have battled my heart black and blue to
find a life of peace away from my husband, only to feel the violence
from my own child, my heart shudders as I feel I am too old to
battle life out afresh. Yet I cannot tolerate, even from so small and
pretty a child, such bad behaviour patterns, yet have I the strength
to lead or heal. God how I find loneliness around me tonight. My
nightly prison. Where are you, my lover, you should be holding my
hand tonight. You have all the power.

❧

As a music critic my father could be quite controversial, and that
certainly was the case in early July when the Victorian Symphony
Orchestra threatened not to play if he was in the audience. A week
later the visiting French conductor, Georges Tzipine, wanted all

49

critics locked out of his concerts. It made for an exceptionally busy and stressful time for my father, so his letters of the time were brief and mainly about practical things such as whether we were coping on the money he sent fortnightly. My mother had an intense distaste for discussing finances so for the most part his questions went unanswered, as did his letters.

Excerpt from my mother's journal:

Tuesday 18th July

Three weeks have passed since we were together alone. Many times since I have seen you socially. Many times you have squeezed my hand secretly and many times you have slyly looked at me through the crowds of friends. But I am bitter and sad and feel most cross with you. I am so tired, so terribly exhausted that I scarcely know which way to turn. I am working myself into a state of hysteria, and out of exhaustion comes insecurity. I so want help from you. I so want attention from you and you have been so busy. Now it is over, your show is underway. Today it opened and three paintings were sold.

I am sad, I am always sad when I see you in public, but today was even harder as your paintings move me so very much that I cannot keep the tears out of my eyes. I know that you are the greatest of them all. There is no-one to compare with you as a painter and I so wanted to tell you but you didn't believe me. O.K. It's true I love your love, but still it is that I know about your paintings. You don't understand, I just know. Also the framing. I told you last week the frames weren't good enough and it's true. But what a joy to find "The Bridegroom waiting for the Bride to grow up". That's truly the most lovely painting. I just love it. Your painting is so very romantic, so full of love, so rich, so very, very passionate, the colour, the texture.

Darling you are great, greater, greatest. I know it and one day everybody will know. I love you yet I am so lonely, so sad, so in need of you. I get so jealous at social functions, I am sorry I worry you. It was so obvious today that you knew I was in a state and you wanted to help but it is impossible. I am cross and too much in love, I feel trapped, frantic, Please my Darling come to me soon, soon, soon. I love you, I love you, I am crying again. Today I cannot manage to live it all out. I want your comfort. You owe me so much. Please be gentle until I feel better. I cry, I cry, because I cannot stop loving.

Having received no response from his previous letters, my father wrote again, repeating his question of whether we were getting by on the 18 pounds English he was sending fortnightly. He also asked if my mother had found a job, and wanted to know about my first day at school. He ended with:

> But would you give me some rough idea of your own
> plans - when do you intend to come back? Even if
> you stay another two months you would have to be
> thinking of booking a passage now and it would be
> of real use to me to have some idea. Please don't
> scream at me when you write. Just give me some
> simple outline of things, and please tell me where
> and how I can help. Please give Jane a kiss from
> me.

My mother couldn't give him an idea of her plans as she had none. She knew she wanted to come home one day and that was as far as she had thought. She found herself a small cleaning job but, when offered a temporary job selling catalogues for the big Picasso exhibition at the Tate Gallery, she took that on as well. It wasn't long before it all became too much for her. She wrote a distressed letter to my father about it but he didn't receive it. By the time she wrote again she had left both jobs.

Excerpts from my mother's journal:

Saturday 23rd July

My Dear man, tonight I am more in hate than in love, I scarcely know anymore whether I love or hate, I hardly have the energy to push the pen and my heart is as heavy as my poor aching body. Is there no relief for fatigue? My back aches, my heart aches, my legs ache, my eyes sore with crying and my head swims with bitterness. Tonight coming home from your house I got on a bus hoping that the bus would crash in its journey and end my thoughts, my love, my heart aches for all time. It is not reasonable to love you so, it is not profitable and I fear it will kill me sooner or later as I feel so completely worn out and helpless. I so want to fight with you. I am in a fury, a passion, a rage of love and hate that burns and burns and I feel I must either destroy myself or make you pay.

Tomorrow you are to have another birthday. I remember so well your birthday last year when you came so full of love for me in the middle of the night. God, how can I forget these things that have happened between us. If only I could recover myself and end it all before my heart breaks, but I am in a terrible state of fatigue with these two jobs going. Really working nine hours a day and then being a mother into the bargain. I am fed up with being a mother and hope to goodness I can keep my balance. I must give up one of my jobs soon as I shall go nutty if I do not get a rest. I should love to go out into the country. If only I could just lie amongst some flowers and regain my composure. But I am so heartbroken. I am not sure what you are feeling but I feel you are too careless and a little afraid, you didn't turn up at the Picasso show on Friday. O.K, it was a terrible storm but I would have gone through a storm for you, My Darling. In four more days you will be heading for Italy and then I shan't see you for six weeks. In my pure heart I want you to enjoy yourself but I am furious that you care so little about assuring me. Darling, if only you knew how tired and sad I am, I dare not tell you, I dare not worry you, yet I am in a rage. I will see you tomorrow night. I love you too much. What now?

<hr />

In the next entry my mother uses the word "slut" which has changed its meaning over time. Then it was commonly used to describe a woman who is lazy and slovenly. At the time, Yvonne was probably working part-time in a local solicitor's office, a job she got not long after the family found a house to rent in Highgate six months earlier. At home she provided food and hospitality to an increasing number of visitors as well as helping Arthur with the more mundane tasks needed to further his career such as letter-writing, bookkeeping and organising paintings for exhibitions. The youngest of their children, Lucy-Ellen, was only two. Polly was thirteen and Jamie eleven. Yet with such a lot going on in her own life, Yvonne was still willing to help my mother by sometimes adding me to their crowded household while my mother was at work. If some of Yvonne's wages went towards hiring some domestic help it would have been money well spent.

Wednesday 27th July

Tonight there are many tears. It is more than I can bear, you expect too much of me. I am cross and full of hatred. If only you would be more gentle with me. Does it not enter your head that I need you sometimes just as moral support? Why do I write? Why do I go on? You have all the power. It is I who is too much in love. But the hatred of the situation causes me the most awful pain and sorrow. I just feel furious as you are so careless. You know I am sad yet you always break promises. You said you would come before you went to Italy. Now in twenty four hours you will be gone and I will not see you for six weeks or more.

I am so bitter, so sharp and tight and furious. I hate your filthy slut of a wife. How dare she let you go on that picnic without ironing your shirt? How dare she? It is more than I could bear. I, who would wash your feet, I, who would devote my life to your comfort. My tears are so full of hatred for her and for you because you are so tolerant of the lazy creature. She has a girl to do all her work. She is a stupid, lazy, good-for-nothing slut and I hate her. One day I will have the strength to tell her what I think of her and I hope it chokes her.

My Darling one, I am so sad, so sorry, I love you so terribly and cannot bear the thought of another man in my life. But you should not leave me to suffer for so long alone. Please, please drive carefully. I looked at your car tonight and prayed and hoped it will get you back safely. I wish you a happy holiday in my pure heart but I do feel you could have made some attempt to come and wish me some peace. I am furious with your weakness in regards these matters. You do so hurt me so often. Yet you say you love me well. I wonder sometimes. I am sorry. I do not care what anybody thinks, I only know that I love you and am proud of it. Proud to have been your Darling Mistress for so long, in such happiness as we have had together. But why, why have you been so careless these last two weeks? Your exhibition is hardly a good enough excuse when you are going out of London for six weeks. My Darling. I am still crying, crying, crying. I love you. My God I do love you so badly. I hate the fact. I hate being so imprisoned with this only love. Why am I not more in control? How will it end?

⌘

The next day my mother was in a much better mood after finding out that Arthur had dropped by several times when she wasn't home. Ironically, it was Yvonne who came to say goodbye before the family left for Italy. My mother writes that she wasn't at all encouraging when Yvonne suggested the visit but said they parted like old friends, "the falsehood lying heavily and mutually between us." Although my mother and Yvonne weren't particularly close, it seems unlikely Yvonne was aware of any falsehood between them.

Tuesday, 2nd August

Dear lovely, sad treasure, I feel gently, quietly, sweetly towards you tonight. I love you so truly. It is even easier when you are not here to understand my feeling, as it is not so much that I want or need you, but that I love you and love you I do. I hope you will drive carefully. I hope you are enjoying yourself and feasting your eyes and soul on all the beautiful things of the Continent, things that are so remote from our Australian background. I wish I were with you. I will never be with you and so best I adjust myself.

I am happy for you. I am proud of you and sure that you are truly a great man and feel ashamed to think of the many, many times I have troubled you with my ordinary female feelings that flare into anger and dissatisfaction of my lot and fear my lack of power over your extraordinary, unmovable barrier that rises many times to irk me. All this makes me ashamed now that you are so far away from me again. I know you left with gentle thoughts of me in your head and I feel ungracious to have performed like a schoolgirl because I felt hurt at what I thought was careless behaviour on your part. But Darling I know you forgive me my little tantrums and I know that when you call me a peach in public that you really are saying that you love me well, but it irritates me at the time as I feel that our love is a little more poetic than that of a man and a "Peach". Yet your words are not your heart, I know well.

You never like using words and I should know that your heart is expressed in your beautiful paintings and your beautiful loving. Why should I expect beautiful words too? Sometimes I look at your sensual, romantic half-caste bride and I see she has certainly got my hair. When I see those hands caught in that hair, I know that they are your hands in my hair. I can feel it, I know I am the bride and what more beautiful compliment can a woman want. Why do I react when you call me a peach? Is not a peach a warm and beautiful thing? If it is that I am a peach to you then I am glad and proud to be your peach and I am ashamed that I thought myself anything else. I am flattered really and there is no excuse for my annoyance. Your peach is still warm and pink and awaiting your return and love. It is a pleasure to serve you, I would do anything for you. A peach by any other name.

But nonsense aside. Your show is roaring with success and you have won great acclaim and I feel proud of you. Dear one, I love your painting and I love you. You should have made a bit of money now. If only it is enough for you to stay in London longer. I have

had a terrible row with that egocentric old bore, Bert Tucker, he is
eaten up with jealousy and feels very cheated. I don't like him or
what he says about your painting so I'm afraid I quarrelled with
him. You will be cross with me but I cannot sit on the fence as you
do. I have to react with words. I love words. I am thinking of you.
Drive carefully my Dearest. I love you so tenderly.

❧

Wednesday

Dear Sweetheart, If only I could post these words on to you, if only
it was something I have the right to write. I love you dearly and
as I know you are far away there is no point in standing at the
window and sending my darling thoughts into the balmy midnight
air as I usually do, knowing that you will probably be thinking
and picking up my love like the marvellous human love radar.
But you are a long way away on the exciting continent and have
probably forgotten to dream of me, with so many other beautiful
surroundings. These London nights are so very magical that I feel
it is a great cheat that we are not in each other's arms where our
hearts could be at peace.

❧

Almost a month after his last letter my father wrote again asking
about my school and whether we intend coming home soon. He also
offered to send extra money so we could do a quick trip to Scotland
or Paris. A week later, after receiving some drawings from me that
included a note from my mother indicating she had sent a couple of
letters, he wrote to tell her he hadn't received them.

In the next letter my mother talked of visiting her father's relatives in Cambridge. My grandfather had left the UK as a young man,
never to return. He was training for the Christian ministry at Ridley
Anglican College in Cambridge when he "converted" to Atheism
after reading Rationalist material. Much to the horror of his family, he turned his back on religion and sailed to Australia where he
became head of the Melbourne branch of the Rationalists. It was in

this organisation that he met and married my grandmother. Apart from a few letters to one of his sisters, he had no further contact with his family in England.

42 Belsize Square London NW3

Dear John, It is to me, quite incredible that you say you haven't had a letter since Jane started school. What evil force exists between you and I, that always there is trouble. It was to me, just fantastic that you never ever answered my last letter and every night when I struggled home so weary and ill and still no letter from you and I felt my heart burn with hatred that you would use me so ill. I do not know, you say you haven't had a letter, well where do they go? Do you tell me the truth? It is a great puzzle that even thousands of miles apart and nothing is easy between us. Anyhow, you must see Bobby and know that nobody has had a letter except Sun.

Anyhow I have had the worst six weeks of my life and am now in a state of complete collapse. I told you in that letter long ago about Jane starting school and the difficulties that would occur during six weeks school holidays while I was working. Unfortunately things have been most difficult, as I got sick. Jane is still on holidays, and I had to take two weeks off from my job. I was supposed to go back on Monday but I still couldn't do anything with Jane. I will have to find a nursery school next week. It is not easy and I am very tired. I love London very much and so does Jane. I have done everything in my power to make Jane happy and happy she is. She just adores everything. She loves being here and gets along famously.

I tackled too much and now I am paying for it. I got myself a job doing housework in the mornings. I never seem to learn that in fact I am not strong enough for this sort of work. I had only been started a week when somebody offered me a job selling catalogues at the Picasso exhibition at The Tate Gallery for the Arts Council. As the Picasso job was only for eight weeks I thought I'd tackle both as to make some capital. It didn't work out and I have paid for my foolishness in pain. I had to take Jane to school, then do my housework job, rush back home and change into city clothes, rush down to the Tate Gallery by one o'clock, work until seven at night. Rush back to my friend Eva who had collected Jane from school and then take Jane home and think about food. Like a fool I worked very hard and well at the Picasso and so they put me on with the permanent girls selling tickets which is awfully strenuous. They asked me if I was used to handling money, so always eager to please, I said yes. Forgetting that I was only used to Australian money. They put me on a desk with a queue larger than I have ever seen in my life. Did I secretly panic, I couldn't as then tell the difference between their two shillings piece and their two and sixpence piece. I nearly went mad but my God I never knew I had such a good brain. It works most beautifully on figures. Anyhow I've been on tickets ever since and everyone says I'm extremely quick witted but God it just wrecked me.

But this was not so bad. When Jane broke up for her holidays I had to take her every day to somebody, sometimes Eva (my German friend from the ship), sometimes Yvonne who lives two bus rides away, even Barry Humphries had her for one day. I would collapse every night too tired to even wash my stockings. This was just wearing me out until something awful happened to my legs. Similar sort of pain as I have had before but in extreme. Such agony I couldn't stand. My housework job consisted largely of polishing floors on my knees and cleaning stairs (three flights). I think it was the being on my knees for two or three hours at a stretch, I have to admit I've never been on my knees before in my life. Doctor said it was Panniculitis. I doubt this myself and have seen another Doctor in the same clinic who says Neuritis. Anyhow all their magic pills have done no good at all so now they are a bit worried.

I myself think it is just exhaustion playing havoc on my old weaknesses. Yesterday I had to have a blood test, this seems to remind them of some condition they recognise, as they keep asking me whether I have too many aspirins or whether I drink too much alcohol. I haven't had an aspirin in six years and here nobody drinks much and I am lucky if I get a glass of beer a week. Anyhow it has been an absolute murder to my stay in London and I have had a great struggle to keep myself going. I have now had two weeks off work and five days in the country with my new Aunt, but it has made no difference to the pain and I am like an old woman, so you can be glad you have got rid of me. I can only get up one flight of stairs and even with my feet up I am still in pain. It is hard to take but knowing myself, I would think it nothing serious. I would think it just some sort of collapse from exhaustion, as I really am pretty well worn out. The fact remains I have bitten off more than I can chew. I only hope to goodness that I can recover myself.

Jane goes back to school in another two or three weeks, when I am able to get around easier I shall just have to find a cheaper room. This area is charming but too expensive. I didn't want Jane to get a bad English accent as I find them most unpleasant to listen to. All this is why I was so hurt when you never answered my letter saying my legs were very bad. You alone know the difficulties and you alone know how badly I become affected. If you remember how you had to rub my legs in the old days. I couldn't see how you just ignored me now when I am suffering so much. Yet now it is too bad as I couldn't bear a feather to touch my legs and they are completely insensitive to hot or cold yet so sensitive to touch. Very odd. I think it is not rheumatic as I don't mind the cold. Most odd. Anyhow it just must pass and I am sure it is just an exhaustion condition. The trouble is that when I feel so badly I get depressed and I feel great hatred because life always seems such a struggle and the person who seems to me to be responsible for years of bloody misery just because he is an awful fool.

Unfortunately my mind is a bit affected and my memory is confused and I see so many memories going too far back for reality and I find myself crying over things that are long since gone and buried. In fact I am furious that you have made such a mess as I loved you once very dearly yet you have all my marriage treated me so cruelly and now I feel as if I am not long to be young. I am now old and my life is still a tiring, trying existence. You have blocked my heart off at every move which is convincing to me that peace was not what you wanted. The only reason I am writing all this is because that letter that arrived this morning although it says you are not well, at least you are kindly for the first time in years. At least you say something for the first time to show you care that I have some good time out of my trip. Unfortunately as is always, that would be enough money to go to Paris if there was only me but it is impossible with a child. It really is just like paying twice for everything. I could manage so much without Jane but I feel it is too difficult. It costs me three pounds in rail fares every time I go to Cambridge which is only 60 miles away. So thank you for your kind offer. I would dearly like to accept but it is too difficult.

But you ask, am I coming home soon? I have no money in the bank now. I am ill and tired and I was most unhappy in Melbourne. I quite frankly don't care one way or another at the moment. The thing that most affects my answer is the fact that I couldn't face a ship. I haven't as yet recovered from the trip over here. Prison for all those weeks. I do not know. I love London and the English people. If I bring Jane home it will be with the plan to come back here by myself. I am lonely here and I was lonely there. But here I love the people. If you are sensible you will not push me because I am tempted to send Jane home by herself. I feel too old to cope any more unless I can feel well.

Do not fear I have always perfect movement in my joints. I am not crippled in the joints I just have pain as if someone keeps striking me with a mallet. But I can tell by the lack of concentration of my brain that I am badly run down somewhere and so I shall recover as I always do. It is filthy bad luck and has spoilt my holiday. Yet here I am, telling you. You would have once again been so cruel to me had I been with you. You would have nagged and nagged and made my illness Hell on earth as even simple

pregnancy was for me. But why do I waste words. I care little
these days one way or another. I am tired, made tired by pain and
exhaustion.

It is a great pity as this is a beautiful city and a world of the
past that is lovely indeed. There is so much to see and think about
and I was happy and I loved the Tate Gallery with all the Picassos
and the Constables and Turners etc. I find it a cruel blow to feel
so frail. But I'm sure it doesn't matter and soon I shall feel grand
again. Jane is marvellous. All her English cousins have treated her
like a fairy. My Aunt's husband thinks Jane is the prettiest thing
and treats her like a Princess. I have a girl cousin my own age but
she is not very cultured or intelligent and it is hard for me. My
Aunt is so happy as she sits and tells me tales of their childhood.
She was Dad's special pal and loved him dearly. You should see
the thatched house they all lived in. Large and pretty with flowers
and herbs. The whole of Cambridge is full of thatched roofs etc. It
is glorious. Rather funny, my grandfather looked just like Bob. I
have been given Dad's photos and his bible and a set of Volumes of
the History of the English people presented to Dad as a student for
being the best student in the whole of Cambridgeshire presented by
the King. The family treat these books as if they were made of gold.
These folk are so full of God that I think may regard Atheism and
Communism as some form of sickness of the mind.

It's unlikely my father would have been unduly worried about the
cause of the pain my mother described. He had heard it all before. In
a letter to Sunday Reed dated May 1949, he wrote:

> But in the main, Jean's doctor, as both doctors
> I have had her to, say the pain is largely
> hysterical, that she echoes the pattern of her
> mother who excused all her own failures by vague
> and persistent illnesses.

> The doctor says not to give her any sympathy but
> this of course is difficult. I tend to say, when
> she is in pain, well, accept it, take a Veganin,
> relax by a radiator, and try to take care of the

general organisation of her life and activity
separately. Try to see when she is well, she is
organised, but it is difficult as Jeannie is not a
good organiser. She dreams a lot, and I, of course,
do not dream enough.

Later in this book there is a letter my mother wrote in 1961 in
which she complains to my father that he didn't fulfil his role as
"master" within their marriage. By discussing my mother's "hysteria"
with my father, the doctor is just reflecting the prevailing attitudes
to marriage.

❧

Excerpts from my mother's journal:

24th August

*How this month has flown, has dragged. God knows my body feels
as if it has been through Hell and back, yet my heart says is it really
a month since your birthday? This means you will be back soon.
God, I have had a hell of a six weeks, I must say. I have been so
ill, so tired, so absolutely collapsed. My legs, my beautiful legs that
you love so much, have pained and pained and I can only feel like
a little old woman. Where has my gay love of London gone? I am
tired, tired. The doctor says I am suffering a delayed exhaustion
state, after so much of a struggle of mental and physical hardships.
My God, it has been hard too. I so want to stay in my pretty blue
room but the price is almost crippling me.*

*I sat for two hours on the last day of your exhibition. I was
calm and saw so clearly just how beautiful and moving it all is. It
stirs me to great love and I am more than proud to be part of it.
That new painting with the bride leaning between the bridegroom's
knees is so full of the most romantic loving between male and
female and the glorious white fuzz of the bride's dress and Hell,
everything when I look at it, it is just like being in your arms. It
woes and wins me. I wish I could have been the one to buy it. It
is really my painting. Even though I think the greatest one is the
"Waiting for the Bride to grow up", the other is the most romantic.*

My limbs go to jelly and my knees shake just as they did not two months ago when we were alone in my little blue room and so in love, so stirred, so deep, so rich in passion. How can a painting move me just as you do? But it is so. You paint just as you make love, so sensitive, so romantic, so masculine and loving. God, you are Heaven for me. I must get well and pretty again for your return, for somehow I know you are wanting me badly. Dear love, I wish I could cope, but I am so worn out with anxiety and worry. I am not capable of dealing with so many worries.

The school holidays have just about been my end. Jane is a good child but the burden of rearing her alone and the mad letters from her mad father ... I am lonely for intelligence. My conversations are with fools and there is no music in my life. I must hear some beautiful music. I am starved for music. I am locked up here night after night with nothing to think about except either money worries or love worries. My love worries are that I love you too much. You will be home soon. I hope you are well, I know I am in your heart. I can feel it.

Despite the doctor's harsh advice so many years ago, my father remained sympathetic towards my mother's episodes of pain.

∞

Letter from my father:

Wednesday August 24

Dear Jeannie,

Your long letter was in the Office when I arrived
this afternoon, thank goodness. Now what should
I say? I had no idea of your long, sad story.
All I had heard suggested was that you were
busy and presumably happy and well. True, I had
heard only little bits from Bob, but never the
slightest suggestion of what is apparently your
real position. Do you know this is the first real
glimpse I have had of your life in London since
the letter from the Overseas Visitors Club, and
what a glimpse. Do not blame me too much for not
knowing. How could I? Of course you believed that I

did and I don't blame you for crying at my apparent
cruelty. But that letter never came and do not use
the Herald address again. But what can I do, can
I send my love even if it is only on a typewriter
and I say that in all friendliness and without any
trace of bitterness.

Next Monday I will send you 20 pound English again
and I wish it could be more, but it is not easy
this end, as that costs me nearly 26 pounds. I have
read and re-read the part of your letter devoted
to your pains and I wonder what on earth you can
do. Please believe me that I will do everything I
can to help. You will surely have to abandon the
housecleaning job once and for all, and let me know
how that affects your money position.

Now could I beg you to try to believe that I am
not constantly fighting or trying to be cruel.
Much of your letter makes me terribly sad, because
the letter itself is so terribly sad, and a quite
important part of it seems to me to be the kind of
misunderstanding one finds in the tragic theatre.
When in my last letter but one I mentioned that I
had not heard from you since Jane started school,
you imagined that I was chiding you for that. But
I wasn't, not at all, I just wanted terribly much
to hear, and said so. After all, I had not written
myself for many weeks because, as I said, I have
been very sad and despairing. That at the moment
is just about the last thing I wish to talk about.
Please let it pass without comment. But after
getting your letter today I felt ashamed of my
request to you yesterday to write gently. Now could
we leave all that.

I cannot write as I should tonight because this
is done in the greatest haste to cover my letter
of yesterday, and today I thought of sending you a
cable just to stop you worrying for 24 hours about
me not getting your last letter. But please try to
relax and not to worry and to believe, if you can,
that if I were in London I would not be nagging
you, but doing all I could to help.

I must finish this. I am in the office and have
a concert. I am working very, very badly and it
has been the most difficult and the most hopeless
season since I began. Now I have just about given
up the struggle and Melbourne music can go stuff
itself so far as I am concerned and I am sure that
the feeling is mutual. However, we had the most
marvellous Russian cellist Rostropovich, a week
ago, and everyone woke up, even me. Today has been
warm enough to work in the garden without a shirt.
I will write again before the end of this week so
that you should get it on Monday or Tuesday at the
latest. Please do not feel completely alone and I
send my love - please do not reject it out of hand.
John

❧

Excerpt from my mother's journal:

4th September

*It is nearly two weeks since I wrote in my little book. Tonight is a
full moon, a beautiful full moon which takes my thoughts back a
long way to your last full moon in Melbourne nearly a year ago,
when we stood so closely together on Mentone beach and gazed
lovingly at it. I am sad yet happy tonight. It is one of those moving,
balmy nights when tears linger behind eyes and thoughts melt
into sighs. You are in my heart so fully tonight that I feel sure you
are back in England. I long to see you and feel we love each other
dearly. Tonight I feel sure of your love and when I lean out of my
window, look onto the pretty square and the trees and the little
sweet church I wonder what magic is in these northern lights.
They certainly are something new to me and I feel frustrated that
I am imprisoned by my child. Tonight we should be wandering on
the Heath, as this surely is the place and time for love. My being
is thrilled somewhere and these nights are not solitary occasions,
there have been so many and they all have an atmosphere and
stillness that I have never experienced in all my outdoor walking
or dreaming even in our land down south. No wonder England*

produced great poets as it is the land for poets. If I stay here I shall
change from being a visual artist to a poet as it is the soul that
moved in Merrie England, not the eye.

Yet tonight I am in love with sweet England and my wild
Australian painter both. I am most glad to be here in spite of the
fact that the Northern climate is already playing havoc with my
bones and I am in great suffering and ill and have been for eight
long weeks. I have given up my jobs and am somehow managing on
three pounds a week. I feel better somehow but I cross my fingers
and hope love will cure me when my Darling crosses my threshold
and carries me to bed once more.

❧

Letter from my father. Alan referred to in this letter is Doctor Alan
Jeffrey who was his psychiatrist as well a friend. Doctor Jeffrey also
treated Yvonne during her breakdown.

Monday. Sept. 5

Dear Jeannie, Last night I spent four hours trying
to write to you and gave up exhausted. This must
be simpler, and the only way I can do that is by
abandoning any attempt to write adequately. Can you
understand if I say that your last letter moved me,
and in a loving and sympathetic way? And I assure
you that I await another letter just to learn how
you are and if I can do anything to help. Please
try to believe that and not to interpret anything I
say as springing from a desire to hurt you. Because
over recent months I have become ever increasingly
depressed.

The break-up of our marriage has had its
inevitable consequence, the complete destruction
of my self-confidence, and one of the results of
such destruction is acute depression. At Alan's
suggestion I had a long talk to him about it during
the week and will probably have more in future.
It left me very tired and just as depressed, and
I am neither optimistic nor pessimistic about
the chances of him helping. I will just try. Yet

alongside this I have enough feeling for you, poor girl, who also is tortured, and less justly, by memories of the past, to wish that you did not suffer. You can't believe that of course, but it is true. Now could we leave that. I don't hope for or expect anything from you except patience and no hatred, and I ask you to believe that your last letter made me think of you many, many times with a desire to comfort you, just that and no more.

Anyway, it is important that we should get some idea of what is likely to happen during the next few months. Will you really stay in England during the winter? Everyone tells me it is terribly grim, and I cannot see you making the grade with Jane and all. On the other hand, could you get back even if you wanted to? I have the idea that getting a boat is very difficult. I do not want to put the slightest pressure on you but let me know when you can.

Ever since you left I have never thought of going overseas myself because of all sorts of deep, sad feelings which I could not express briefly. But last Friday I went and saw the editor and told him that I was very worried about my ability to continue next year unless I went abroad this summer. He had no alternative but to believe me and said I should suggest a scheme. This is possible. The paper is unlikely to contribute more than a tiny fraction, if anything, towards my expenses, and the question is whether they will give me three months leave with pay and lend me 400 pounds. Anyway, that I will discover as I go, and for once I will negotiate with the strength that comes from not having something to gain, but from having nothing to lose. I don't really want to go abroad, and so far as happiness is concerned, I would far, far sooner wait for the day when I would meet you and Jane at Port Melbourne, because I feel that one embrace from Jane is a lot closer to the medicine I need, than the diversions of travel.

Please give my love to Jane, I will write to her
later this week and don't tell her but I will make
a record and send it for her birthday.

John

Chapter 7

For Better or Worse: Plans for a Reunion

In September my mother met Daphne, an English woman with a big, friendly personality and a voice to match. Daphne was looking for someone to mind her six-year-old twins after school as she was working full time. They met when my mother applied for the job and Daphne quickly became a good friend as well as an employer. As is the way with children, Mark and Middie (Elizabeth) soon became my best friends. Daphne and the twins lived at 54 Belsize Park Gardens, just around the corner from our flat at 42 Belsize Square.

Jane with the twins, Mark and Elizabeth.

Back in Melbourne my father was busy negotiating the financial arrangements of his trip to Europe, as well as organising a trip to a recording studio, taking several of my friends and cousins to make a small record for my sixth birthday. An added stress was the possibility he may be required to stay in Melbourne to attend court. The ABC had reprinted an article by Charles Mackerras that my father believed defamed him. On my father's behalf, the Herald sent a letter to the ABC demanding an apology in all newspapers within seven days or a writ would be issued. The ABC were refusing to apologise.

During this time my mother wrote two letters to my father which are missing. My father wrote several letters keeping her up to date about his travel plans. His responses suggested neither of her letters was very friendly. He asked her to soften her approach and wrote:

> You have lost none of your power to hurt me, and I
> don't want you to do that, and I don't want to hurt
> you in return.

A letter he wrote on 22nd September started:

> Dear Jeannie, your letter dated Sept. 14 came
> yesterday and saddened me terribly. All day I
> wandered around in a muddle, unable to start
> to think about anything. You really shouldn't
> be so sick and I worry about this more or less
> constantly.

<hr />

My mother was obviously in a better frame of mind the day after writing to my father.

Excerpt from her journal:

15th September

Tonight I sit in my little blue room feeling quite peaceful and resolved at last. Everything is settled now and I think all my decisions are the right ones. I am in much better health and have got myself financially straight with a small job of collecting and minding two extra children, our little playmates, which will enable me to keep my pretty room until Xmas. Then I do not care what will happen. My bloody leg muscles are still in a frightful state and I have been told recovery from muscle fatigue is a slow and dreary business. But my heart is at peace at last after so much confusion and insecurity. I love my Darling so dearly. I want no other. We have now decided not to fight against it ever and I am to remain the sweetest mistress for the rest of my life. Life is perfect now. I know what I want and what makes me happiest in the world. I love so much, my sweet man and I cannot bear another to touch me.

After these last few weeks and the loneliness of my time with my sweet one in Italy and all the parties and people, I know that I belong to one man and there is no point in trying to fight it ever again. My sweet man loves me dearly and things between us are perfect indeed. I am satisfied to live life out on this level for ever. I have tried to find a desire elsewhere and it doesn't work at all. I have two fine admirers and it is cheerful to have such walks and attention and so on from the opposite sex and it means that I can spend time with the Barry Humphries whom I love, without being a solitary woman. Yet all this is fine, and my admirers so admire, that I feel pleased but then that moment always comes sooner or later, the pass is made, the hand is held and the eyes are searched and so on and on and I feel nothing except an embarrassed physical jerk that awakes and becomes frigid immediately the lips come near mine. No, I cannot go away from my heart, my lips can never leave my heart.

❧

Friday 16th September

I am in a dream, I am in love, my life has begun for me all over again. I am in a dream of love, the air is sweet and floats around my head and I walk and talk sweetly to the trees and the flowers and I smile, and even laugh and touch my face, as did my love. I am in love, more than ever before in my life, dream of dreams, I am complete. Oh my Darling sweet one, I have not forgotten you for one second since you left me yesterday and I am so happy, so very happy.

By late September my father's trip had been approved, offering him more than he had dared hope for, five months leave on full pay, fares paid by the Herald Office and even some extra money towards expenses. He planned to spend a few weeks reviewing in New York before flying to London to spend Christmas with us. Then he would buy a car to take us exploring in England before flying to Europe on his own to see as many concerts as possible. Later he would return to collect the car and take my mother with him back to Europe. There was no further talk of a court-case.

My birthday record had been made and was on its way to London, along with 25 pounds Sterling to pay for a party and to help buy some new clothes for my mother and me. So on a grey autumn day in early October, magic happened in London as a flat black disc spun around on a friend's turntable and sunny Australian voices filled the room. I remember my father hamming it up in a deep, resonant voice as he introduced in turn each nervous child while the others giggled in the background. My cousin Russell started tentatively with, "Hello Janie", followed, after an embarrassed pause, by "How's ya dollies?"

In this journal entry my mother's propensity for melodrama is evident. At the end of a small party at the Boyd's house Brian O'Shaughnessy insisted on driving home the remaining three guests, including my mother. She saw a conspiracy to keep her from being alone with Arthur despite the fact that no-one else knew of the affair and Arthur had already disappeared, as he had a tendency to do when the mood took him. There are a couple of clues in this entry that suggest a less dramatic reason Arthur didn't drive her home that night. Towards the end of the party he may well have been feeling too drunk and unwell to do anything other than go to bed.

1st October.

Oh my Dear little book, a more tragic mistress could not be. My dear little one, if only you could wrap your arms around me and lull me to sleep. My heart, my poor tired heart, God have Mercy on me. I am but too sad, Dear little book, give me some peace, give me some peace that I might fall asleep relieved of my sorrow. I dread to live out the moment, the moment of now. I am worn and spent and weary of life. Dearest little book offer me but a wee comfort and allow that I should face the future.

How dare that so called friend of yours sweep me off on your wife's command. My Darling, something went wrong tonight. Suddenly I saw your wife look at us as if she had suddenly seen a great ghost. You were rather drunk and you kept filling my glass and talking to me separately from everyone but you have always done this. You let slip about my room rather badly but I'm sure nobody heard you. Yet your wife suddenly looked at you with unguarded eyes. Oh my God, my Darling, I am sure she guesses something, but what? What?

You said you had been sick these two weeks. My Dear, if only you knew how I worried when you said that, I could not bear for you to be ill. Darling one. I love you. How you love me in return. I could feel you in the room all night. You want so much to touch me, Darling, I know. You sweet beautiful man. I am anxious for you. What Hell on earth awaited you when you came back for me and found not me, the house empty? All your guests suddenly whisked away as if by magic as the force suddenly set to get me out of your way. Darling, the speed with which we were ushered out, to get us out before you returned, as if we were lepers. The Humphries looked astounded, they couldn't understand, they just couldn't understand, they seemed so young and so puzzled as they were ushered into Brian's car as Brian announced like a Parson, that he was taking Jean home and that was that.

I am so frightened, is it all out, is it all over? I so wanted to be with you, I so wanted to hold your darling hand and kiss your sweetness. My Dearest soul, what now? What now? Is it all over? What odds are we up against? Your wife, curse her madness, is on to us and I fear we are lost to each other. My Dear, dear heart, I *love you, I love you, I love you. Why did I go today? Why did she ask me? Hell, Hell, Hell, I am anxious about you, what now, what now, what can we do? Will I ever see you again? What can I do? I want you so badly, I would fight wild horses to be close enough to touch your hand, yet your mad wife is your mad wife and I do not know how to cope. What will she do?*

Dear, dear sweet love, be at peace. I love you so tenderly, I sometimes feel you are not bold enough but I suppose you know what you are doing. If it were me I would go straight around there and tell them all to go to buggery. But I am wild and in love so desperately. I hate your wife tonight. What does it matter to her? What does it matter, she doesn't love you. I wonder what has happened. I am sorry. I hope it is not serious for you. I have stopped crying now. My little book is good for me and soothes me. What have you tonight? You have no little book. Poor Darling one, you so wanted to hold my hand, didn't you, sweetness.

There is a lot to be said for love. We are so in love. Could we but have had a moment together today. What a mess of a party it was. Ye Gods. I hate them all. No, that is not so, I am very, very fond of Rosalind Humphries, and I think our Barry is a genius and I love him madly. They were so puzzled and looked so innocently at you when you kept reappearing and demanding that you, and you alone, were driving Jeannie home. Dearest one, it was too much, but something else happened before that, something made Yvonne's eyes pop. Darling, has someone told her? How did she know we have seen each other? Sweet, sweet treasure. I fear that your life may be made difficult, more difficult, I am sorry. I am sad. I love you. I could hardly bear to be so close to you for so long without stroking your darling head.

Sweetness. I let my hair flow on purpose as I know I look so like your half-caste bride. A fine old monument. Darling, you love my hair don't you? I could see you loving my hair. Was it naughty of me to come to your party with my hair flowing like the bride? Every curl of mine has been painted, hasn't it. It is so obvious my hair you paint these days. Dearest one. I love you, you love me. How dare these people interrupt. How dare even your wife interfere. She is a cold, ungiving frog of a woman, how dare she care if you want some warmth out of life. Sweetest, sweetest. I am your bride for every year of my life but I won't always look so nice. My hair can't go on falling in golden bride ringlets. One day it will be old and grey and my face will be dark and tired.

Sweetness, what can I say. If only I could fall into your arms. Why don't you just come? One of your paintings is worth all their lives put together. If you love me and I make you paint beautiful love paintings like the bride series, how can they dare to interfere if you love me. I know you do. Paint some more love paintings. Paint some more love. Paint, paint, paint. If you need love then I will give it. I love you with all my heart forever more. Forever more. Sweetest.

❧

Monday 10th October

One never knows whether an eruption is the end of a chapter or the beginning of a new one. I am in love tonight, as if it is a magic new beginning of a new chapter. I am so in love and, thank God, the players are the same. Life goes on, my sweet, sweet treasure, how happy I am. Tired and rather remote, but happy. Last week I thought all was over and when you never came to see me and the week passed on, I began to fear that my thoughts were real and true and indeed our affair had been cut off in its prime by the tragic sorrows of your poor mad wife. Yet it seems you did come to see me but lady luck was not with us as each time I was out or had visitors.

In front of the little church opposite our flat was a small square. In daylight hours the church looked welcoming, and in the warmer months the square offered a pleasant place to sit. But at night, when streetlights barely penetrated the gloomy shadows, it was a perfect place to avoid being seen. It was also a good vantage point to see inside our flat if the lights were on. To avoid Arthur having an embarrassing encounter with any mutual friend, my mother left the curtains open if she had a visitor in the evening. Presumably in an attempt to prove that he had come to see her one night, Arthur accurately described where one visitor had sat.

Later in this journal entry, my mother muses on having Arthur and Yvonne at my birthday party.

> How pretty and gay it all was, it cost me more money than I could afford but it was worth it just to see you there and your three children. I am so fond of your children. It is a mad state of affairs, us all being so poor, here am I, wanting more children, loving my own one Sinclair child and loving your half Yvonne children, I enjoy them all so. Yet you are terrified I will become pregnant. How I would like it, but I would never do that to you unless you agreed to it. Poor Darling, you have so much already to worry about, yet I feel sad to have to stop our sweet love from adding yet another little being to our old world. How nice a little half you half me baby would be. It is because I love you so very much. Our loving seems so perfect and life is so ripe when we are together that I feel it should produce something. Yet I know it produces great and beautiful things in paint and that should satisfy me, should it not?
>
> Today was lovely. How wet and grey the day was, yet how happy we were. How shy I am always when you first arrive. It is that strange naughty feeling that we both know the visit is for one purpose, we both know and we both are trembling with passion for each other long before we even see each other. I could melt with love for you hours before you arrived, just because when I think of you coming I just go weak in the knees. When I looked out the window just as you stepped into the entrance and looked up at me, I felt shy and blushing like a schoolgirl about to meet her sweetheart. Our sweet secret meetings, and after all this time we are still so much in love. You say the same things, that you are nearly ill with anticipation of our loving.
>
> Was ever love more sweet, each loving seems more wonderful

than the last, can it go on and on like this? Today you were the most perfect lover, sweet beautiful man. I love you more and more and even more. We seem as if we could never unfold, and even long after love, t'was impossible to move without falling once again into each other, like two crazy unbalanced objects that could not direct movements away from each other. When you touch me after love, is even more beautiful sometimes, as one has a feeling of such perfection of physical harmony and love, pure beautiful love. The touch of a man who loves beyond passion. Darling, darling sweetheart, if one could only retain the sweetness of our nearness, one could go on smiling for the rest of one's days.

When we parted it seemed unreal, I just wanted to drift away from you into the crowded Swiss Cottage world of shoppers and buses and so I did, and you came back as I stood at the crossing and you just touched me and smiled and I think it is so that you love me. Dear painting man of my heart, you are true to love, I am true to you. I want no other. If I could but dream of having you always to come floating with love and passion into my world I would be more than happy. But we can live it out for now. Let us have it while we may and let it sort itself out. Such sweet love. You darling man. I want none other. Could you ever love another? Today was so sweet. I can still feel your arms about me. Sleep with my vision, as I shall sleep with yours. Goodnight.

⤞⤝

Although my parents rejected a lot of the social mores of their era, there was one expectation that neither challenged – that a husband should always support his wife and children. Of course, usually the other side of the bargain was that a wife should fulfil her role as a housewife and "love, honour and obey" her husband. Neither parent subscribed to that part of the deal. My mother preferred not to think about money unless it was absolutely necessary. So the regular amount my father sent was accepted by her as a natural part of the scheme of things, not worthy of gratitude. Even so, I am surprised there is no mention of the extra 25 pounds my father sent for my birthday party in either my mother's letters or her journal.

Tues. 11th October

It is the morning and it is not usual for me to touch this little book at such an early hour but I am carried on such a gentle wing of love as I sit with my little cup of coffee in the sunshine. My nearness to you, my dearness to you, my complete love for you, finds me today so glad, so terribly glad with warm human satisfaction and tenderness. I sip my coffee out of the cup you had for your tea, I look at the chair you sat in, and I have just eaten the delicious continental bun I bought especially for you, and in my muddlely melting way, so warm and full of love and glory, I forgot all about it. See, you shouldn't love me so well, it made me forget to offer you food. It is true, dearest heart, I do so want you to tell me what to do, tell me, boss me, let me sublimate my personality into your marvellous one. I just want to exist for you alone, so completely, you don't really mind do you? My love, my dear, dear love, how lucky I am that you love me too. How tenderly, how sweetly you touch me, how passionately you love me, My Darling one. I am glad to be alive this morning. You are here with me in my heart. My life is not always so good.

⸙

Excerpt from my mother's journal:

Tuesday night

Twice I write in my little book in one day. How sweetly my little book brings me relief from all the joys and sorrows. Tonight I have had such a wonderful time that I must record it somewhere, and where better than my book. My second concert in London. Heaven-sent music, beautifully performed, has left my heart even richer than it was this morning. I went by myself. A perfect companion, I must in future go to concerts by myself. No interference, no embarrassment, just me and the most marvellous music.

Classical music was one area of deep understanding between my parents. After my father's death, my mother told me many times how much she missed being able to talk with him about the music they both loved so passionately. Yet for many years before his death, she vehemently refused to talk to him at all. Over the decades my parents made several more attempts to live together as man and wife, but each reconciliation brought with it more pain, resentment and anger ready to boil over at the slightest mishap. Any sensible person would be mystified as to why they kept trying. The romantically inclined may call it love, the world of psychiatry may have a different interpretation.

∽

Letter from my father:

Tuesday October 11, 1960

Dear Jeannie,

Your letter, the second part of which was dated October 6, came this morning, and sad to tell it was all worries and no fun. Not a word about Jane's birthday, or the record, or the fact that I sent you 25 pounds English - and I was just bursting to hear some cheerful news. That no doubt will come in another letter perhaps before you even get this, but today I felt rather burdened down with worries and as a result I felt very disappointed. Anyway I don't want to complain, and the real trouble is that I am worried about all sorts of problems involved with me leaving here.

Firstly the few points in the earlier part of your letter. Don't bother to think about advising me regarding clothes etc. because the point is I am buying virtually nothing here and if I buy a new overcoat it will be done in London. The simple fact of flying means that I can bring very little beyond a spare suit and a dinner suit, which is of course required in all European opera houses. I will of course, bring my velvet jacket if I can, but would prefer to buy a new one in London. That thought might well be abandoned now as too expensive.

But you are a funny thing, at least you have funny

ideas about my attitude to clothes and clothing
conventions. The reason I so seldom wore my velvet
jacket is not that I thought it was too arty and
improper but simply because it is not really
comfortable. It looks comfortable but it isn't.
It is a question of tailoring, of having made the
joins and so on, very thick and padding everything.
Such a jacket as Dorian has for instance, is just
what I want and when you put it on you can scarcely
feel it. Mine feels like a horse rug.

I don't quite understand your comment on no airport
at Tahiti because here they quote prices on the
trip via Tahiti instead of via Honolulu. Anyway I
will check.

It is almost humorous the way my father tries to avoid directly contradicting my mother. Maybe it was because he knew there was an argument brewing that had nothing to do with whether or not Tahiti had an airport. He needed to find someone to collect and bank the rent from Rose Cottage as well as deal with any unforeseen problems while he was overseas. His brother in law, Christopher Sidway, had offered and was an obvious choice. The Sidways were respectably middle-class and reliable but in a previous letter [missing] my mother had responded angrily to that suggestion. My father knew he may have no alternative than to accept Chris's offer so the rest of his letter is an attempt to get my mother to understand the difficulties he faced. Rent money from Rose Cottage was essential to cover some of the extra expenses during his trip.

Another delicate subject was that my mother's possessions would have to be cleared out of Rose Cottage before it could be rented. My mother wasn't going to be happy with the idea of my father touching her belongings but there was no alternative. He promised to pack it all up most carefully before putting it in the little storeroom at Rose Cottage and locking it. He ends his letter with:

Anyway let me know if you have any bright ideas
[about who could collect the rent] and, of course,
I cannot wait to hear something of Jane's birthday.
Yours, John

My mother's next letter is missing, but if my father's bewildered response to it is anything to go by, some parts were intense.

Dear Jeannie, why oh why did my last letter distress you? It was not meant to do that, and I tried to make one tiny complaint - that I had no news of the birthday or the record, gently and without ill will. Of course there was an undertone of anxiety, because I was worried about Rose Cottage and you must remember that my letter was in response to a very violent one of yours about the Sidways, which tended to worry me even more, even though I agreed with every word you wrote. Anyway, please try to be patient - to understand, and not to tear me to shreds as unjustly as you did in this letter which came today.

The rest of his letter would have brought my mother much relief. He had arranged for one of her friends to collect the money and her sister, Betty, was to rent half of Rose Cottage. My father went on to give details of his flight to New York, including a 36-hour stopover in Tahiti. He urged my mother to explore every possibility of leaving me in England while they toured Europe and talked of the possibility of them visiting Moscow. At the end of the letter he tells her how glad he was that the record was a success and thanked her for "the lovely details of the sort of party only you could arrange". Obviously my mother's letter contained some lighter moments.

My father basically agreed with my mother that his sister, Lillian Sidway, was bossy and suburban in taste, but he underestimated the intensity of her fear that the Sidways would somehow interfere with Rose Cottage or the tenants. To my knowledge, my mother's in-laws had no idea of her hostility towards them. Despite his dismissive attitude, his sister Lillian was very good to my father, especially in the last years of his life.

⌘

Excerpts from my mother's journal:

18th October

I am in a strange state tonight. Somewhat unreal. Did you really come today? Somehow our relationship seemed vague, although happy and surely most loving and perfectly sweet, but somehow I feel as if I dreamt today. Perhaps it was the fog that began the day and the strange sunlight that filtered into our bodies as we lay in peace. Somehow it was so sure a piece of heaven, so smooth, so calm, so easy. You were quiet afterwards. I was vague and quiet. Actually I rather liked the quietness of both our moods.

It is nice to have you sitting having a nice cup of tea with me after we have proved once again we belong to each other. Yesterday, you were so nice and so naughty. I really thought when we passed each other on the stairs that you would love me there and then, and whenever you come near me to offer me a drink my being tingles with love for you and I know by your face that it is the same for you. Surely I was good yesterday. I kept my attention on the conversation always and never looked at you. After all, I knew you were coming today and I could see no reason for being impatient. When we called at my place yesterday you were wild for me like a crazy man and I felt slightly frightened of you. But in your sweet arms today everything seemed perfect again. I love you Dear one. How long can this go on? You are worried about it. Perhaps I had better go away soon. Goodness knows what will happen.

John, my poor irritable, yet pathetic husband is arriving soon and wanting to take me to the continent. Charlie Blackman arriving to live in your house. Where will it all end? Frankly, tonight I don't care. If you want me to go on being your mistress, then I shall, as I love you very much and find it hard to let you go home to your wife's pillow. I wonder will you really come again on Friday. But I am still vague and somewhere tonight am at peace with the world and find I don't like living very much. I could just sit and stare now. Just let me sit and stare.

❦

Saturday, 22nd October
Tonight I am frightened that maybe I am not only a neurotic lonely female, as when I got a fright when a great loud noise suddenly

burst from the wireless, my heart gave an even worse fright to me as I felt as if indeed I was swaying between life and death and as if my heart is in a frail condition. Is it possible that I am really ill? It is not my good day and I have had a terrible battle with Jane and I am tired and frail and ill but then this feeling as if my heart was not able to continue with such frights in life. It suddenly occurs to me that I may really be ill. I have never considered such things as I have been taught to consider my ailments basically neurotic. I feel strange and fearful! My Darling, what if I should die? I feel so strange, calm and strange. Like someone looking in a window. I know what dying is like because I nearly died once. It is calm and strange. Just like watching someone else. I don't want to die, not tonight. I hope it is that I am neurotic or tired or some such.

I was so happy as you nursed me in your arms yesterday. You used to do that to me at Rose Cottage. Just like a father nursing a babe. You nursed me and I loved you. I feel quite odd. I feel hot and breathless and a bit sick in the tummy. All because I got a fright. I never thought much about my heart. Surely I have a strong heart. This couldn't be. Yet something has happened to my body. Just because I got a fright. Oh My Darling, I love you so, so terribly. If anything happens to me just paint beautiful paintings for ever. I love you terribly much and wish you more happiness than life has given you. Surely I am just neurotic. I wouldn't leave you as Doris did. I am young and in love. Terribly in love, yet I feel so queer as if I just have to be terribly still. I will go to bed. Funny feelings now up the back of my neck. Breathless, tired, queer. Darling, Darling. I don't want to be worn out yet. My life is too hard for me. I am killing myself.

As it turned out the fright wasn't responsible for her feelings of ill-health, nor was it the result of a weak heart. She was coming down with something. Luckily for her, she felt well enough the next morning to walk me to school, because Arthur came to visit that afternoon. Most of their secret liaisons were during my school hours. Luckily for Arthur, he didn't catch my mother's illness.

23rd October

Sweet, sweet. Goodnight. How many more little happy meetings like today will we be allowed? I am sitting now in my little room with a hot water bottle to keep me warm. It is late and I must go to bed now as the hour is late and I am tired. I am tired and happy, a pleasant combination. Our time is running out. I do not care as I feel it will always come back again. You were so sweet to me today. I loved you dearly. Thank you for not putting that awful oil on your hair, you looked so sweet, so terribly sweet, your hair is so grey but I like it grey. I love grey hair and it suits you so. Poor Darling, you are so concerned about your looks. Sweet, sweet face, if only you knew how I loved it. We were happy, so very happy together today. I so love it when you come for tea. So nice to make tea for you and so happy to talk to you, to tell you all the things I feel about life. To talk to you about Dylan Thomas is so wonderful because I know you know and feel what I feel and I then don't feel so lonely. To talk to you about anything. To have you all to myself. You were so nice and loving to me today and so happy because you had finished some work. You are painting again. This is happy for me too as I love to think of you working. I am so happy as you were so thoughtful about me today. Come what may! You love me well. Goodnight.

<hr>

In a letter to my father dated 24 October my mother made several suggestions as to where I could stay while she and my father travelled in Europe. Leaving me with Daphne was one possibility, if my father would pay for a nanny to look after me and the twins while Daphne was at work. Or I could stay at Highgate with the Boyd family, but for some reason my mother thought I wouldn't get enough care there. Her favoured possibility was a small county boarding school. She went on to describe in detail the fright she got when the radio made a loud noise and her "strange and instinctive feeling" that she hadn't long to live. (In fact, as time would tell, she lived another fifty-seven years.) The long letter ended with:

I am either a terrible neurotic or I am ill or tired out or completely exhausted. I do not know. I have been very happy in London and some very good things have happened to me. I can see no reason for my condition. There is but one question we never answered. Could I possibly have caught my father's illness those many long years ago? Not a happy thought. Harry said we were all suspect.* I am ill, John. I know it. Somewhere I am ill. There is no pain. Perhaps I am just a wreck of human emotions, as I have had a great share of both good and bad. But why should I go off the beam now, things are good and I am working well and sure of my talents. My reaction to frights has been becoming increasingly bad over the last five years. Is such a condition an emotional condition or a physical one? For God's sake, when you get here be nice to me and gentle. Look after me, I do not want to die. I must get over this and get on my feet properly. I cannot endure this exhaustion and fatigue. I shall probably be all right in a day or two. Is this any sort of nervous breakdown? How can one breakdown before one is broke? I am frightened. Keep your fingers crossed.

Jean

❧

Letter from my mother to Sunday Reed (the earlier letter to Sunday to which my mother refers is missing):

25th October 1960

---

*   In 1959 my maternal grandfather died of untreated tertiary syphilis in Kew Mental Hospital in Melbourne. By all accounts he was a highly principled man and probably refused life-saving treatment due to a sense of guilt and shame. He contracted the disease later in life, long after the birth of his children, and at the time of his death this was known to all his immediate family. Although my grandparents had an open marriage it would have come as a nasty shock to find he had infected his wife. My grandmother received treatment and survived. Harry Edhouse was studying to become a psychiatrist at the time and was married to my mother's older sister Margaret. I doubt that he would have seen any reason to blame any illness or mental instability in the Langley family on his father-in-law's illness.

Dear Sun, I have had you very much in my mind today as I have spent half the morning in the Bendix shop doing my washing. It's such a mad new way of life. They now have a great new machine which dries for 6 pence extra. I always remember your new Bendix and you doing my washing when Jane was a baby. Anyhow, I've just come home with my laundry all washed. I get a complete Bendix load into that marvellous shoulder bag you gave me. It is impossible to wash sheets any other way and as Jane is still a bedwetter doing the laundry is a great task even with the Bendix shop. Even running this little two-roomed household seems to take too much time. I am still working every afternoon. But I have strayed away from the reason for another letter so soon. I sent you such a mad terrible letter the other night. I was frightened, so I thought I'd better write quickly and say all is well.

Strangely enough I am very happy as I have complete faith in the people I love and this to me is heaven. This I think has been a preoccupation with me since I was a child in a strange way. It is easy to love people as people are so charming or beautiful or clever or entertaining. I love people but I have now found several (at least two) people, I have complete faith in. Yes, I am very happy, I consider myself lucky to have human relationships of quality. Both have lives of their own but what does it matter. The fact that they exist is what matters.

The only regret is that I have spent so little of my life with you, my one true friend in this very sad world full of people who are all struggling against one another. Now that we are so far apart I cannot understand why we saw so little of each other. I hope when I come back to Australia one day to have a little car and spend time in the bush and with you. I always thought of life as a very long, long time. I wonder now whether I will have a very long life. Something seems urgent.

Never let us quarrel. I am through with quarrelling. I just want to be quietly with my friends and the wildflowers. I will try to live out some of my life in the bush. I have had great feelings as if

I want to stand on top of Mt. Dandenong. Arthur says I am just homesick and it will pass soon.

> *Poor Sun, bear with me and forgive me sometimes. I am looking forward to getting out of London for a bit. John says he will take me to Russia if he can. I would like that. I am going to try very, very hard to be patient with John. He has been very, very brave about my honesty. I have stated some pretty hard facts. Did I tell you about the bread I get? Called the Howard loaf. Compost grown, stone ground wholemeal. It is just the best bread I've ever tasted. I wish I could send you some. Sorry Sorry Sorry. Love Love Love*
> *Jean*

It wasn't long before the mystery of my mother's confusing symptoms became obvious.

Thursday

How I would love that you would come to see me tonight as I am sick. Yet it would be bad as you would catch my infection. It seems that in fact I have some real influenza and that I was on the way down last weekend when I felt so queer and awful. Tonight my head is leaden and aching and my chest and back tight and painful as I have a shocking congestion. This is odd for me as I am not a chesty type. I feel so lonely and tired and I will have to go to bed now as I cannot cope. If only I could spend a day in bed but this is not possible. Next week is school holidays. I cannot be bothered with children but what can I do. Soon my husband will be leaving Melbourne. In a month he will be here. What then? How can we be parted? Yet it is to be. We shall have such little time together. Sweet, sweet Darling. I love you so dearly and wish for you so many, many times. I am patient really. We have our precious moments. We do love each other. At least we have love. I wish I was in your arms tonight. I would like to fall asleep close to you. I feel simply awful.

Letter from my father:

Monday October 31 1960

87

Dear, dear Jeannie, Was there ever such a sad letter as your last one. I read it in Rose Cottage garden and once again wanted to rush straight to an aeroplane, and to London. What can I say to help? I look forward to next week with joy, but I regard even Tahiti, and certainly New York, as hindrances, because I want to get to London. Do you not think that I understand? So much of what you write is known to me from my own experience, and when I say that I cannot wait to get to London, it is not to nag or worry you, but to offer you every bit of affection and help I can. Your reaction to frights for instance, I know backwards, and it is inseparably related to emotional tension. I know it so well ... One is perhaps even unconsciously, or partly consciously, anxious or tense, and there is a sudden noise and one goes off like a breaking fiddle string. It is not sickness which does it because when one is sick, one's response is, if anything, more lethargic, but when one is really tense it is not funny, and I understand very, very well. But please try to relax and certainly stop worrying whether you are a neurotic or a hysteric. We all are, surely, in varying degrees, and so what. One does one's best to come to terms with oneself and one's neuroses.

I write badly but I do want to beg you to take life as easily as you can, and please, please try to enjoy yourself and forget. This is not at all as good a letter as I had hoped to write but you must believe me that at present my life is such that it would be comparatively easy to write in a rowing boat in a rough sea. Another week, however, and it will be all over and I will be on my way.

My plane booking from New York to London is for a flight departing from NY at 10 am on Sunday November 27, and arriving at London 7.30 pm the same night - Sunday three weeks! It is too exciting to think about.

My mother was obviously not happy with my father's explanation for her extreme reaction to loud sounds in this letter. Upon re-reading it after his death she wrote across the top, "JEAN INCUBATING MUMPS CAUGHT FROM JANE. STILL SICK WHEN JOHN ARRIVED". But it was influenza she came down with four days later. She came down with mumps four weeks later.

My mother's younger siblings, Betty and Bob, were twins. Both struggled financially; Bob in particular found it hard to find a regular source of income. My mother was very sympathetic and didn't want either of them put under pressure to pay the rent, if they were having difficulties. This was one reason she objected to the Sidways as rent collectors. She worried they might be ruthlessly efficient. My father was caught between my mother's desire to help her unreliable and impecunious relatives and his need for extra money to avoid returning to Australia with considerable debt. He thought he had it worked out, until Betty pulled out of the arrangement seven days before he was due to leave. He tells my mother the latest news in the rest of his letter but asks her not to worry and to trust him to deal with it in a reasonable manner. No doubt it caused him several sleepless nights. There is no further mention of rent or rent collection until after my father's return from overseas.

❧

Entry from my mother's journal:

4th November 1960

So I have been really ill. A whole week in bed, ghastly prison my room has become. How I loathe illness. But I am now coping and improving slowly. Tomorrow I will go out and do the necessary shopping. Now Jane is home again I shall just have to improve.
Life is strange. How funny that my dear one, you have been caring for Jane. It had to happen, there was no one for me to send her to. After all, you have three women in the house to help cope and I was so ill. I just couldn't care for my own child. Now it seems to be clear again.

You came to take her away and I was so pale and ill. I felt sure you would come back to see me within many hours. You were so sweet with your dear little bit of heather for me and you took my hand as you left with your friend and although it was not possible to speak love or caress each other, your hand said to me a million sweet things. But I have waited and waited and lay dreaming of your return in my feverish state of ill health and despair. But you never came and there I was ill and tired and sick of heart.

My soul so torn in its sudden hating of London. Suddenly I want to be out in the wilds of Aussie bush and tramping through the scrub. I hated you in my loneliness, in my anxiety and illness, I loved, wanted and hated you in turn. My feverish nightmare world, no energy, no spirit, just raging loneliness. But the week has passed and I managed to feed myself, to survive, to cope with life again. I seem to be all right but I am weak.

But tonight you both came. How strange a night. I am too outspoken and we two so agree that we always seem to be against the lady. But how irritable she makes me, how crazy she is, what does she think, she does nothing, says nothing and yet expects London to treat her like a celebrity. She is bored to be a wife. What on earth will she do to cheer up her sad ego? She is but a child, she should grow up. The world is marvellous if you ask for nothing. The world is rich and full, to be consumed and loved. But she wants to be admired, but for what?

What a shock you got to find that John arrives in three weeks. Ha, that tricks you, does it not? It tricks me too! Poor John. Poor Darling, poor us! We are doomed! Yet I love you most madly. I love you more than ever. I couldn't look at you tonight. It is so easy for us to fall into each other's arms that I felt we would do so any moment. I feel you all the time. You kept feeling my head and my pulse to see how ill I was. You can't keep your hands off me and I know exactly how that is and what it means. It means we love each other very much. Yet there you are, saddled to a mad fool of a beautiful woman who is so cold and boring and selfish. Poor Darling one.

Monday 7th November

Nearly, I am at the end of this little comforting journal Why do I continue to need this little book to tell my thoughts, feelings and needs to? Goodness knows. Does it matter? Perhaps it helps. One cannot whisper into a pillow all one's life. Last night we whispered into my pillow together. This morning the sun is glorious and shining over me as I sit on my little balcony. The trees in the square are bare now and expose much of the ugliness, so typical of London. I am tired of London and so very anxious to clear out to the sea or someplace where I can be at one with nature. Yes I am weary of the great city. But my Darling the sun is shining, I feel cheerful again, I am well again, thank goodness.

I was so depressed at your party last night and felt we would never rid ourselves of those infuriating people to find ourselves alone. But finally, long after midnight, we fell into each other's arms. Such joy. You loved me so beautifully last night that you have brought life back into my limbs and joy back into my heart. I love you so very much. We need not say these things. I hope you are sitting in the sun this morning. Did I really inspire your last painting, or were you just trying to butter me up, so to speak? Yes, it is worth all my loneliness. I love you, that is all. As you have said, there is no need to stop. Love is all.

Sunday 13th November

If most of my words in this book are sad, desperate, bitter ones, the reason is good. I use the book as a safety valve and mostly write when my life seems desperately futile and unbelievably heavy. It doesn't mean that all my life is spent in this state of mind. Many times, and perhaps most often, I am bright and cheerful and generally constructive, so that I don't even think of my book. London has been too big a burden for me in so many ways, yet I wouldn't have missed it for the world. My love and I are closer than ever and are pledged to love whenever we can. Yes, I should be content. There is no other answer. Yet my heart is not still today. I feel I am more bitter than is fit for one such as me. It is not my natural response to life. My reason tells me to curb my feelings.

Soon my husband with all his neurotic emotions will be here with me, and even though in many ways I fear his first tantrum which is bound to follow on two or three weeks after his arrival, there is good reason to be glad to see him as I am surely at my wits end in need of relief of caring for Jane. Poor child is now sitting in bed with a swollen face wrapped in a blue woollen scarf and destined to be in bed at least another five days, and then home from school another two weeks, as she has mumps. Cheerful thought I must say. After two weeks of being ill myself and bored to death of these few walls that are my prison, now the third week because of Jane and the thought of another two weeks. Sweet and all as my flat is, it has now become hateful to me.

The winter is with us and most days are grey and dark. The square is now bleak and cheerless and people hurry in the coldness. No, I am sick at heart with the difficulties of London. So my happiness is blackened.

Friday night my love was supposed to come and he didn't. This leaves me hateful, against my better judgment. I loathe and detest his stupid sick wife whose speech last week sickened me. She is far from noble, and a fool. What sort of illness is it that makes her unable to see what a distasteful collection of statements such as her snobbish little schoolgirl mind conjures up. Does she not know she shocks me with this talk? Does she not know she is making a fool of herself? Why does she say these things? It worries me so much, so terribly much. She is surely an ego-maniac but she is so limited. If only she could do something, maybe she would feel better. She does nothing. Nothing, nothing, nothing … oh the agony. She doesn't even know she has nothing to offer. She doesn't know what other people give. She doesn't understand. Poor, poor fool. She is so caught up in her fantasy about her position in her imaginary society, or the top, as she calls it. She is blind to what is going on under her own nose. Poor fool. Why does she tell me, does she not know I find that talk most distasteful? She is so ordinary and so untalented and yet cannot see why she is not treated as a Duchess.

My poor Darling. My God. My God. Where will it end?

Chapter 8

Up, Up and Away!

Letter from my father:

Wednesday 9th November

Dear Jeannie, For the last week - oh, what does
one say? A heart so full of something like love,
anxiety and all sorts of things and a head full of
a thousand problems. Anyway, last night I saw one
of the sights of the world - Sydney from the air
by night. Now, I am through customs and await my
call for the aircraft to take me to Tahiti. I will
get there at 7 am Wednesday, and it is now 8.50 am
Wednesday in Sydney. I got your last letter, thank
you, and Jane's drawings, and if ONLY this plane
was going straight to London.
Love, I am off,
John

For most of his time in New York my father stayed with a friend,
Paul Byer, who lived in White Plains. He included Paul's address in
this letter.

New York, November 15, 1960

Dear, Dear Jeannie, This note is many days late
and should have been written from Papeete, where I
thought of you so often and failed to write because
after two wonderful days on the island, I boarded
the aircraft so exhausted and in such a rage with
American tourists and stupid people that I fell
asleep. Then I was in Honolulu and then in so short

and crowded a time I am in New York and this is
written from a (very good) cafe just near Grand
Central station.

But, ah, Papeete. How often I thought of you and
wished you were with me to share the joys of that
madly disordered and charming town - the Chinese
end - what must it have been like when Gaugin found
it? I hired a push-bike and rode most of the way
round the island. New York, where I have not yet
even begun to get going on the music, is staggering
- and so far much more pleasant than I anticipated.
Paul's home is at the equivalent of Fern Tree
Gully and in a very pretty, hilly area, with high
gables, six-panelled windows and no fences - all
like the covers of the [illegible] Home Journals. But
I am rushed - please write quickly - and unless I
find myself caught by musical events I will see you
Monday week at 8.30 (November 28). Already I feel
I may have to stay four days longer to hear the
Israeli Philharmonic Orchestra, and the weather is
so mild and pleasant that I thought of trying to
persuade you to come over by boat. But that would
probably be silly. But forgive my confusion and may
this note get to you very, very quickly. Please
write, no matter how shortly, by return mail.

Yours, John

Dear Jane, Here I am, Sweetie, in New York where
the buildings are higher than you would ever
believe. They seem to go right into the top of the
sky. Now I must hurry and go to a concert - and it
will not be long now before I see you.

Your Dad XX

Three days later my father wrote that he had decided to stay a
few more days to attend the concert by the Israeli Philharmonic
on the 30th. He also told my mother he had come down with "a
filthy cold come flu". By the time he wrote his next letter his cold
had progressed to acute bronchitis, requiring drugs and bed-rest,
and putting him way behind schedule. He now planned to spend an
extra week in New York. He had already received the news that I had

the mumps and ended a little note to me with a drawing of a sick man in bed in New York and a young girl with a very swollen neck in bed in London.

My father's good friend and fellow music critic, Dorian Le Gallienne, was highly educated and cultured, unlike my father who felt that he had talked his way into a job for which he was not qualified. Rubbing shoulders with the music world's elite must have rubbed somewhat against his nervous sense of inferiority. Trying to review music in a city such as New York with his strength drained by illness must have been quite daunting. It didn't take much to cause my father anxiety, sometimes resulting in a disorganised muddle that he struggled to overcome.

My mother couldn't tolerate this. She needed him to be strong, confident and in control of his life, to be her rock of last resort when she found herself in danger of drowning. So when he wrote that he felt "a bit lost and disorientated", and worried about "the big problem of New York", she reacted badly despite his otherwise chatty and friendly letter. Once again he starts a letter asking why my mother gets so easily distressed by what he writes, and pleads with her to understand that he "didn't mean to convey anything more than a normal amount of concern". He went on to say he had found much to enjoy, and described visiting a violinist who lived ten miles out of the city in a house filled with beautiful early American furniture. He ended with:

> Thank goodness you did not get the mumps because until this [time] I would have been in poor shape as a nurse for Jane.

Unfortunately he spoke too soon. Five days later he was in the middle of writing to inform my mother that he had once again delayed his flight, when he received her letter telling him she now had the mumps. The news sent him spiralling into indecision. He waited until the next day when he could make enquiries about possible flights to London before completing the letter. By then he realised that my mother would probably be over the worst of it before he could get there. He asked her to send a cable if she wanted him to come urgently.

Dec. 6, 1960, White Plains, New York

Tuesday evening

Dear Jeannie, Needless to say I have worried about you like hell during the past week. Both yesterday and today I hoped for a letter or a card but none came. If only I had not got sick in N.Y. this would not have happened and I would have been with you when you most needed me. The only thing that comforts me is the thought that if you were really desperate you would have sent me a telegram. But at least on Friday you will at last have someone to take the load from your shoulders, and at long last you will get some help and assistance to enjoy yourself. Believe me I have come too far, and the months have been too sad, for me to arrive with anything but a peaceful and open heart and all I beg is that you should try to look forward to Friday with the same gladness that I do. I will of course be bursting with excitement and happiness and will be just as happy and lively as you wish. If only I could be sure that you are reasonably well - that is the worry.

Today I enquired about a telephone call but it would cost $9 and I then thought of a telegram which I did not send because I realised it would be midnight in England when it arrived. Have you enough money? That has worried me a bit as that 60 pounds was at least a month ago. If you are well enough by Friday I would of course love you to come to the airport BY TAXI FROM BELSIZE SQUARE and I will pay. That would be a great joy for me, and Jane, and you too if you are well enough to do so - but I do not ask you to do it if you feel unable. Otherwise I will get a taxi straight to Belsize Square and leap up the stairs like a boy.

I am on B.O.A.C Flight 582 which leaves N.Y at ¼ past 12 Thursday night and gets to London International Airport at 2.45 p.m. Friday London

time. Can it be true? Oh I hope you have not had
too much suffering in the past weeks,

Love John

PS. I will have about 30 pounds in cash when I
arrive.

FOR JANE XXX three big kisses from her Daddy.

Over the previous couple of months Sunday Reed had sent several letters to my mother apologising for her tardiness in responding to the many letters from my mother. In one, written at the end of September, she explained that she has been spending a lot of time visiting her old nursemaid, Doodie, who was seriously unwell in hospital. In the same letter she thanked my mother for sending a springtime greeting:

> When I read your letter I looked out the window and waved
> to you and saw the pear blossom drifting down like snow in
> the first warm wind and forget-me-nots everywhere as if the
> sky had fallen down, yes I thought, Jean is right, it is truly
> springtime.

Sun also expresses concern for my mother's wellbeing, explaining:

> I am often anxious about you and sometimes I am almost sea-
> sick darling, going up and down at such a rate on your mad
> old heart's see-saw.

But it was Sun's poor old heart that was soon to be wrapped in sorrow. By the end of November another of her closest friends lay dying in hospital. Joy Hester had survived the cancer many years longer than expected but finally her body was succumbing.

On 4 December Sunday wrote a letter to my mother that started with:

> Dear Jean, I want to tell someone I love that I have lost
> someone I love. Joy died last Sunday. For Joy, I can't imagine
> anything more dreadful and terrifying than her last week in
> hospital.

My mother hadn't yet received it when she wrote to Sun four days later. In Sun's previous letter she had told her how much she treasured my mother's letters and assured her that my mother's face did not look tired, as she had claimed. Sun suggested she should get a new mirror.

In this letter my mother told Sun about her financial position. She had been earning two pounds ten shillings a week minding Daphne's twins after school. Throughout our time in the UK my father continued to send an average of 10 English pounds a week.

8th December 1960. 42 Belsize Square

My dearest Sun, Your letter arrived at a moment when I needed a friend and so glad I was indeed to read your most loving words. I got a new mirror all right but it told me something worse, and as I stared hard at Tweedle Dee and Tweedle Dum in the reflection my heart sank heavily and I cried and cried – there was Jeannie's nose sitting in the middle of a great pink pumpkin. I had the mumps.

After spending three weeks caring for Jane like an angel of mercy and being cheerful in our quarantine, I just couldn't believe it was true. Too true in fact. The week that has followed has been Hell us I have been very ill indeed and most miserable. It is a fearsome thing for adults and there was nothing the Doctor could do but it all worked out finally and here I am today able to sit up and write to you.

Your letter arrived while I was in a bad fever and I felt lonely indeed and thanked you so deeply for having chosen so needy a moment. It cheered me up and I felt not quite so terrible. Arthur took Jane home to his place and she has been there ever since. John was supposed to have arrived here last weekend but then he postponed it until this week and now he has postponed it again until next weekend. God knows. Only he could really have been of some use.

Actually I am not looking forward to seeing him really even his letters drive me up the wall. Heaven knows how it will work out. I am sorry somehow as Jane is very, very excited, I will try somehow, in many ways it will make a great difference as it will give me some freedom from time to time. I shouldn't think John will want to go out every night so I expect him to babysit sometimes.

As for going to the continent, we shall wait and see how things go. But I am a little frail and let's hope I get cheerful about things when he gets here. Yet how badly Jane and I need a Bloke to look after us as I do not see how to deal with some things.

Funny, I have been thinking lately so much about the idea of a boarding school as the only solution. I haven't much idea but I thought a nice country school IF one could find one that doesn't feed children on white bread and margarine and suet pudding. This I think is the major problem.

I don't mind continuing to earn my living but being a mother as well as having jobs is just killing and I feel it's got to be one way or another now. I've now lost my afternoon job, so unless John pays my rent I will have to give up this cheerful room. I've seen enough of it these last three weeks. It is time I moved on in any case. I want so much to see wilderness.

Several days have passed now and I must report that I am getting better. I got up for an hour or two today and seem well enough, my face has gone down and the only remaining signs are two strange bags hanging down under my chin. My tummy seems badly poisoned which is odd as I went onto nothing but orange juice right from the beginning. It is now ten days and I am fed up with the mumps.

I received a card from John whose heart has been torn with a desire to come and nurse me, search me why. Instead of coming he cancelled his plane twice, he is all talk. I really needed a boy scout these last ten days as I don't think I will ever forget being alone with Mumps. But how full of my troubles I am.

It is nearly over and Xmas is coming. Winter is with us. It is not fearfully cold but it is the darkness and greyness that seems hard to take. All day today it was too dark to see without a light.

My little friends on the windowsill seem hungry, they seem to like my crumbs of wholemeal bread. I saw a seagull yesterday which cheered my heart. Your news about Aspendale is marvellous.* How glad I am for you. I think I know just what it means to you, it is wonderful news.

I have lots of homesick feelings but I plan to stay in Europe just as long as I can manage. I have no idea how I am going to manage. The way I see it, is that once I get home I'll never be brave enough to set out again so I had better do and see whatever I want to now while I'm here. I want to go to places like Portugal and Spain and then as well as seeing the continent I would like very much to go home via Burma and Siam. Ambitious, aren't I? It's all vague in my mind and depends on so many things. Sometimes I wish John would take Jane home with him. It's hard to save any money in England as wages are terribly low. I'm not against this really because the people here, although they are poorly clad and without luxury, they have happier faces and seem to enjoy their lives. You see, I still like the funny old English people. Also I'm determined to get to Wales and Scotland next summer. Here I am talking about summer and the winter has only just begun. I'm hoping it will snow for Xmas. It doesn't seem cold enough to me. I've never seen snow fall. Apparently it doesn't often snow in London.

This is a pretty awful letter, you must forgive me. I am not myself. Another couple of days and life should be back to normal. Give little Wishnu boy a special hug.** I miss him very much. Is he still very beautiful? I still haven't written to Ethel. I shall have to do something. I shall use Xmas to send Pappy my love. If only I could whisper in her ear. Dear Sun, I miss so much, so very much.

---

* The Reeds had bought a property on the foreshore at Aspendale with the intention of building a very modern beach house there. The architect-designed house was completed by the following summer.

** Wishnu (sometimes spelt Vishnu) was Sun's pedigree Siamese cat. My mother's friend, Ethel, was minding our cat, Pappy (sometimes spelt Pappie).

Perhaps I am too old for all this adventure. I will write a proper letter when I am up and about. My love to you, my love to the Aussie sky,

Love Jean.

Chapter 9

The Reunion

I still have a bluebell that I picked as a child from Buckles Wood near the small English village of Leiston. There is no longer even a hint of blue – it is brown like the stain of an old teabag, thinner than paper and more delicate than the dried wing of a butterfly. At the time I was six and living at Summerhill, the progressive boarding school just out of Leiston my parents chose for me. It was founded and run by Alexander Sutherland Neill, better known as A.S. Neill, whose progressive approach to education is considered radical to this day. The school was run on the principles of democracy, equality and freedom. The rules were created democratically, were open to challenge, and everybody's vote had equal weight regardless of age or position. The few rules imposed by Mr and Mrs Neill related to safety. Attending lessons was voluntary at any age and I suspect the only "lessons" I chose to attend were mucking around with paint or clay.

In the six months I was there I certainly didn't learn to read or write so the little letter sent to my mother in which I enclosed the pressed bluebell was dictated to my "house mother". It was posted on 19 May 1961, after my parents had returned from their trip to Europe and when my father was back in Australia. My mother was then living with her friend Daphne at 54 Belsize Park Gardens and once again minding the twins while Daphne was at work.

Dear Mummy, Could you come soon? Here is a bluebell from

Buckle's Wood. I hope the twins are happy. I got your card today with a picture of a girl painting easter eggs. I hope you are happy.

Love Jane

But when my mother wrote her first letter of the year, my father had only recently arrived in London to join us at 42 Belsize Square and the thousands and thousands of bluebell bulbs lay still dormant in the frozen winter ground of Buckles Wood.

1 January 1961

Dearest Sun,

Just to wish you a Happy New Year. I hope nice cheerful days on the beach are your delights at the moment. How I wish I was allowed a day in the hot sunshine. But all things told London is pretty good. The weather has been beautiful. Lovely sunny days with cold mornings. No snow as yet. We are not feeling the cold really although my nose seems to be my most sensitive part and I think I will have to knit myself a little woollen hat for my nose. It is very cold but still, and so if one is wrapped up well the cold can't get in. Rose Cottage was so draughty and all the ceilings leaked so badly that one had to put a mackintosh over one's bed, whereas this carpeted heavily curtained room with cosy chairs heats up with the little gas fire in no time, and with a constant flow of hot water, winter seems less difficult than at Mentone. I must say I miss my Mallee root fire. One of the things I loved to do best in the world was gathering twigs in the garden in the winter.

John has bought an old car. I love it, it has nice old leather seats and heavy doors. So far we have had several short trips into the country and plan to go to Cornwall soon. The forests look just marvellous in the mad, bare, grey, still world. It all looks a bit like a backdrop for the Swan Lake ballet but I find it quite enchanting. The silver birches are a great surprise as they look so lovely. I have such awful associations with suburban lawns etc.

We went one day in a fog and it was all like a magic land. John and I are good travelling companions because we like to see the same things. We call at old churches and pubs and admire the dear little mushroom cottages. We found one little old cottage, so small, as if for fairy people. It was quite round with a round mushroom thatched roof, but the thatch was covered in beautiful green moss. We went to Abbott's Langley and King's Langley and found the most beautiful little very ancient church with the outside walls made out of old bricks and pebbles and the whole thing patterned like a draughtsboard. Inside the ceiling was wooden like the inside of a rowing boat (rather Norwegian in style). Apart from the most lovely and old stained-glass window was a mad fresco of two angels. It was all so unlike English churches. I suppose you have seen hundreds like it on the continent.

Jane is bored with sightseeing so we are going to try to get her into a progressive school for the next term. She is keen and I think will like it. We plan to go soon to France and Italy but are not as yet sure how or when. John seems all right but personalities don't change much. I am not very well as yet. Seems the mumps have sent me off the rails again. I despair of myself. I must be very neurotic these days. John is not very well and has had a bad cough all the time. He isn't writing at all and is getting very fussed about this. I only hope that we get on to the continent. We will take the car if it's still working well and the plan so far is to travel through Italy with a German girlfriend of mine who has lived a lot of her life in Italy and speaks Italian. We may go to Greece to meet up with Dorian. France we will probably do alone. John can go to Germany on his own later as I think I would find it hard to leave Jane long enough to go with him. Besides, I doubt if we will still be speaking to each other by then.

I find myself less tolerant than I used to be. We saw Dorian when he spent three weeks in London. He made us jolly to start with so that was good. John really needs someone like Dorian around all the time. He slumps into a sort of muddle and inability to function and it is most heavy to live with for me as it makes me feel as if the sky is dark with cloud. Dorian looked very thin and

*tired and was quite wild with frustration about English people and
can scarcely wait to get back to Eltham. I alone seem to like the
English. I feel this is a socialist country and I think the bulk of the
people very happy. I don't know anything to complain about. Yet in
spite of all this I would adore to be down on Wilson's Promontory
with real fresh air. I dare not get homesick.*

A Happy New Year to Heide.

Love Jean.

⌘

In this next letter my mother told Sun that she and my father were
going out to dinner with his boss and Arthur and Yvonne. According
to my mother, my father knew of her affair with Arthur from the
beginning. Certainly his first reference to it later that year indicated
that he had long accepted Arthur's place in my mother's heart.

1 February

Dearest Sun,

*So many hours seem to have passed since I wrote you a letter and
even now just an infuriating sheet of airmail letter. Just to say I
never forget you and that you are always an invisible companion.
I suppose John loves you as much as I do, even though he is so odd
about human beings these days. But it is constantly you that we
both think of whenever we see or hear some beautiful moment.*

*Everything is going very well. John and I are getting along well
on some levels and it is very easy to see why we ever got married
and it is strangely just as easy to see why we shall never be able to
stay married. This is not a marriage now, it is a strange holiday in
a strange and wonderful world where certain realities are ignored.
Enough of that. All is well and nobody has any illusions.*

*Jane is settled into the school and I am a great A.S. Neill fan. I
think it is all wonderful. I am so relieved to have been so happily
relieved of Jane that I feel quite young and enthusiastic about life. I
didn't know how heavily she weighed me down. Yet I love her very
dearly.*

We have seen a good bit of country and I adore it, even in this cold grey state. The forests look magical and it is a joy to stand in a forest and loosen the earth and smell the soil and hear the birds. I am no city girl. Also our passion for Aldeburgh is great and to be near the sea I adore as my heart is at peace when I stand on the edge of the sea. Can't get used to the pebble beaches to walk on but they have settled in my vision.

Having got Jane settled after great effort, we are now planning the next months. John leaves for Germany on the sixth of Feb. I am giving up this room as it is too expensive to keep going all the time. I do not know as yet what I will be doing when John is in Germany. I may go to Paris or I may stay in Cornwall. We begin our car trip to France and Italy on about the sixth of March. There has been this last week a sudden drop in the temperature and the weather has become a bit wild and I'm afraid I don't like it much now. I have really felt cold this last week. Still no snow. Those few flakes that fell Xmas week will probably be the lot.

The Boyds are all very well and Arthur has had a crew cut which is simply awful. They are having a struggle to remain and are living on their return fare, which is a worry. It's all rather funny yet in one way sad. I feel sometimes it is so very mad, the way we all live. Yet I am so very sure on the other hand that it is not possible for me to manipulate any change. All I know is that it is impossible for people to invent love when it doesn't exist and just as impossible for people to stop loving when they do love. It is all a great delight for me to find love is constant in spite of barriers of time, space or hostility. If it is not possible to live with people one loves, then the next best thing is to go on loving. I am afraid I will go on loving even if love is withdrawn. I am so sure that I consider myself lucky to experience a constant love level. A relationship that is as easy as the song of a bird.

Speaking of relationships, I received a terrible shock when I heard that my mad little brother Robbie has gone and married Margaret Crowe. Never did I dream of this happening. I like

107

Maggie myself but theirs has been the most erratic relationship. It has never brought happiness. It reminds me so much of John and I, with that, on again, off again, madness. That mad compelling love, hate type sadness. Just awful and so depressing to me now, when I am so convinced that love must be constant and sweet. Those two feared getting old and being unmarried,* here am I, thirty-five and no longer pretty, yet I am more starry-eyed and in love than ever before in my life and, what is more wonderful, I am more passionately and truly loved than I ever imagined possible.

Do not be cross with my talk. I am being very nice to John and what I realise so much now is that most people don't care much for anything too complex. John is happier without too much involvement. Love is not John's food. He doesn't care much where my heart is. What a terrible girl I am when I write. I do not mean to say all these things. Do not think me dishonest. I never cheat. All is well. Everybody quite happy and coping. John looks very well and boyish and jolly. He is enjoying himself and is pleasant most of the time. He has a chronic cough, yet otherwise seems very fit. We are living on special compost-grown vegs, bread and eggs. Marvellous oranges very cheap. Worse thing is we aren't getting free seats to concerts etc. Forgive all this muddled emotional stuff. Do not worry, all is well if not perfect. Am quite a bit homesick from time to time. Is Wishnu OK? Give him a kiss. What size espadrilles do you and John take? My love to you. How is Aspendale? Love. Love. Love. God my heart is full.

Love Jean.

I'm fairly sure my father wasn't aware that my mother held no hope for their marriage, as she stated at the beginning of her letter, but occasionally her belief in her own honesty was well-founded. Admitting to feeling so happily relieved of the burden of her child was nothing if not candid. If she had second thoughts about

---

* My mother was as yet unaware that Bob's marriage to Margaret Crowe had nothing to do with fear of being old and single and everything to do with the new life growing in Maggie's womb.

expressing herself so freely, it didn't stop her writing to Sun again with more descriptions of the joy of her newfound freedom, and using a strange comparison to explain herself.

Upon reading it for the first time it brought a surprised and mildly sardonic smile to my face. I find it sad to think of a six-year-old child being sent to boarding school but in this case it was me, and if I felt any sense of abandonment at the time, it is long forgotten.

<hr/>

Belsize Square, Sunday 5th Feb.

My dear Sun,

Time has flown since John has been here, for two reasons. One, we have done so much more and secondly, with John, one seems to also muddle so much more and so time has been burnt up one way or another. Getting Jane off to school found me spending my spare time darning socks etc. One begrudges the domestic chores which seem endless wherever one is. But now Jane has gone, I heave a sigh of relief. What a mother? God knows I adore the little pet and miss her fearfully and struggle with my heart to remember her sweet little features, but yet I am relieved. I feel as if a great weight has been taken from my shoulders. I am sure this is what Victoria used to feel when her families were removed – firstly she would be very fussed and search and cry and carry on as if she didn't feel it to be true that the little worries weren't hiding behind a geranium bush, her personality that carried responsibility, even though the kittens would be well over three months and perfectly capable, would be tuned to her job. Then suddenly she would forget all about them and dance around the garden and chase butterflies as if she had never had a care in the world. I am afraid to admit but the truth is I feel so different without Jane. I feel as if I have the old personality back and my driving force seems first class. I have great plans and feel most frighteningly creative. My vision seems so alive and my eyes are feasting and my heart full and cheerful. I feel life is pretty good even though it has several big difficulties.

In spite of all this however, I have the flu. So has half of England. I have been so well these last weeks that I cannot see how it crept up on me. The main worry is that John leaves for Germany on Tuesday and, needless to say, it would completely bugger up his plans if he got it. However we both have fingers crossed. He has had a perpetual cough ever since he arrived but in spite of this he looks extremely well and relaxed. He is enjoying himself even though he is in a constant flap about what he hasn't written. He hasn't changed much, I'm afraid, and there are times when I cannot bear to be in the same room as him. He seems to have drops of some sort whereby he goes into a melancholy state of mind and behaves like a sad sack and truly it is worse than a wet week. When he is in these moods I have no patience. However when he cheers up, he cheers up and we get along quite well. Apart from the fact that he is constantly an old woman domestically, he appears much younger on the whole and more cheerful than he has been for ten years. I like John even now, yet something curdles in my head when he gives in so easily to his moods. I feel despair is not something to be forced on others and I want to reject everything, as there was a time when I would become infected with John's despair and yet even then I felt it was foreign to my natural mood, even in those days I could always see some sunshine in the back of my mind. Now it doesn't worry me badly as I live very much on my own rules and values and John couldn't possibly swamp my boat.

Even great sadness and loneliness have never really brought me despair. I do not really know what terrible thing is in John's heart that creates this thing I name despair. This was to have been a letter of news, events etc. rather than my vague feelings. The best news is that Jane's school is first class. I am more than happy about it. We were supposed to make our first visit today but I am still in bed and infectious. Both telephone talks with Mr. Neill proves that not only does Jane think the school is very good but that Mr. Neill thinks that Jane is very good and complimented John on her upbringing. I was very pleased as she certainly is a dear strongminded little girl.

She has become so pretty even though toothless. She has very long hair worn like Alice and although she is a wild tomboy she has most gracious movements. She asked me with earnest eyes to please be nice to Daddy as he was her best person. She really adores him. The sad thing is that she won't understand me until she is thirty-five.

Anyhow, all is well at the moment. I would like to keep Jane at this school next term also as I feel that when John goes back I would like to stay and work a lot before I go home. John wants me to go straight home but I refuse. This is my last week at this room and I am not sure where I will be while John is in Germany. I will try to spend some time in Aldeburgh to be near Jane and my beloved sea. I may stay with the English girl I worked for or, if I can afford it, I may take myself off with a sketchbook and my little blue case to Cornwall. It would be silly to get another room in London as on March the 7th we set off for the continent and I look forward to enjoying myself immensely. The latest plans are to swap cars with Arthur for the trip as he has a caravan car fitted with everything and this will save us hotel expenses all the way.

Tomorrow night I'm going to wrap up my flu in vitamin pills and cough drops as we have seats for the "Midsummer Night's Dream". Poor John, for the first time we are having to pay for some concerts and operas. These seats cost a fiver and we are both determined to go hail, flu or shine. John saw the rehearsal and has just sent off an article to Melbourne. He is very keen and seems to think friend Benjamin the truest of souls. We are looking forward to it immensely.

We met Barry Humphries one day and they are both well and very busy indeed. Rosalind is working in a Pantomime. I shall go and see them as soon as John leaves. Arthur is painting. I saw one last week that made me melt but I am an easy victim. It seems the lovers in the creek world goes on and on, but to me each one has a special magic. The lovers get vague and the bush more romantic but the colour seems to me beautiful and the brushwork so light *and yet so sensual. I wish I could describe them. I am hopeless with words but they seem to me to be so very beautiful that I want to tell you about them. They are sweet paintings. Romantic and sweet and yet so passionate and so full of Aussie dark creek life. The last one finished had become so vague that it was hard to see what was creek and what was bush but the lovers were covered by the sweetest yellow dress. The yellow seemed more than yellow. It seemed to me to be the most beautiful yellow I had ever seen. Then there was a bird as there is always a bird or something but the blue of the bird seemed again to me to be more beautiful than blue can be. It was a painting of love. It was to me most beautiful. It made me very happy.*

All the paintings these days seem to me to be quieter in mood yet cleaner and brighter in colour. Sweet and tender, caressing and sensuality that seems to jump out of the canvas but different somehow from the Bride series. Not the anguish and cry of pain anymore.

There has arrived some peace into a heart I think. I tell you all this because most of these paintings have been sold and gone into some strange English world never to be seen again. I am sad as I wish I could hold them back for myself. I have heard them called lighter paintings but maybe this is so. They do not cry out to the world in great shapes. The brushwork is fantastic and makes me amazed. There is lightness of brush rather than lightness of feeling. It all makes me terribly happy and full in my heart.

Peace and love reign and I'm off to the continent. Jane is happy with other children. All is well but no snow yet in London. My love to little Wishnu – when I wrote his name I saw his face for an instant. I am a little homesick for Aussie air and gardens and friends. I hope all that talk of mine doesn't drive you mad. I go around in circles but it all really means something important. Whatever works is good regardless.

My love to you. Are you well? Now I post this off with love two days later. "Midsummers Night Dream" was simply marvellous.

God bless Benjamin Britten. Enjoyed myself immensely. Sweet
world of sweet music. Darling man. Is there anything else I can get
in France for you? Be well. Happy Summer. Love to Heide. I am
leaving my little blue room.

   Love Jean

⊚᎒⊙

On 10 February 1961 my father left my mother and headed to
Germany for several weeks of intensive concert-going and review-
ing. After leaving her little blue room, my mother moved in with
Daphne and took weekend trips to Aldeburg, a seaside town close
to Leiston. From Aldeburgh it was a short bus trip to visit me at
Summerhill.

My father wrote his first letter from Stuttgart after spending a day
in Heidelberg.

```
It was such a lovely day, a light fog cleared
slowly about mid-day and I saw this fairytale town
in a veil of misty sunlight.
```

Not everything was to his liking though. The German Embassy
in London hadn't told him he would be arriving at Carnival time
in southern Germany, and he complained to my mother that all he
had seen so far was "one outsized Moomba". He wrote again the following day, mainly about practical details around swapping his car
for Arthur's van for the trip to Italy and France with my mother. He
wrote this letter four days later.

```
Vienna. Sunday morning. Feb. 19
Dear Jeannie, during the last two days I have
almost gone batty with excitement and here I am
in Vienna this morning, rather like a child who
has come down a slide, flat on its bum. Last
night, after travelling all day I rushed into
this pub, and out again to hear Cosi, in the tiny
theatre here where Mozart worked (seats 250).
Got to the theatre to find that the repertoire
had been changed and there was no performance. So
rather crestfallen, I went off to the Staatsoper,
I thought to hear Ariadne. It turned out to be
```

Traviata with an unknown cast so I came home and to bed.

The information given to me by the Austrian people in Munich was out of date and it was just bad luck. But last night I felt at the point of tears and that I would stay at the door of that beautiful little theatre until I heard what I wanted. But I have gone mad with desire in a way which I didn't really foresee. The first days in Cologne and Frankfurt were cruelly barren and depressing. But then Stuttgart was good and Munich was marvellous, and as I say I have become possessed by a feeling that I want to hear some things just once before I die, Cosi in Italian and by Mozartian singers, and Bach in a German church with first-rate performers, and all these things are possible here but the dates are all wrong for me.

But the great joy of Munich was Figaro in the Cuvilliés Theatre and nothing one had read, and no number of photographs could have given one the slightest preparation for the moment of entering that theatre. It was perhaps like the vision young children have of fairy palaces. It is supposed to be the most beautiful rococo theatre in the world and it may well be. As I entered my box (it is all boxes) the doors of all the boxes were open and one had a vision into and across the theatre. It looked like what a rose in the sunlight must look like to a bee ... An absolute dream of pink, white and gold with little candles (electric) in the boxes and eight glorious little crystal chandeliers. The performance, in German, was not good for much of the first two acts but the third act was so grave and serious and so very beautifully felt that I was constantly in tears.

Then the following night there was at the Munich Staatsoper, a shattering performance of Strauss's "The Woman without a Shadow", a big Wagnerian work but devastatingly powerful and what a performance ... it becomes any Englishman to dip his lid. But the pressure on me is fierce. The language barrier

114

```
remains a great problem in dealing with opera
people, and with the daily round of packing, trying
to plan my next move and executing my present one,
there is scarcely time to eat and even in the train
one cannot rest because the view is so constantly
fascinating.
```

The rest of the letter contained a vague idea of his plans but admitted he might not be able to complete his trip on time and might not return until 2 March. A week later he wrote again after receiving two nice letters from my mother. He suggested that she come by plane to Berlin rather than wait for his return. Knowing she had never flown and was frightened by the idea, he suggested a quick whiskey before departure. He wrote:

```
Then you could look Nefretete* in her one glorious
eye (she has lost the left one) as well as spending
a few hours in paradise in the opera.
```

A couple of ecstatic descriptions of opera singers he had heard was added to encourage her but I doubt she would have been tempted enough to board an airplane. It would be many years before she found the courage to fly. And his letter contained another little story that would have left her less than enthusiastic. Arriving at Munich station early one morning, he put his two cases and his typewriter on board the Berlin Express train and went to have coffee. When he returned, the train had already left. After much confusion, the staff at Munich rang through to Nuremburg station to get his luggage taken off when the train stopped there. It was 24 hours until the next train to Nuremburg so my father spent a sleepless night at Munich station. He could be infuriatingly vague and forgetful sometimes, which drove my mother crazy, as she was quite a competent and efficient traveller.

He wrote two more letters before returning to London, explaining that he was delaying his return by three days because of a couple of important operatic productions he wanted to see.

---

*   An Egyptian Queen whose bust is housed in the Museum of Berlin.

After my father's arrival, my parents spent almost two weeks in England. They visited me at Summerhill before leaving for their trip.

There is a little story my mother told me about this visit. After the initial joyful reunion, I climbed into the back of the big old car my father had bought and we drove off for our special day out. All was quiet for a while as I sat sucking my thumb alone in the middle of the large leather seat, absentmindedly watching the passing scenery.

Suddenly I pulled my thumb out and uttered my first real swearword: "Fuck!"

In the front seat my parents exchanged surprised looks but said nothing. I continued. "Fuck, fuck, fuck!" I waited, but the response didn't come. I'm sure both parents had slightly stunned smiles creeping around the corners of their mouths as we drove on in silence. Summerhill had taught me something after all.

Another thing I presume I learnt at Summerhill was what a penis looks like when erect. My mother was true to her word and kept most of my childhood drawings. I have them to this day. Somewhere between six and seven I drew quite a few scenes of obvious sexual play between males with erections and females, sometimes smiling, sometimes not. These days I suspect such drawings would furrow the brow of even the most relaxed and libertine of parents. I know if my sweet daughter had drawn such things at the tender age of six I would have been nearly hysterical with worry, whereas my parents just thought I was the next Picasso.

Time has proved them wrong about my artistic genius. But time, I believe, also suggests they were right not to panic about how I acquired my precocious sexual knowledge.

Unsurprisingly there were times of intense friction between my parents on their travels. How much of the trip was marred by this is a question of perspective, but my father obviously thought all was well when he bade my mother farewell to return briefly to the continent on his way back to Australia. After three days in Venice he went to Greece to visit his dear friend, Dorian Le Gallienne, before heading off to Istanbul where he spent a couple of days with Nan Gooderham, an old friend of my mother's, who was living there with her partner.

⟨≈⟩

Back in London my mother was left alone with her thoughts, and when it came to her feelings about my father, time did not heal nor did absence make the heart grow fonder. She forgot all but the very worst of times during their travel, and her bitterness increased with each passing day. It took my father quite a while to hear the cold, angry silence from across the seas.

```
Friday. Venice

Darling Jeannie, firstly, thank you very much for
being so sweet patient and helpful with my getaway.
I got the plane without any difficulty and the last
I saw of England was a collection of great houses,
with immense green parks, somewhere between London
and Tunbridge Wells. The country, by the way, is
becoming very green indeed, much more noticeably
than it is in London, and you should take a quick
train or bus somewhere like Epping Forest, as
soon as you can. Lunch on the Swiss aircraft was
beautiful, finishing up with a little flat rum cake
with a tiny bunch of flowers worked so beautifully
in the icing it was a pity to eat it. And how
strange to fly over France at 500 mph. to cover
in half an hour country which it took us days
to traverse. O.K. I got to Zurich, was terribly
tempted to buy a musical box, but they were not
really cheap and the cheapest of the good ones was
5 pounds and it was just not good enough.

And guess how I got from Zurich to Milan - by
train. The plane from Zurich to Milan was over-
booked and there were about six of us in the same
boat. And even though it was vital for me to get
to La Scala, I was (and it should not surprise
you) by far the most pleasant and easy-going about
the trouble. So with the choice of spending the
afternoon at the airport or proceeding by train,
I took the train. Had at least another peep at
```

Switzerland which is just like one great lawn as
you know, with tiny, immaculately clean houses and
roads running through it. I thought of you the very
moment the bus from the airport got on the road
because all my European driving was done with you,
and I wished once again that we were starting our
European trip again and this time with me free of
the stupid burden of worry which almost, but not
quite, ruined your, and our, three weeks. And of
course, I thought of you more than ever as I stood
outside La Scala where we stopped the car and
wished ever so much that you were with me as I wish
it now.

Anyway, I got to the opera, straight from the
station, bags and all, just in time for the
performance which began, thank god, at 9. p.m. Joan
Sutherland was magnificent, a glorious quality
and faultless accuracy. Spoke to her afterwards
briefly. She is rather reserved, she may be
considered conceited perhaps, but I think the
fact is that she knows she is good and she simply
concentrates on her job, before, during and after
a performance and doesn't waste time on nonsense
with anyone. She has a lovely face. Anyway, after
the performance I got a taxi back to the station
(not having a pub) found a train ready to depart
for Venice (at 1.15 a.m.) and got it. Got here at
5.30 and saw the Doge's Palace, the most delicate
creamy pink in the early morning sunlight. The
whole place at this stage is very beautiful but
almost unbelievably scabby and decrepit so far as
the preservation of the buildings is concerned.
I am not sure what you would think, not sure how
your nose would react to the special aroma, if
that is the word, of the place. As one watches
the thick green waters of the canals, you notice
every now and then a cloud of muddy stuff mushroom
from the sides under the waterline. Does this mean
that someone up the street has pulled the chain?
I wouldn't mind a ride in a gondola but by Jesus I
would hate to fall out.

But I must be off as I have not yet even seen this
place. Goodness knows what kind of music is on
Jane's record but when I saw it I decided to give
it a go as you had suggested that we sent one from
France or somewhere ...

Love XXX John

My father typed the first part of his next letter on the plane between Istanbul and New Delhi. Typing a letter on an aeroplane flight
seems a strange thing to do these days, and may have been a little unfair on the person sitting in the next seat. Unlike the modern laptop
computer, typewriters were quite noisy when in use. The letter starts
with, *Somewhere over Persia. Monday? Night. 1.5.61*. Enclosed in it
was a small pressed flower with flattened, almost transparent petals
that are now a soft purple, and on the back of the letter my father
used a biro to write, *a red poppy from the hills of Athens*.

Darling Jeannie, How I wish you were with me, and
how glad you are, no doubt, that you are not.
Writing on the red ribbon because the black is
getting a bit pale.

Left Istanbul this afternoon. It was hot and humid.
Now it is cool and quite dark. It is astonishing
how nightfall is accelerated when one flies at 500
mph away from the sun. In Istanbul at this moment
it would still be light. Anyway, Nan was very nice
and of course very excited to see me. Sad to tell I
arrived a day late because when I arrived at Athens
airport I discovered, to my horror, that I had left
my passport at the bank in Athens and so missed the
plane. Poor Nan ... I sent a telegram immediately
but of course it did not get there until the next
morning in typical Greek and Turkish style. Dorian
warned me that I must never expect them to do
anything in less than a week and now I understand
what he meant.

Anyway, Nan has a flat which almost might be at
Elizabeth Bay, Sydney. The front room has a large
window and at night one can see the lights of half
of Istanbul and the ferries going to and fro across

the Bosporus. Istanbul, however, is interesting
but disappointing. These days it is a huge
industrialised port with lots of smoke, and if you
imagine an immense kind of Port Melbourne with the
dilapidated, unpainted weather board houses black
with age, decay and smoke, and stacks of concrete-
surfaced blackish grey flats and buildings, you
will not be far wrong. Of course in the middle and
all through this there are the old women in old
Turkish dresses, the water and drink sellers, and
public-letter writers, the donkeys, the dhow-like
boats and so on. But it is not a city for you, or
really I think for Nan. It is terribly hilly and
the roads of dreadfully bad cobble-stones are just
plain cruel to walk on. I think poor Nan feels that
life is sometimes a bit hard. That is, I think she
just finds it hard to do the amount of walking she
has to do in such conditions.

Her girl friend is an absolute shocker, a German
who is incapable of being anything but extremely
and consistently rude, flatly contradicts
everything you say, says what she has to say as
though it was an eternal and unquestionable fact
and indeed represents all the German national
failings at their very worst. Her name, serves her
right, is Charlotte ... But what use is there in
such thoughts. Do write to her, she would be very
glad if you did.

The mosques of Istanbul at first glance from
outside are disappointing because they are all made
from the same grey stone which looks just like
old weathered concrete and the same goes for the
Sultan's Palace. But inside they are very beautiful
in an Oriental way, covered with a lace of ornament
which I was astonished to find was not mosaic
tile but simply hand painted. But I liked their
atmosphere and, after all the stinking churches
of Christendom, I loved the gentle, quiet ritual
of taking off one's shoes. They have a few badly
preserved mosaics which are supposed to be, but I
think are not, equal to those in Ravenna. But I saw

them with Charlotte as a guide and I can't imagine
a worse handicap.

We are losing height ready to come into Tehran so I
will try to finish this later.

Off again. Had three good days in Greece with
Dorian who sends his love and he also took
your address. Like Istanbul, and unlike the
Italian cities we saw, the signs of the past
are surprisingly few. It is mainly a new city,
not beautiful in detail but beautiful as a whole
because all the houses (flat roofs) and buildings
are simply white cubes and in the brilliant light
of Greece the effect is wonderful. Dorian's place
is 10 miles out, a new house, with an orchard
for a garden and one might almost be at Mildura
or Shepparton. But he drove me out to several
villages, quite unspoilt with peasants riding on
donkeys, women in folk dresses working in the
fields and wonderful stony hills covered in thyme,
poppies and all kinds of tough shrubby growths
I did not know. But speaking Greek, Dorian took
me amongst real Greeks and they were adorable,
very, very poor but gentle, charming and with such
radiant smiles as I think I have never seen before.

I thought very much of you trying to come home
on a Greek boat, not for the boat, but so you
could travel through Italy to Athens. The ideal
answer would be for you to do this and for Jane to
fly to Rome or Athens and that is not absolutely
impossible, although it would be very difficult
to arrange. I thought perhaps of you contacting
Qantas, for example, finding a nice hostess,
introducing Jane to her and getting her to take
Jane under her wing, so to speak. Do not dismiss
this idea, think about it, plan and scheme, it is
a long shot but it is not quite impossible. Apart
from the very complex problem of you getting home
- and I pray dear Jeannie that you do not think of
the prospect too unhappily - the one thing I would
like you to do, and quickly before the full flood
of tourists, is go to Paris for say a week. The

very moment I get back I will send you another 20 pounds and a week in Paris, fares and all, should be possible on that. Try to do it the moment Jane goes back to school.

But are you well? All this writing and I have not asked that, which does not mean that I have not wondered and hoped many, many times. And how is darling sweet Jane? Poor girl, I suppose the dentist got busy with that drill. Indeed, as I write this (we are now over India) you may well be on your way to or from the dentist. Please give her a special hug for me, a big one. You may perhaps, with me gone, find from her a rising pressure to return to Australia. Perhaps not but in any case you will deal with that sensibly.

I have thought often since leaving London what you felt. Most likely I thought that despite all the bad things, you missed me as I miss you. God knows it would have been so much better if I had spent less time getting into panics and more time giving you the support and love you need. Or did you say that? Anyway here comes New Delhi.

Since writing that we have come down right over India and are approaching Singapore. I am in a Qantas plane, and how strange, and how good to see Aussie faces and hear good Aussie voices. They are excellent these stewards, without a trace of the yes sir no sir servility of the English but open, simple, friendly and very good at their job.

New Delhi was very hot. Calcutta was simply a steam bath and so was Bangkok. If I stayed on this plane I would be home at mid-day tomorrow but I have decided to sneak one more day by breaking at Singapore.

Off now, please give my regards to Daphne and the twins. And please, please try to get really busy on solving the problem of getting a passage home, see Mr. Tokimassa,* for instance. As soon as possible I will send you enough money to cover the deposits,

---

* A travel agent.

but really the problem begins your end. Off now,
love and another letter, shorter no doubt, next
week.

XX John

⚬⚬⚬

Traditionally a Christmas pudding is made four or five weeks before
25 December. On the day of the feast it would be served with rich
brandy butter or brandy cream. Another tradition was to insert silver
sixpences into the pudding. By the end of Christmas dinner, each
otherwise empty bowl contained a small collection of coins, sucked
clean of pudding. Adults had to eat carefully to avoid cracking a
tooth, but it was worth it to see the joy with which children pulled
another sticky sixpence out of their mouth to add to their collection.

For weeks afterwards many a sweetshop owner stood impatiently
with a small paper bag cupped in one hand, waiting for yet another
child customer to decide which sweet to add next to the sixpenny
mix. It was always a hard decision, requiring a lot of careful thought.

In those days English sweetshops had to be seen to be believed.
Everywhere you looked were tempting sweets of all shapes, sizes and
colours. At Christmas adults may have been in danger of cracking
a tooth on a sixpence but the danger to children's teeth was much
slower to show itself.

I had my first taste of brandy shortly after my father arrived in
London, but it had nothing to do with Christmas. At the age of six,
it was gently dripped into a hole in one of my back molars. I have a
vague memory of the intensity of the pain, and the strange warmth
that accompanied the disgusting taste of the brandy. And I remember crying a lot.

My father's long-awaited reunion with his wife and daughter may
have been a bit more stressful than he anticipated. But by the time
my father was writing these letters, I had forgotten about toothache
and remembered my love of sugar, if I ever forgot. Such is the care-
lessness of a child.

Chapter 10

Differing Perspectives

8th of May

Darling Jeannie, home again - or at least, in
Melbourne again and I would be much happier if
I had been able to go straight to Rose Cottage.
Instead, I am staying with Lillian which is
impossible and I must get away to South Melbourne
or anywhere until I can move into R.C. in a
fortnight's time. Anyway, in this quite artificial
situation I am too confused - and it is in any
case too early - to give you any impression of what
it feels like - except that Melbourne, as never
before, seems very, very small.

I arrived on Thursday morning after flying straight
from Singapore, Darwin and Sydney. Had dinner
that night at the Balzac with Sun who I greeted
spontaneously with wet eyes. Told her and John all
about our trip in quick outline - how happy you
were at times, how good you were at reading maps,
how depressed and horrible I was for much of the
time and how sad I was that it was my depression
that alone spoilt what should have been paradise.
Anyway Sun asked me if you were returning to
Australia and to me and I told her that I hoped you
were, and God knows how I hope you are.

Dear Jeannie, on this score I am an optimist. I
well know the victory I failed to win - but then
when I remember my first days in London and then
some of our moments in Paris and Europe, I feel

glad, much happier and very much more your husband
than for years past. But at present I miss both you
and Jane terribly, and tonight all I wish is that I
could put my arms around you.

Poor Sun is rather worn out and it was good to be
able to distract her for one evening with the story
of our adventures. Her stories of Sweeney, however,
were quite terrifying, and there is not much you or
I or anyone can do at this stage except hope that
Sweeney does not finish up in jail pretty soon.
He has left school. Got a job in Heidelberg which
lasted a fortnight. Now he seems to have taken over
Heide where he entertains the local larrikins. He
lies in bed most mornings - pours out tirades of
abuse at Sun and John. Takes Sun's car when he
likes (by joining the ignition wires whenever she
takes the ignition key). When she complains he
calls her a fucking old bitch, and after a good
lot of this stuff retires in tears to his bedroom -
writes a "poem" and drops it into Sun's lap. Jesus!
Now please believe that I will do everything I can
to help Sun - but there is very little one can do -
in fact there is NOTHING one can do about the basic
situation. Certainly I saw, as you did, trouble
sooner or later, but it is sooner and more serious
(at least it appears so) than I expected.

I gave her your present only as we parted and I was
very happy to be able to give her such a joyous
parcel. Now believe me, I will do everything I can
which is simply to give Sun love and moral support.
But I will write again later, and of course by then
I will have seen Sun again. Tomorrow I hope to get
to Mentone and that will be good as that is home
and I want to see it.

Please write soon and tell me how you are - and how
happily or sadly Jane returned to school. How are
your legs? Oh Jeannie, I would rub them gently and
gladly. And please, please what have you done about
enquiring about a passage home? Please come - and
please try very hard to get the passage arranged.

Love and another letter soon, XX John

Posted 9 May 1961:

Darling Jeannie, as I write there is a sound which
you have not heard for a very long time ... the
sound of rain on a galvanised iron roof. At first I
wondered why it sounded so interesting and familiar
and then in a second I realised. I have before me
the map of Europe which we folded and unfolded so
often. Rather than waste time with useless regrets,
I prefer to think of the many happy moments and
they leap at me off the map.

John and Sun were astonished that we went over the
Simplon Pass. They did not think it would be open
yet and all things told, they were very impressed.
There you are, a heroine.

Anyway, I went to Heide last night. The Percevals
were there and Georges and Moya.* I told John
[Perceval] that you wanted to organise a fund to
send him to Europe. Georges of course knows every
inch of Paris and said several interesting things.
For instance the Moulin Rouge is not the original,
it is not even in the same place. And as soon as
I told him where we had walked that morning we
saw those poor miserable prostitutes, Georges said
yes, they are there for the market workers, they
are there all day from early morning, and they
represent Paris at its poorest and worst.

Sun, of course, loved the parcel in total and the
cat and the combs in particular. She took the cat
to bed the very first night and I must say you
are a genius, because as I looked at it with that
lovely heart from Florence pinned on its front I
was envious that I was not clever enough to do
anything as good.

I hope I did sound too alarming about Sweeney in
my last hastily scribbled letter. Saw him last
night and he is just a huge boring lout. But I am
pessimistic about the whole situation. There seems

---

* Georges Mora and Moya Dyring, who was married to Sam Atyeo (one of
Sunday Reed's lovers before Nolan).

to be no real relationship between him and John
and Sun, and Sun's attitude to him is a mixture of
real insight and the wildest and most dangerous
nonsense. There is very little one can say and
nothing one can do. Keeping your fingers crossed is
as good as anything.

Anyway, I went to Rose Cottage yesterday which
looked really very nice. The Kirks are very nice
and they have kept the garden beautifully and
without cutting a twig. Betty, Mrs. K, is enough of
a gardener to know what you were after and she has
respected that. Bob was not home worse luck but I
will see him next week. Poor Bob, I do feel sorry.
There is credit control from the Government here
now and things are tough and Bob could not have
picked a worse time to become a father. Anyway,
enough of difficult problems.

I never knew whether a Mr Kirk was living with the Mrs Kirk
mentioned in this last letter. And I have no memory of her, but I
came to dread hearing the name Betty Kirk. My father's affair with
her must have started sometime after she and her family rented half
of Rose Cottage. I have no idea how long it lasted but the reper-
cussions went on for many years. My mother used to tell me that
the difference between her affairs and my father's was that she was
always separated from him at the time and was completely honest,
whereas my father cheated during the marriage and lied. This may
have been partly true but it certainly wasn't as clear cut as my mother
suggested. However long it lasted, my father's affair with Betty Kirk
wasn't one of the heart, for him at least.

Decades later, in more forgiving moments, my mother would
express some sympathy for Betty, commenting that my father would
never have taken Betty to a concert or introduce her to any of his
friends. She dyed and permed her hair, according to my mother, and
had no taste or style. My father liked to be seen with "classy" women.
It was rare for me to hear my mother say Betty Kirk's name calmly
– usually it was spat out in hatred during arguments with my father.

It was always "Betty Kirk!" Betty alone is too soft a word to be used in anger. The abrupt nature of the name Kirk is needed to deliver the furious verbal punch my mother required.

⌘

Posted 15th May 1961:

Dear Jeannie, it seems a long time since I left
London. It is in fact nearly a month and I do so
much want a letter. Do you wonder why I am anxious.
On the one hand I fear that perhaps I made you sad
so often that you do not want to write, let alone
think of coming home. On the other hand I wonder
if you are well, if you can cope without me, if
there is anything I could do and of course how Jane
is and how she feels about going back to school.
Do not think too unhappily, if you do, of the sad
moments of our time together. Think also of the
happy ones which were just as real and I think more
important. At least does it not mean something that
I get back to Australia looking, so I am told, ten
years younger? That basically was you and Jane, not
Europe.

At least I know that that the memorable moments
of Europe were those with you, that I missed you
acutely the moment I left London and that I am more
in love with you today than ever before. So when
you think of coming home, think also that I will
be there to meet you with the greatest joy and that
you will be tied to me only so much as you want to
be. But I must stop this. Perhaps a letter from
you will cross this one and if so I will be glad.
At last I feel at home. Melbourne at first was
bewilderingly small and very ugly. Now after two or
three perfect days it has all taken shape again and
not too badly.

The rest of this letter contained the news that the Kirks had moved out of Rose Cottage. It also gave the exact details of the Summerhill fees account, reminding my mother of the payments he had made and instructing her to tell the Neills that from now on she would be paying the fees.

In a letter written on 22 May my father sent another unhappy letter. He suggested she make inquiries about a ship sailing from Southampton in September. While admitting some uncertainty, he presumed she wished to return and sent an extra 30 pounds sterling for a deposit. His financial situation was not good. Now that the Kirks had left, there was no rent coming in from Rose Cottage, Bob was four months behind in payment, and my father had returned with a debt of 150 pounds. He told my mother not to worry, that it was his job to find money when necessary but it would help a lot if he had some idea of her plans. He ended the letter with news from Heide:

> Sun is pretty worn out with Doodie, her old
> nursemaid, dying in hospital and the Sweeney
> problem on her hands 24 hours a day. But of course
> she sent her love many, many times. If you do
> write you could mention, if you wished, that I had
> told you that Sweeney was proving something of
> a problem, but I would stick to the most general
> references, as you know there is very little one
> can usefully say. I am sorry for the generally
> gloomy tone of this letter, but my past letters
> were not so and before you get too cross with me,
> please do try to be just. It is your silence which
> has saddened and hurt me. Maybe you will say that
> it is nothing but what I deserve and perhaps that
> is so. But whether it is just or not, it still
> fills my head with thoughts which it hurts to
> think.
>
> I'm sorry. Do not be cross. I will write again, and
> I hope more cheerfully, when I hear from you.
>
> Yours John

Monday May 22
Dear Jeannie, I have just spoken to Sun who says
she has a letter from you in which you say that
you are terrible unhappy and that nothing will

ever make you come back to Australia. Is it TRUE?
Is it TRUE? Is it true that my growing anxiety
over the past weeks is to end in this nightmare as
a reality? Please, dear Jeannie, I would beg and
implore you - for all our sakes - please, please
try to - oh what can I ask? Indeed I can talk only
to myself - and I cannot face the possibility that
you will never return to me. It is hard to write
it - and just as hard to think of living with it.
There has been enough sadness in our lives - some
things so sad and painful that I have never spoken
to you about them - and for you, of course, it is
the same only more so.

And what about my darling Jane - please, I beg
you, I cannot think, but if you do not intend
coming home then I would ask your permission to
sell Rose Cottage. I would then resign and come
to England. That is not quite a matter of choice
because since returning, I have realised that I
could not possibly continue on the Herald without
you and Jane here, and during the past week my
ever increasing worries about you have caused me
to think very seriously. When I said in an earlier
letter that the good thing about Europe for me was
you and Jane I meant it. By returning to England
I could not compel you to be happy or love me but
I believe that I could, given a little time, do
so because there is nothing else I want to do.
Jeannie, I beg you for all our sakes to think
carefully. I cannot do so at present but I have
only one life, like you, and I am quite certain
that I will not spend it here and alone.

I don't want to be a music critic. I want to be
your husband, Forgive me I cannot think any more

XX John

P.S. Think of the gap which separated us when I
arrived in England. Were there not many times in
Europe when that did not exist? Does that mean
nothing?

The following day he wrote again. It was much longer, with as much sadness but less panic. Again he tried to explain the pressures of his job. I don't think my father ever felt successful as a critic. He knew he could be good at it and had earned a degree of respect, but he never stopped sweating and struggling over each review, and consequently often came far too close to the paper's deadlines. The pressure of being the *Herald*'s "star" writer overseas had exacerbated his fear of failure and all the paralysing anxiety it produced.

He ended the letter with:

We have Jane whom we both love and do you want to break my heart for ever. Must I wait until she is a woman? Already I have suffered enough for the years with her I have lost. She loves me, but even now as much like an uncle as a father, I suspect. But I am very tired, dear Jeannie, do you think that I am not anguished by the knowledge that your silence means that you are tormented almost beyond endurance. Until I hear from you I do not know what to do but you cannot expect me to continue here in Melbourne alone. But did I hurt you so much? I did not mean to. I can't bear to think that I did, I love you more than you have ever allowed yourself to believe and I beg you dear Jeannie to try to realise it and to see its signs in amongst the many unhappy things of the past.

But I am too tired to write now. What I will do depends on your letter when it comes. I am terribly sad but I send you my love.

XX John

∽

Wednesday May 31. 61

Dear Jeannie, If you are even sadder and more lonely than I am, and I'm afraid you are, then please God help you. For days on end now I have thought about the past, the immediate past and the distant, in infinite detail and as a whole, and if my heart has not bled for you it has thumped away for many long hours of sleepless nights. For myself

I have been terribly sad; for you I have been not
only sad but frantic with worry. Did I make you so
unhappy? Do I have to say that for the times when I
know I cannot forgive myself? Yet on the other hand
I am anguished by the memory of those many, many
times when you misunderstood very badly and were as
a result cruelly unjust. For those moments I bear
you no resentment. How could I? Because they hurt
us both equally. But the hard thing is that they
were untrue.

He went on to plead with my mother to write to him, and begged her to return, offering her Rose Cottage with no demands from him. He told her there were people in Melbourne who loved and missed her, then reminded her that he had agreed to me attending Summerhill on a temporary basis only, pointing out that the difficulty I would have when transitioning to ordinary schooling would increase with age. He asked if I was happy at Summerhill and told her that thinking about me was, for him, the "bitterest thing of all" and "like a knife in the guts".

A few years before my mother's death, she and I were having a disagreement over things that happened in the past. My mother didn't take kindly to anyone disputing her version of events so she was already quite cross with me when she told me that, as she remembered it, she and my father "got on extremely well" during their trip to Europe in 1961.

I had read these letters when she gave them to me a year or so before, so her comment brought tears to my eyes. Spontaneously I blurted out, "Oh, Mum, if only he had known that!"

My mother reacted as if a small electric current had shot through her body, then glared at me with a mixture of confusion and anger. "You think he didn't know?" she said.

"No," I answered sadly, "I don't think he knew."

The incredible, unnecessary sadness of it all drained me of my strength, my shoulders slumped and I put my head in my hands and cried a little. She regarded me quizzically for a moment before appearing to reject any further thought on the matter and changed the subject.

⁂

Finally my mother replied to my father's distraught letters. At the time she was living with her friend Daphne and earning a little extra money by taking the twins to and from school. I was still at Summerhill and my mother would have recently received my little letter with the pressed bluebell from Buckles Wood. Ironically, it may have been the gentle tone of my father's expressed sadness and affection that sparked the already glowing coals of her anger into flames of fury. He had reminded her of her shattered dreams of a beautiful marriage, and maybe even disturbed some latent feeling of guilt she had fought hard to ignore. When replying to my father's letter, her incandescent rage left little room for reason.

> Dear John,
>
> It seems to me impossible to communicate my mind to you. You speak many words that go around and around your needs and your anxieties your unhappiness, your inabilities, your fears, your heart, your demands even. I TOO am a living thing. What do you offer me? I am no Florence Nightingale, you offer me a cause, not a life, you need me. You need me, that is what you have said five thousand times. Have you questioned what I need or what Jane needs or what three people need? You need me, you do not love me. What do you offer me? A hell of a prison with a neurotic dog that bites the hand that feeds it. You have a great blank in your mind. When you think you are thinking of other people, you are thinking through an impossible neurotic condition of you own self. I am more than homesick, more than insecure, more than depressed. The difference between you and me is that I have a strong character, I carry out my intentions, I give love truly and live by a sense of responsibility rather than just talk about one.
>
> When you left I didn't have any clarity of mind or ideas or dreams, I wanted to be left alone true enough, to think to feel, to

133

know. But when you had really gone there was a great void. A real void. Once again I was alone. The battle was on but worse than that, those terrible ice picks of long ago were lodged again in my heart. Hurting, hurting, terribly, just terrible frustrating heartache. All the energy I gave out to human relationships and there is no return, no love no nothing, just great sharp ice picks. They had been still a long time and they were dislodged by me giving my body and heart again to the careless keeper, the husband who knows nought of human love but only a great egocentric need of body and soul. I am bored with your needs.

But there are other things to consider. I find you too unrelaxed, too neurotic, too irritable, too selfish (apart from the boy scout act that is put on to please your conscience). Then there is the awful fact that I like you. Yes I like your brain, I like your person, I like so much but the conflict must end for me. No woman of my sensitivity can possibly be a prostitute for bread and butter. The real fact is I cannot sleep with you and so, as you are such a demanding and ungenerous and bullying parasite of human love, there is no other answer. My body will kill me if I misuse it. I am confused by my own thoughts and worried about everything and everybody.

I adored my own father and so I cheat Jane. Do you think I will enjoy that? You are terrible and shock me when you say you are no more than an uncle to Jane. You are so blindingly in need that you want to be a parasite with your own child even. Never have I seen a purer little child in terms of love. What you judge, you judge through neurotic adult eyes. Do you want to eat your child or love her? It all makes me fear for her future. You are sick. You are badly sick and I suggest that you show this letter to Alan Jeffrey and make arrangements to have some analysis or treatment immediately.

I am not a strong woman and what you ask me to do is out of the question, you ask me to sacrifice my life for yours. You are a parasite. Do you understand? Also there are other signs that worry me. You have no power to clear your mind. Your confusion is too great. There is a junk room of needs and fears acting instead of

your high intelligence. What is to be done? I know you are unwell.
You must believe me. It would be irresponsible to just give in to
you. I have no life worth living but I will not live in Hell. Please
go and see Alan. If only you would break down and really show
your anxieties to him and try to get back your dignity and live by
responsibility rather than this childlike need. I am not your mother,
I am your wife, a fellow human being, not to be trodden on, hated
or choked of all personality. I am me. You offer me only a hard and
thankless job of being your keeper. I know you need me but you
would kill me. You freeze my heart and body and leave me like a
zombie. Any man not so obsessed with his own needs would see.
I suspect you hate with a greater passion than love ever had but
we will give you the benefit of the doubt. I am amongst strangers
in a land that, although entertaining, is not my home. I have had
over these last three weeks a terrible flu wog that has added to my
depression.

Forgive me if you think I am cruel. I am determined to live,
to be alive on my own terms. You will not kill unless you do it by
force. How well I see the satisfied John, my husband, weeping over
my grave, telling himself this is why he is in a muddle because
Jeannie, darling Jeannie is dead. No, it will not be so. You forget
that I alone know you well. I spent three hellish years with you
when you used the excuse that it was my love for you that was the
cause of your mental anxieties. Now it is because I don't love you.
Always you need some justification for your anguish. I will not be
in my grave. You are sick and in need of someone to receive all your
violence. Better to ask Alan to find some way to release it, so that it
won't hurt either Jane or I. I am deadly serious and can accept no
responsibility. After all, Alan can send you to someone.

Your threat to sell Rose Cottage went home and nearly broke
my heart. Please do not. If you really loved me your letters would
be very different. You cannot demand love. I have been more than
generous. Have you? What have you offered me for the future?
Not even ownership of my own body. I love Jane very much. I

consider her to be a wonderful gifted and pure child. She is with the tribe now. She doesn't need to be tied up emotionally with us, she is consuming the great world, the tribe, she is with the tribe. She is complete and has greater potential as a human being than either of her parents. She is absolutely secure and I adore her. You adore her too, I know, but do not expect or demand a neurotic relationship with her. We are just wonderful love figureheads to her. She worries about our need of her. This is wrong. We should be too busy to demand love. She does love us very much but she is adult and out in the world, quite full of mother love, she has had a feast in infancy. She has had mother love and now she is secure, she will cope whatever happens. Her love for us is pure and complete, she is not in need – you are in need, desperately but try to be a pure father. Jane will soon need you more than me. If you get yourself well, you shall have your Jane but you have no right to demand while you are in this confused and violent state.

It may also have touched a nerve when my mother read my plea for her to come to Summerhill that accompanied the bluebell I sent. Describing me to my father as an "adult" out in the world, secure and confident thanks to an early abundance of mother-love, was likely an attempt to convince herself as well as my father. Too many decades had passed by the time I read these letters for me to identify with the little girl at boarding school who missed her mother dreadfully. As an adult, reading her defensive conviction that I was somehow "complete" at the age of six, elicited not much more than a chuckle at the patent absurdity of the claim.

She went on:

I don't give a stuff about the Herald, your job, or any such. I care only about happiness. You are a cheat. You constantly cheat me and you would do it again because you have no control. You must get control. You must learn to act according to your intelligence. Your muddle is nothing to do with me and you know it. You are using me as an excuse. Get rid of your hate. You are ridden with hate.

It is horrible. The fact that you wrap it up and label it love means nothing.

See Alan, I beg of you. You are not capable of dealing with it alone. It is not to be taken lightly. You have no right to refuse me my right. You are not in a position to demand my whole self. You have not offered me anything but suffering and Hell. If you are not sick then you are hateful. I beg of you. Go for help. Take up drink. Do what you will but get rid of the anxieties. Anxieties do not come from loving too much. It is not love that worries you. Cleanse your brain. My God it is too heavy for me. I want peace. I am sorry I ever met you. I'm sorry if I sound hard, it is not so, I am confronted with a very serious problem. I am not very strong and these days I feel old and tired. I am sick of having to worry about everything. You are the husband, not me, I am the wife, not you. You would feel better if you carried the responsibilities instead of crying and wailing like a child. I am not one to want a son in bed with me. Either you are a master or not. Do not mistake the word master with the word bully. Master is by right of superiority of brain and justice or some such, the master of responsibilities.

I would, by nature, prefer to be left to dream, grow flowers, have babies, do little drawings and make a sweet nest. It is you who have made me powerful because I had to be responsible where you were weak and muddled. I am haunted by this awful feeling that it doesn't matter what I do, you will chop it down. You are so much in hate with me, you are jealous of my good qualities and embarrassed by my bad ones, that is not love. You compete against me, yet I am innocent of deliberate personality. I am me and you don't love it so you bitch me socially constantly and illtreat me privately. This you call love. You give me no love, save a physical desire, yet you demand that I live for you, with you. You are tedious in your self-centred ways. I had to accept a way of life, why shouldn't you? It is childish to say you cannot live without me. In any case, I strongly suspect you are happy being unhappy. You wallow too obviously. Why should you play my fondness of you? It is a great big cheat. What I gave you *in London meant very little. You are ungrateful in the extreme and cannot really bear peace and love. It is not your environment really. You like a battleground. You thrive on war alone. Is that not the crux of the matter? Yet my heart is disappointed. I married you in good faith. I am not callous of heart, I am tired of heart. Yes, there were nice moments. Please talk to Alan and be honest for God's sake. I beg of you.*

Jeannie

If my father had shown this letter to Dr Jeffrey as my mother suggested, I doubt he would have thought it evidence of my father's instability. My father didn't shy away from his mental weaknesses which is why he sometimes sought help. My mother, on the other hand, seemed oblivious to her wild misinterpretations of my father's words and of the many contradictions within her letter. It did not occur to her that the psychiatrist might raise his eyebrows about the state of mind of the letter-writer rather than its recipient. Her belief that the nature of her heart was peaceful was contradicted by her history of furious arguments or periods of resentful silence, not just with my father, but also with her siblings on occasion, and most of her friends.

Even Sunday managed to unwittingly offend my mother. In a letter written in 1955, Sun talked of being deeply wounded by "this silent, withdrawing thing" that my mother did, and wrote that she "can't trace the source of the shadow that had fallen between us." Whereas my father's only other fights, as far as I know, were in relation to his job, not his personal life.

His response to her extraordinary onslaught is surprisingly muted. Maybe, as he said in a previous letter, her silence was the worst thing of all.

Tuesday June. 6. 61

Dear Jeannie, Your letter arrived last night. It was of course, terribly sad and distraught and at the moment I have not time to reply adequately –

yet I do want to say three things which I hope may
help, even if only a little. Firstly, I thank you
for writing - and I mean that absolutely sincerely
(need I say?). Secondly, to repeat what I said in
my cable - to beg you not to fret. And that message
- no matter what you say - was sent out of love and
terrible concern for you. Thirdly, to repeat what
I said in my last letter - that you are free to
return to Australia ON YOUR OWN TERMS. Now this is
a message rather than a letter, but it is sent with
love and the ONLY thing I would like to persuade
you to do is be calm and - for God's sake - go to
Paris or somewhere. A letter soon,
Yours XX John.

Saturday July 8
Dear Jeannie, I'm sorry not to have written before
this but (although it's not much of an excuse) I
have been frantically busy. And even now I write
not slowly and at leisure as I had hoped to do
but in very great haste just before I go to town.
Because after thinking about you and your last
letter, I now realise that it should have been
answered quickly because, apart from anything else,
you could scarcely have sounded more tormented and
distraught. Yet it was not easy for me to find
an answer because it was not so much a question
of what to say but what to do. If you find it
difficult to communicate your mind to me then you
must believe that I find it equally difficult to
communicate my mind to you. I have never ceased
thinking about you and Jane since I left England
and while that might mean little or nothing it is a
simple fact.

My mother seemed not to have noticed the words, "ask your permission" before he suggested the possibility of selling Rose Cottage
in his letter of 22 May. In this letter he reassured her that it wasn't
meant as a threat. He begged her to see that she added unnecessary
sadness by imagining hostile intentions when there were none. He

139

also told her that Bob and Mag's baby had been born, a bit early but doing well.

> The only thing I want to say in this letter is that if you have not got a husband in Australia then for God's sake believe you have a friend and think of me and approach me as one. Love X John.

Meanwhile my mother had found something better than a trip to Paris to calm her anger.

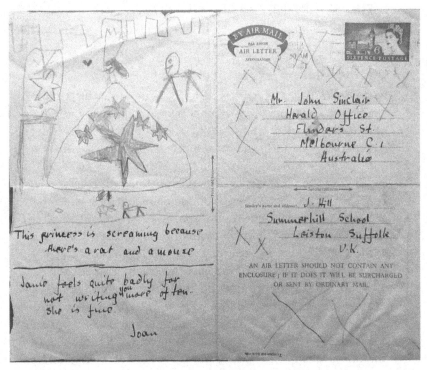

Letter from Jane written by Joan Hill, her house mother at Summerhill.

Chapter 11

A New Romance

This letter to Sunday was never posted and not completed. It was not dated but was probably written sometime between 10 and 18 July 1961. I was still at Summerhill and my mother had just moved from Daphne's flat in Hampstead to 27 B Jacksons Lane, Highgate.

Dearest Sun, I am writing at a little lady's desk, on a sweet dark green velvet chair looking out French doors over the sweetest garden, my garden. My first English garden and so this is really my first completely happy letter. My long silence bears witness to the fact that my life has been depressing and emotionally unfit to write home about. I was so low of spirit and tired of heart that I could scarce bear to communicate with remote shopkeepers.

Now all that is past and many things have happened to me and I am very happy. I write to you now because at last I can bear to tell news of myself. Yet all this time my thoughts about you and your Heide world have worried me. Your silence is too great. I have had no word since Joy* died and I sometimes think maybe you are cross with me, and then I wonder whether you are as sad and distraught as I was that stopped me being able to lay pen to paper. Forgive me asking, my dearest friend, I wonder so many things… Is everything all right??? You once said that if somebody loved me he would send a leaf over the ocean to me to communicate love if he

---

*   Joy Hester

couldn't write a letter. There is no letter from Sun, no leaf, nothing
but vague messages from my poor John.

    But I am over my crisis and am happy and settled and
managing at last. Do not think I am scolding you but I am worried.
John said you were tired, and then Doodie, and goodness knows
I have no real news. I take it Doodie is really dying. I am sorry. It
seems to have been a bad year since I left you. Please if I can say a
few warm words to you to tell you that I miss you more than you
would ever believe. Your face and your voice sometimes come so
purely and fully into my memory that I cannot understand that
you are not with me. I love you very much, and in my fading love
for human beings my faith and heart are constant to you. If you
think me a poor and hopeless human being in dealing with my own
life, do not judge me thus, as it is impossible to tell you how difficult
my life has been to steer into any calm seas at all. God knows I am
sometimes very silly and muddled, but I have one constant and
maybe foolish characteristic, that is that I have courage. So it is
that fools rush in and Jeannie rushes in but things usually work out
all right. I have taken the bull by the horns once again and God
knows what I had to lose.

    My poor John Sinclair whose memory is softening in my
mind will be furious with me. I have written to John. I was still
desperately unhappy at the time and it was a sad but cruel letter.
He would be able to stand that as my unhappiness would calm his
temper somewhat. I am about to write him a letter to tell him I am
happy, that will be terrible for him to bear.

    It is a sweet little modern fairy tale that has become my life
out of a state of chaos. I met a strange handsome Englishman, he
was sick with alcohol but I didn't know. We became friends and I
wanted to help him as he seemed a poetic soul and was deeply sad
and alone. He became very ill and I nursed him through shivers
and shakes and alcoholic sweatings and ugliness and sadness and
loss of human dignity. I found it awful but was urged on by some

*desire to fulfil a Doris-like role and so this young man became my Merric.**

Several weeks passed and aided by great doses of vitamins and good food and the cutting down of alcohol, the cure worked. Then comes the fairy tale part, the beast turned into a handsome prince and adores his Australian friend. Well, he gave up the drink and wants to live happily ever after with me. While all this was being acted out my heart was being melted for this poetic man with great sad eyes. One day he came and asked me to live with him and as I said yes the phone rang and Barbara Blackman asked me was I interested in a garden flat underneath them. It was previously too expensive for me to consider.

However here we are in the most beautiful little flat. It has all happened so very quickly and goodness knows I don't know really what I think except that I really was close to giving up the ghost several weeks ago myself. My new man hasn't as yet completely moved in with me and so I am here by myself trying to sort out my feelings, relax and get some beautiful sunshine on to my limbs. There are many corners of my heart that find the whole idea impossible. Yet I find my heart really a big and full-flowing thing if there are enough gentle people for it to love.

Love is such a big word. I do not know whether I love or what. I love everything sometimes. My constant heart is steadfast like a rock and I weep a little inside to have to share it at this stage. I was so lonely and my dearest love struggled and worried and was torn betwixt and between, suffering through my suffering. I had promised to be as strong as an ox, but since John went back to Australia my loneliness and despair were too great and I yearned to sleep side by side with my love night in night out, and because the world was too much for me, I withered and became tired and ugly, I could live no more. Then fate sees me so decided and sends me a

---

* Doris was Arthur's mother. She spent several years looking after her husband Merric before he died.

143

*new gentle soul to look into my eyes. Poor young poetic man five
years younger than me, sees eyes sadder than his own and now it
is he who is the Florence Nightingale. He loves me very deeply and
moves me to quite girlish thoughts. I am happy. How strange. I will
not be lonely now. I feel almost young and carefree.*

*Another day now. My letter was interrupted. My thoughts are
strange today, perhaps not quite so romantic. Yet I do not know. I
am well content with happenings. There must always be something,
someone left out. I feel greatly about John and Rose Cottage. Jane
doesn't worry me as she strikes me as being such a complete little
being, so full of good loving gentle thoughts and wisdom for one
so little. She will be all right. She and I get along so terribly well
together. Whatever happens Jane will be all right. There is a great
and beautiful relationship with Jane and I feel sure that she must
and will stay with me whatever happens. So it is John who is the
lonely sad one and destined to be more lonely. Somewhere I feel
ruthless about him, as his behaviour during his stay in London
was enough for me to leave him on the roadside forever. Yet one
has this awful twisting turning heart that remembers so much and
wants to do the right thing by everybody. My God, how can I go
on considering John as part of my life, yet he has to be because he
demands so much. What right he has to demand, I do not know.
What terrible weakness of personality have I that …*

It's probably just as well my mother didn't post this letter. With so
much sadness and trouble in Sun's life, she may not have been in the
mood to read about my mother's "sweet little modern fairy tale" and
her beautiful relationship with her absent daughter. Sunday knew
how much easier it was to get along well with a child when contact
was restricted to school holidays and the occasional weekend visit.

When Sweeney was nine years of age he was also sent off to boarding school. There was no further talk of my mother sending me back
to Australia as she suggested in an earlier, angry letter to my father.
Now she wanted me to stay with her whatever happened, which was

just as well. My father's job often required very long nocturnal hours, and the Single Parenting Payment hadn't been introduced yet.

❧

My mother sent a postcard from Glyndebourne to tell my father of her new address but he didn't receive it until several weeks had passed.

> Dear John,
>
> Thought of you many times on my great trip to Glyndebourne. Saw Mozart's "Il Geralio". Loved it very much. Beautiful Mattawilde Dobbs. Haven't paid for it yet. Patti Hanna lent me the dough. Hated the audience. Ghastly snob value of middle-class type. Buildings ugly but gardens superb. Very expensive but worth it musically. Best Mozart I've ever heard. Loved it. Thought of you. Letter following. Sorry I've been in a great silence but so have you.
>
> Your letter arrived yesterday but I haven't digested it yet. Give Bob and Mag my love. What about the school fees? I am struggling financially and working on and off. I had to find somewhere for Jane to have her holidays. New Flat. New address 27B Jacksons Lane, Highgate N.6. It is underneath the Blackman's flat with garden.

Truth is sometimes hard to grasp. It can be slippery and tends to change with perspective and time. A lie on the other hand is much more solid. By definition we know when we tell one, otherwise it is just a mistake. My mother believed honesty was one of the most important of virtues. But somewhere between shining truth and dreadful lies there is a fuzzy, grey middle ground of omission. It was in this middle ground that my mother's new love, with his poetic soul and sad eyes, became her paying lodger in this letter to my father.

I have no memory of the months John Folkard lived with us, nor do I know how my mother explained his presence to me upon my return from boarding school. Possibly, like my mother, I was too caught up in my own world of make-believe to take much notice of the real world around me.

18th July

Dear John,

I have had a letter from Mrs. Neill and it seems the account is worrying them. I didn't feel she was very friendly to me but you know how very unreliable I am on these affairs. However it seems that only the 25 pounds that I paid early in the term is the money they have received. However the account runs like this. 81 pounds 9/6, 25 pounds paid 13/5/61, 56 pounds 9/6 outstanding. It is terribly depressing. God knows money is unbearable and I am constantly in a state of anxiety and see no possible means of coping with anything. You say there is no rent from Rose Cottage. This is news to me, terrible news as I have always justified myself somewhat on the score of R.C. rent. Where are all those tenants? What is the news of Rose Cottage? Is there no income there? God almighty. I cannot bear the thought.

Jane is home in two weeks. I saw her on Saturday. She is splendid and adorable as ever. I miss her in the most terrible way. I cannot live without her. After all, I have only had a little of Jane since you left. However, she will be home for eight weeks and I cherish the thought, so because of this I have taken a flat underneath Charles Blackman for twelve weeks. What then I do not know? It is 7½ Gns [guineas] a week but I have a paying lodger, an English bloke I know well. I have worked on Windows in Regent St. with Daphne but have let her take most of the profits because she is in queer St. Also I have been charring for Barbara Blackman, and so even with this it is a constant struggle to buy toothpaste. Unfortunately my legs collapse from time to time so I couldn't cope with working full time. In any case, Jane is more important. It is a perfect flat for Jane's holidays. French doors opening onto my own garden which is charming. Very near the Highgate woods, and yet even with a garden I am homesick beyond measure. You may be shocked at the price but I had to take the step as I was worried sick about the holidays. I couldn't bear Daphne's place a moment longer.

My new landlady is an artist and I got the flat as I am a cat lover and I have a cat to care for. Jane has made a friend. A real friend at school. I have made Jane very happy by offering to have her friend in London with us for most of the holidays. They are wild with excitement at the prospect. Strangely, the eight-year-old girl Jane looked at on her first day, she said, looked like Lulu. Her name is Katey and although she is eight, they are great buddies. Jane follows her around adoringly and Kate is a crazy scholar and tells Jane great tales of History. Jane gazes in wonder at such knowledge. Strangely also, Kate's mother and I had coffee together after seeing the children on the train. We got along famously. She is a writer and looks very much like me. Kate says we look exactly the same. The children are delighted that we mothers like each other. Kate's father is an Australian who is an actor at Stratford. Her parents are separated. It has all worked out very well as it has counteracted the terrible Bobby situation.* Jane is as happy as Larry. She is so proud of her big friend Kate. Joan cut Jane's hair, and she looks very like you around the eyes now.

Did you get my card from Glyndebourne? The other night I heard the Monteverdi Vespers in Westminster Abbey. It was wonderful. Also at Kenwood I heard the Hall's Chamber Orchestra with Sir John Barbirolli. I had a front seat and I think the old boy was drunk. He was half an hour late. His wife played the oboe. He is a funny little man with a fierce brown eye and pansy hands and feet. He behaves like a Spanish dancer. He was grunting like a sleeping man. I didn't really like his face. Also at Kenwood we heard Campoli who I thought was a lovely bloke, so charmingly devoid of mannerisms and nonsense. He played the Kreutzer Sonata which I hated (sorry). One night I heard the Philharmonic Ensemble play a Schubert Octet in F. Major which I loved very, very much. One

---

* Bobby was a boy of my own age at Summerhill. I don't know of any particular problem with him. As far as I can recall, my only complaint was his infuriating ability to save his weekly ration of sweets to eat in front of me, long after I had greedily devoured all of mine.

Kenwood concert was Carl Dolmetsch consort. I was in heaven. He
had two beautiful smiling daughters in with him. They all smiled.
It was the most smiling music-making I have ever seen or heard.
What a lovely family. The festival of Haulmere is on this very week
but I cannot afford to go.

It is hateful to be poor these days. I am too old. However, I do
not know what to do. I am in a stupor of worry and indecision.
I know not which way to turn. I wish I was at home. So many
thought worry me as to the future. I am glad you want to be my
friend. I am tired of emotion. I hate London these days, it is heavy
around my soul. I am Australian. I have stayed too long.

Jean

My father had written about the Summerhill fees two months
before but my mother didn't seem to understand that paying only 25
pounds at the beginning of the school term would leave a substan-
tial amount owing by the end of term. Nor had she considered the
financial implications when my father told her that the Kirks had
left Rose Cottage. The house had been divided into two, with my
father living on one side and the Kirks on the other. Bob, with his
new bride and baby, lived in the Tram Cottage but had paid no rent
since 9 February.

⌾

Letters between Australia and the United Kingdom took a minimum
of three days to reach their destination at the time. My mother was
obviously in a panic and not thinking clearly because she wrote this
letter three days later.

21st. July

Dear John, I do not quite understand why I haven't as yet heard
from you about the school fees. I told you I was embarrassed and
worried and no word of instruction or explanation. I have written
to Mrs. Neill myself with a lot of embarrassed words about the
situation and told her I have no idea whether Jane will be going
back next term or not. I do not want to part with Jane ever again

myself. However, I do not care for London from her point of view. I have no idea what to do.

Obviously you are furious with me but by what right may I ask? For Christ's sake write to me about the fees. God knows you are cheerless and busy and frantic but what the Hell! I write you a large letter with very serious thoughts and you don't even answer that, what are you thinking about.

One good thing … I went to Glyndebourne again. I haven't paid for either ticket yet. Patti had a spare one and so I went to "Elegy for Young Lovers" by the modern German [composer] Henze. Words by Auden. I adored it. Thought it marvellous opera, theatre or poetry or whatever. Simply enjoyed it all immensely. Thought some of the arias were marvellous and although lots of the music was modern, I loved it and thrilled and my hair stood on end as the symbols clashed and so on. You probably read about it. Ah well. Also the audience was more serious and highbrow and sympathetic. Obviously the social ladies were frightened.

There is no other thing to report, I am just so happy that Jane is coming to me in just two more days. I will let you know how she is. Ah well, I am tired of struggle and what do I care, except for Jane. Please be nice to Bob as he is very sad in spite of the baby. It was not his idea. Just fate. Please write.

Jean

❧

Replying to my mother's letter of the 18th:

July 26.

Dear Jeannie, needless to say I was glad to get your letter. I wanted to reply immediately and would have done so but I've been frantically busy with Rose Cottage, and after weeks of work the new tenants moved into the yellow room side during the weekend. O.K. that's 3 pound 15 to the good. But I must write fast and briefly and I can only beg you to believe that not one word or thought contains anything but care and affection, if not love.

And you must reply very promptly because all the
matters now are very urgent.

In the rest of the letter he begs my mother to make sure I see a dentist regularly. He tells her that Mag is "radiant" and Bob seems happy with the baby but they have paid no rent since the 9th of February. My father worries about how Bob is going to cope with a new baby and no income. My mother's description of the Dolmetsch Consort performance in her letter touched the sadness in my father's heart. He writes:

It is a tragedy that your hatred of me is so
terribly deep-seated, because your mind and
heart run so close to mine that I understand you
perfectly so often and so easily, and of course you
know that I do.

∞

Wednesday Aug. 2.
Dear Jeannie, you poor silly girl ... And now you
had best stop getting hot flushes of anger and
work out how it is that a man writes this phrase
affectionately. Your second letter from J's land
(your third since I left) came yesterday and this
is almost by return mail. I take it that our
letters have crossed, yours seems to be postmarked
July 23 and you would not by then have got mine
which was sent, I think, on that day. And in any
case, poor Jeannie, you must be very panicked
because only five days had passed since you posted
your other letter on July 18. Fortunately I sent
you on July 24 another 20 pounds English and I
will send another 20 pounds this Friday so that it
should be at your bank by say Monday Aug. 14.
Your letter simply tears at my heart and I beg
you to believe that I am not, and have not been,
"furious" with you and that I would love nothing so
much as to be able to send you 1000 pounds and tell
you to work it out yourself. Can you believe me,
quite simply and completely? If not then please try
to. Gods knows I know how you feel and how you feel

150

about Jane, and if you think that any sentence of
mine is meant to chide you then you misunderstand.
I repeat, because I feel it is desperately
necessary to be clear, that I write, think and
worry not with hostility in the slightest but with
care and affection.

But what on earth, Jeannie, is the answer? No doubt
your next letter will cross this, and will help to
answer that. Since I have left England I have given
you 152 pounds English, 172 with next Friday's
amount. Now I am not shocked, and not cross, and
not resentful, but I am alarmed by the financial
position. That is I think over 10 pounds a week
Eng. And true, if Jane's school fees had been paid
in full it would have left you little, indeed not
enough to live on, but if Jane's fees are only one-
third paid then, Jeannie, for the first time in
your life you seem to have spent more money than we
could afford. Even if you have, so what. But the
point is, where on earth do we go from here? I have
nothing in reserve and if you are to return, my
first problem will be to find the deposit for your
fare. And this will be done, without worry. But if
Jane returns to S for another term, then how do we
begin to get the fare home?

On 8 August my father wrote again, mainly to tell my mother that by
waiting a few days before sending her money, he could overdraw on
his wages and send her 50 pounds rather than 20 pounds. He ended
with news from Heide:

Sun's old nurse Doody died a week or so ago after
a very bad long drawn-out sickness in which Sun
and John did all the hard work. Sweeney so far as I
know is still doing nothing except what he wants to
do and a month or so ago poor old John was trying
to get him a job, and there are easier things to
do than find a job for a disinterested boy with no
education when unemployment is at its highest peak
since before the war.

Anyway I am sorry, this is a terribly dull letter,
not because I feel dull but simply because it is
late, I am tired and all I wanted to do was advise
you of the 50 pounds as quickly as possible. Coming
up in the car today I thought how very much I miss
you, how nice it would be, if all the emotional
problems could be kept back, to talk to you for a
night, but now I am just too tired to even think of
that as the reality it was this afternoon and will
be again tomorrow. But I wait for a letter. Forgive
this terrible effort and please give Jane a big
kiss for me.
X John

11th August

*Dear John, Your letter arrived this morning 11th August. Thank
you. I am sorry about the muddle about money and school fees.
As soon as I have notice from the bank I shall send a cheque to A.S
Neill. I cannot possibly send it all. God knows where money has
gone. I feel very depressed about it. I am sorry. I somehow hadn't
understood. Anyhow I'm glad I'm here and glad I took the law into
my own hands.*

*Two weeks of my feeding and Jane has put on weight and looks
wonderful. She is very happy and simply loves the garden and the
flat. There was no alternative. I am not concerned about Jane's
not going back to Summerhill. I don't think she ate her meals as
she was very thin when she arrived in London. I am spending
money on an extra special diet for her, to fatten her up. She is
very cooperative. I do not indulge myself but living is difficult. My
landlady came to London yesterday and she has offered me the
same flat but sharing the kitchen with her for 5 pounds a week.
This would begin in a month's time when the lease with the agent is
up. If Jane doesn't go to Summerhill then this will be well worth it.*

*One of the thrills of our stay in Highgate is that one day a
Siamese male [cat] walked through the garden. I talked to him and*

he came several times. Now he lives here and we call him "Wishnu telly poo poo" as Jane cannot call him anything else. He is very like Wishnu and sleeps around Jane's neck. He is beautiful. He belongs to some family down the street and according to my landlady nobody loves him as we do. He is sitting behind me on the chair at this very moment. We also have the landlady's cat, a marmalade lady. Jane is very happy. We had her girlfriend Kate for five days but I was very glad when she went home as I really didn't care for her or her influence on Jane. She was ten years old and inclined to be bored with life.* This is one reason why I don't want Jane to go back to Summerhill as they are great buddies. Jane is, as always, Jane. Witty, pretty, imaginative, drawing and playing by herself all day. She talked a lot about you when she first came back. She quite bluntly says that you are always very nice to me and that I am always horrible to you and that it's all my fault; it hurts rather.

I hate London these days. I find it ugly depressing and airless. There are no concerts now and the holidays are on and London is unbearably crowded with tourists. I am sorry Robbie owes you so much money. I do not know if you have any idea how unhappy he is. If you have any feelings for me, please extend some kindness towards him as he is heavy with a sense of failure. He didn't want to marry Mag. Wish I'd been home at the time. Apparently the pressure from all sides was too much for him. He had planned to leave her when the babe was born but says now he has fallen for the babe. It's an old story. He is very unhappy. He is my brother, even if you are intolerant of his personality, and I am very fond of him as you know. Could you imagine how his marriage, against his better judgement and heart, worries me. Do not forget he is a lot younger than you are. Anyhow I can't bear to think about it all but I feel it is a terrible story. His letters are low and dispirited. For God's sake, be kind to him if you possibly can.

As for Sun, I haven't heard a word since Joy died and I begin

---

* In a previous letter my mother had written that Kate was eight rather than ten.

to wonder if she still loves me. I write very little these days. I write to no one really. I think constantly of everybody but I feel very removed. Give Sun my love. I will write to her soon.

I had quite a long talk to [Sidney] Nolan one night after a party given by the Whitechapel Galleries for the Aussies. I liked him ever so much more and he sent his regards to you. I was a bit drunk and passionate and I told him everything I feel about his paintings. He took it very sweetly and promised faithfully to paint me some more Dimboola landscapes. He said the moment would come back. He squeezed my hand several times with great warmth and gentleness and sincerity. Cynthia was not there, needless to say. All this was after buckets of champagne provided by the Beauts (B.B.B. Mattresses). Sid is a sad man, I will swear. When I looked at his eyes they were very lonely. He looks very, very old and thin and tired.

Thank you for the money. God knows I don't spend a penny I don't have to. Jane is well cared for. She is in bad need of shoes and socks etc. It is not easy. I am sorry.

Love from Jane and Jean

⟡

Living with a hypersensitive, emotionally fragile woman wasn't easy, as my father well knew. But actually being the woman so easily hurt can be devastating, as I know only too well. In many ways I am like my mother, and unfortunately this is one of them. As a child I wouldn't have noticed my father's potentially hurtful comments, probably unintentional, or the glum face and depressing sighs that sparked my mother's angry response. The first thing I would see would be her shrill, spontaneous attack that caught both him and me by surprise. His initial reaction was usually to try, unsuccessfully, to calm her down. He might not have always been as nice to my mother as I had apparently claimed, but he was consistently very nice to me. He could be teasingly playful at times and I loved him dearly back then. My mother's letter is surprisingly honest and quite sad but, once again, she fails to answer my father's questions.

Tuesday Aug. 15

Dear Jeannie, your letter of Aug. 11 came this
morning, thank goodness and I am very glad. I
came into the city especially tonight to reply at
length, to try to convey truly and accurately some
of the many thoughts that have gone through my
head today and previously ... but on the way in I
called into Allen's, had too much wine with dinner,
and now feel just overwhelmingly tired and with a
headache for good measure. It's a pity because I
feel I want to write to you at great length and to
beg you to read it carefully, and that I will do,
I hope tomorrow or certainly this week, because
the time is terribly urgent and I feel it is very
important that you should know something of what I
think and feel. But your letter meant a lot to me.
It did not allay my worries about Jane's schooling
etc. or about any other practical problem but it
was good to hear some domestic news of how you and
she were.

Of course I was interested in your talk with Nolan
and deeply touched that he sent his regards. So
far as Sun is concerned, I would remind you of my
earlier letter of my description of the Sweeney
problem and now Doody's death after months of
lingering. She has often asked me to send you her
love, and in writing to her I would suggest that
you did not add to her worries. I'm sorry that
sounds a horrible and stupid thing to say but you
will know what I mean. Sure, I will be kind to Bob,
as I have been. You tend to still lecture me on the
point but there is no real need to.

But I must stop writing. I am just too tired and it
is not coming easily and not the right way.

He asks once again if my mother plans to return this year, em-
phasising that it will be on her own terms, and repeats his question
about whether I have seen a dentist. He ends with:

Thank you very much for writing as nicely as you
did and I read the final sentence many times,

155

```
because it said love from Jane and Jean and that
was nice and warm to read.
XX John
```

Ten days later my father still hadn't received answers to his questions so he wrote again, offering to share Rose Cottage or for him to live elsewhere if that were a condition for us to return. He urgently requested a decision and asked permission to return to the UK to see us and work as a freelance journalist if my mother planned to stay. More questions followed about my teeth and whether I still wet the bed. He told her that Sun had offered to pay for another term at Summerhill but he was not keen on the idea as he still owed her money he borrowed while overseas. The letter ended:

```
But I must finish this. Sun of course sent her
love. She is worn out these days, largely by worry
about Sweeney, as I would be if he were my son.
But that is a long and depressing story and I don't
think anyone can do much really to help. Please
give Jane a kiss and a hug for me and tell her I
will write her very, very soon a long letter. But
please write yourself quickly because, as I say,
the problems about Jane's school and your plans are
urgent.
XX John
```

Knowing my bedwetting was probably due to childhood stress must have made it a sensitive subject for both parents. From a very young age I witnessed many of their loud and often violent arguments. Theirs was a scrambling sort of violence which mostly involved pushing, shoving and flailing of arms, and was usually initiated by my mother. At least that was the case in the early years. Sometimes, as I slept, my dreams would be interrupted by increasingly loud, angry voices, followed by huffing, puffing and grunting noises as the fight turned physical, and finally my mother's loud, distraught crying. It was too much for a child to bear alone in her dark bedroom. The knowledge of what I had seen and heard would have created a dark smudge of guilt in each parent's heart. My father's response was to add it to his existing depression, while my mother just attempted to ignore it.

⚬

Saturday Aug. 26

Dear Jeannie, Yesterday I wrote you a long letter which just wasn't much good. It said some of the things I meant to say but it did not say them well. Last night I stayed at Heide and got back here this morning tired, worried about you and more worried about Sun, and then, joy of joys, there awaited me your cards from Glyndebourne. Thank you, they were very sweet and thank you for thinking about me. Ah, what I would give to be able to hear Seraglio. Of course, your comments about being able to see Jane so seldom tore at my heart, but of course that is a long time ago now and silly girl, you sent them by ordinary mail. No wonder they did not arrive.

In bed at Heide last night I had a few bad pangs and wondered how long this dreadful business of you and Jane living on the other side of the world will go on. But please, in thinking about me and about what to do, I beg you to think straight and realise that since I left Eng. I might have written you a lot of maudlin and silly words but there has not been one angry word or the faintest trace of hostility or resentment from me. You can if you wish call that boy scout stuff ... but finally without being vain, stupid or egocentric, I know that interpretation is not true.

Why do I talk about myself like this? Simply because one suffers enough with the knowledge of one's failings that it is necessary to living to sometimes believe one is not just a hateful useless bastard. Anyway, your words on the Glyndebourne card were very sweet and if they had cost a pound to send they would have been worth it. The story about Sun is not a happy one but I feel I should give you the general picture. I might say that I am not being either a boy scout or good fellow about

157

it. I was out there last night because John had
gone to Sydney and Sun cannot be left alone. Most
likely I will go back there tonight. I talked for
hours to Sun last night and of course this morning.
Although she was very nice (she is much too tired
to be anything else these days), she really wanted
me to go because, as she said, she felt I was
"deeply critical" of her relationship with Sweeney.
And of course I am, as you are and a whole lot
of her friends are. But the answer is of course
that we are not so critical of the relationship as
Sweeney is. The fact is that he hates and loathes
John, Sun, Heide and all that goes with it. That's
the basis and it's often also the surface. This
year he refused to return to school. Got a job and
stuck it out a week. Stays out all night with the
riff raff of West Heidelberg or brings them all to
Heide for parties, installs them in the cottage,
supplies them with food, cigarettes, blankets and
anything else they require from the house.

He is of course only 16 and not a licensed driver,
but he takes Sun's car when he wants it. He took
it a month ago and cleared out to Sydney for a
week with a prostitute and another boy just out
of jail. John and Sun were woken up at 3.30 the
other morning by three leather jacketed louts in
the hall, looking for Sweeney and looking for a gun
that the jail bird boy pinched and took to Sydney.
A few weeks earlier they had been wakened at 4 a.m.
by a police patrol flashing torches around the
garden. There had been a hit and run accident and
they were looking for Sween. They dragged him out
of bed and questioned him.

He was in the clear this time but you see he is
getting pretty well known. Yesterday he took the
car and then again last night. Oh, it goes on and
on, you have no conception. But it is going to kill
John and Sun, I am afraid, and that is not just a
figure of speech. John was in Sydney in fact to get
a few days spell. Sun just tries to go on living
and there is a limit to how much longer even she

can go. I know I don't have to tell you anything
about this, that is, about the causes and so on.
But there is just no answer. I talked to Sun last
night, trying to get her to see that her present
attitude was simply giving Sweeney the kiss of
death. And it is. And she will do just that and
there is nothing that you or I or the cleverest
doctor alive could do about it.

And my only thought this morning about my talk
with Sun is that I must stop trying to think
constructively because in the first place to be
constructive now is almost impossible and in the
second place, no matter how hard one tries to
conceal it, what comes out is a critical attitude
towards Sweeney's upbringing, which of course
simply adds to her tension without really helping.
Sun is, of course, quite mad at one level. At
another, as you know, she is marvellously lucid and
knows quite well that there is nothing much she can
do now without changing her whole relationship with
Sweeney. She is not going to do that. It's going
to go on and on until something blows up. All this
has happened in six months. What are the prospects
for the next six months and indeed the next year?
There is constant talk of moving out of Heide and
it's serious talk. Constant talk of more and more
retreats.

I'm sorry. This is terribly depressing but as one
of Sun's closest friends I think you should know
it. All you can do is give her your love, and other
things to think about. Hug our daughter and think
how lucky you are. Forgive me. The day is glorious
and I must spray the peaches because the buds are
swelling.

P. S. Rang Sun a few minutes ago. As soon as I left
this morning, Sweeney pinched 4 pounds from her
purse and pinched the car once again. Sorry, this
is the most depressing letter ever.

Love XX John

Sweeney was a little under two years of age when his life turned upside down. The Reeds weren't strangers to him but nor were they the parents he had bonded with, the parents that just seemed to disappear from his young life.

Not long after Sweeney was left with the Reeds at Heide, Nolan left, never to return, and Sunday collapsed in complete despair. It is likely young Sweeney's needs were temporarily forgotten while Sun recovered slowly and patched up her broken heart. It would be a while before Heide became the peaceful, stable environment Sweeney needed, and by then he was creating his own disturbance.

After a few years of home-schooling, in desperation the Reeds sent him to a strict boarding school but were horrified when they discovered he had been caned for misbehaviour. John Reed wrote an angry letter to the headmaster explaining the evils of corporal punishment. As it turned out, Sweeney showed signs of responding quite well to the sort of discipline he had never before experienced, yet the Reeds decided to remove him from boarding school and send him to Preshil, a free school based on similar principles to Summerhill. It wasn't a good idea.

When my father was writing these letters it was only eight months since Joy Hester, Sweeney's biological mother, had died. It was no wonder Sweeney was proving difficult.

⟡

Tuesday Aug. 29

Dear Jeannie, On Sunday I posted you a long letter
mainly about the Sweeney problem. I hope that
it did not go astray and, as I said, I told you
because I felt that, depressing though it was, that
as a friend of Sun's you should know. I saw John
yesterday and talked to him about it at length but
to no real purpose. Sweeney was due to go to court
today for driving without a licence but I do not
know the result. There is once again talk of S.
leaving home but it is wishful thinking, and so far
as I can see, John and Sun have no resistance, no
control and in fact nothing to offer but hope that

160

he will change, and I can see no reason to believe
that he will. John, I think, knows pretty much what
it is all about but Sun asks if he is nutty and
says she cannot see the point of such behaviour.
The point is all too clear, but make sure you don't
make it clear to Sun.

Anyway I think your only chance of getting a letter
from Sun is if Sw. does leave home temporarily.
Otherwise I cannot see her getting time free enough
of worry to write. No doubt it was this background
that made me so pleased with your cards from
Glyndebourne and the one from Aldeburgh. Perhaps
I made too much fuss about them but I was pleased
that you thought of me while at Glyndebourne.

Last night however I had a bad night. Went to
bed around midnight and then woke sharply after
dreaming that I was swimming and wading against
a difficult river with Jane behind and holding
onto my neck. I asked her if she was all right and
she replied, "Yeah, I'm all right". That is all.
But I was then horribly awake, it was only 2.30
and I stayed awake until nearly dawn, tormented
by a thousand memories and reflecting, rather
bitterly I afraid, on your long letter in which
you dispose of every word I had written in one
sentence, underlined, although often accurately,
my weaknesses and then disposed of all my good
qualities as the result of a guilty conscience.
Today, of course, I am very depressed and I don't
think that is unnatural. Yet I know that my bitter
reflections last night were only half the story and
often unjust to you.* But it takes two people to
break a marriage, and I sometimes feel that I am
today not as bad a husband as you believe I am. I
had hoped not to write this way to you again but I
confess my present thoughts because for once I feel
it best to be simply truthful. But it is equally

---

* The long letter my father refers to is the undated abusive one my mother
  sent in response to the increasingly worried letters he wrote upon his return
  to Australia.

truthful to say that my first reaction and no doubt
my last reaction to that letter is a feeling FOR
the woman who wrote it.

My father then asked about my mother's plans regarding my schooling and apologises for the general trend of his letter, which he acknowledges will annoy her. Yet it was not the general trend of my father's letter that would upset my mother this time, but something quite specific. He had suggested that if she didn't intend returning then he would be back in England by early October. His talk of returning in previous letters was sufficiently vague as to not worry her unduly. At the time of writing this next letter, she hadn't received his letter informing her of his intention. Her panicked response was yet to come.

Living with John Folkard wasn't turning out to be the sweet little modern fairytale my mother had imagined, as her ardour was cooling. His, by contrast, was increasing and he was keen to introduce her to his parents, so a weekend in the small seaside village where they lived was arranged. My mother's passion for Folkard may have been waning but her passion for the sea was life-long. Never before had she lived more than a short stroll away from it and she missed it dreadfully. Her desire to stand on the edge of an ocean and look to the horizon, whatever the weather, was like a hunger deep in her soul. But there is one type of weather condition that can frustrate the ability to appreciate the beauty of any vista, and England is renowned for it. Fog, thick, enveloping, isolating fog.

The thought of a weekend breathing sea air with her young lover was not enough to keep my mother in good spirits when writing to my father.

⁂

31 August 1961

Dear John,

All this talk, backwards and forwards. All this talk about money.
All this talk about love, all this talk about what you are and what I

John Folkard. He had grown a beard by the time he lived with us.

am. So what, so what. All I know is that what you say has nothing to do with what you do. As for money, God knows I sit down and stare at my cheque book. It gives me no pleasure. Do you know that I have never ever in Jane's life ever bought her a dress? Not even as an infant. Here I am still patching up Glynis's old fat dresses.

We are having a late heat wave and are off to spend the weekend at the sea for the first time. I am so frustrated for the sea and at first was so thrilled at the invitation. But here today I can't find one dress fit for Jane to wear. Last week I had to buy her new shoes. I got them in a sale for 1 pound. You tell me I have become bad with money. Rental is the killer. I spend very little. I had to have the Doctor last week as I was so ill. Once again my blood count. All this because I am very poor. Jane has been cared for with all my heart and energy. She is superb. I have never seen her so well and happy. She is quite well covered for the first time. She has charming double chins* and round face and looks like Sarah used too. She has two great new front teeth very like yours. Her diet is excellent. She hasn't wet the bed since you left and it is never likely to happen again.

OK. This flat is madly expensive but there was no alternative. Jane is healthy and happy. Her drawings are marvellous. The future is hard to deal with. I am terribly homesick. More than I can account for. London bores me. I have no money to spend on the few things of interest. What to do I do not know. I cannot live with you as your wife. Coming home frightens me as all your promises mean little. You have never allowed me the freedom you talk about. I cannot trust you on this score. I would like a divorce and then I could be a friend with you and to you. I like you very much and even miss you but I cannot live with you or love you. I feel deeply the fact that you are Jane's father and that is enough to make me come home, apart from homesickness, but how to cope with your heavy and complex personality, let alone your masculinity beats me. I haven't the courage to fight you nor the heart to love you. After all why shouldn't you miss me and be sad about my life? I have always been very nice to you but have you been fair to me?

Do not come to London. I will not be here if you do. I will not live here long. I have a boyfriend who wants to marry me. I do not know what to do about it. It is too soon to know. He threatens to follow me to Australia if I go. Also my other boyfriend from Melbourne who had three daughters and was in love with me before I left writes that his wife has died.** Goodness knows, life

---

* I don't appear to have lost or gained weight in any of the photos from our time in London. I was a fussy eater so I suppose it's possible I lost some weight at Summerhill but I suspect this is a just case of exaggeration.

** Stuart King had written my mother a rather strange letter on 4 June. It was

never stands still. Do not think you are in a position of great power over me, as I have several alternatives before I take to the streets. At the moment I am Jane's mother and my life is spent caring for her and guiding her to womanhood. I think her worth much energy.

This isn't a carefully thought out letter. I cannot think clearly. I will write in greater detail with more clarity in a few days. As for Jane's schooling, I do not know. If I can I will do my best. I am sorry about Sun's troubles. I have to make lots of decisions in this next week. Do not think you alone worry about life. I feel trapped. I just am sick to death of love, emotion and human relationships. Maybe I am getting old but I care little, I just want peace.

I will write soon. Jane sends her love. Jean

Although my mother's letter was nowhere near as vitriolic as the long angry one mentioned in my father's last letter, it was enough to upset him. Adding to his hurt may have been my mother's first mention of an English boyfriend.

❧

```
Monday Sept. 4. 61.
Dear Jeannie,
On Monday I sent you some photos taken last weekend
of the garden and baby. That night your letter
arrived and although I was fearful, because your
silence had made me so, I suppose there was one
```

only on the second page that he informed her of his wife's sudden death on 4 April. The story, as my mother told it, was that Stuart's wife killed herself after finding out about the affair. But Stuart's letter suggested he and his wife were getting along reasonably well and the marriage had survived his infidelity. Also he ended his letter saying, "Please don't think that Bettye took her own life, that is not so, she was worried about a possible pregnancy which in fact was not the case, and weakened herself to a point where she apparently could not recover. I could not reason with her. It all happened within a few hours. I did not recognise how bad she was." Stuart was hoping my mother might come to him in New Guinea. I don't know whether she contemplated such a move, nor do I know what she said when she wrote back, but in his letter a couple of weeks later he sadly wished her much happiness with her new man.

small lingering thread of hope that it would not be
too bad. Well, it was terrible. At first I reacted
badly because of the hurt but after a few hours
thinking about your life, my own and Jane's, such
foolishness vanished and I just felt hopeless and
sad.

Today I still feel sad (and I say this for the
record and not with a desire for sympathy) but
absolutely calm, quiet and I think more resigned
than ever in my life before. And it would not be
strange if this were so because if one is in a
fire long enough a lot of useless stuff gets burnt
away. No letter that I have ever written has had
the slightest real meaning to you (I think) and I
have no illusions about this one being different. I
don't quite know why I write but I do so. If I were
to ask you anything I suppose it would be not to
stop hating me but at least try to realise how much
and how often that hatred distorts your vision.

In this letter you say that you like and even miss
me and then you say later, "Do not think you are
in a position of great power over me" and add a
few threats about your "alternatives", as though
vindictiveness was my most likely reaction. It
was not at any stage my reaction and it is not so
now, and you could have spared yourself, me and
Jane the thought because such thoughts affect us
all. You say you have a new lover. Do you think
that surprises me? I knew it in my own heart and
mind weeks ago, and although the knowledge was the
result of the way I constantly and intensely think
of you, it was not very clever of me. O.K. you have
another lover whose wife has died and you say life
does not stand still. No, Jeannie, all that stands
still is your image of your husband. It is not
that you think of me always as a "neurotic dog that
bites the hand that feeds it and as a demanding
bullying parasite of human love" because I know,
thank God, that you often think of me differently.
But overall, when it comes to me, you are alone
in two ways, in the extent of your knowledge but

166

also in your inability to distinguish truth from falsehood.

This letter means nothing, will change nothing, not even one heartbeat. Well, you are free to do as you wish and in saying that, I give you nothing because as you know I am powerless to influence you even if I wanted to. It is you who is in a position of great power and I find it hard to believe that you don't know it. Sad, tormented, desperate, to be sure, but in a position of great power with me.

Well, life is what it is, a comedy for he who thinks and a tragedy for he who feels. Perhaps in 10 years' time you will see that for all my awful bloody faults, I paid a very high price and even so my mind was a lot better and my heart by no means as empty as you thought it was.

I'm sorry about all this. I must hurry to a concert.

X John

Two practical points please. Re Jane's education. It is not a question of doing your best, Jeannie, it is a matter of fact and of law that Jane simply must go to some approved school for the next term and constantly after that. And please, I want, and you have no reason to refuse, exact answers to the following questions. Did Jane keep her two appointments with the dentist the week I left London? What did he do? What did he say? When has she seen the dentist since then and what work has been done? I'm sorry to sound bossy about this but I am now in a terrible hurry and I have asked for this kind of information many, many times before.

My mother used to laughingly suggest that all my father really cared about was my teeth. His insistence on regular visits to the dentist continued into my early adulthood so naturally I would laughingly agree with her. Now I realise I have him to thank for the fact that I still have most of my own teeth, and I know that part of being a good parent involves such practical things as dental visits, vaccinations and facilitating your child's education.

On the same day my father wrote his letter, my mother was writing him another, even angrier letter. He was about to discover that her last terrible letter could easily be outdone. Our weekend by the sea hadn't improved her mood.

4th September

Dear John, Your urgent request for a decision awaited my seaside weekend. Jane was thrilled with her letter but I'm not so sure that I was thrilled with mine. You ask what I am planning to do. I do not know, but I am amazed at your talk of being in London in October. I never heard such annoying talk. Why should you come to London? It is pointless. I will be home as soon as I can bring myself to it. I greeted you pleasantly and generously once in London. I would never again. If we meet again it will be in Australia. I want to go home as you well know but nothing you say convinces me that I would be free of your demanding emotional personality.

Nobody has any right to be so obstinate as you. You worry me frantically. I feel like a cat that has left its home base and doesn't know how to sneak back into a good position of safety from some enemy. I will not be your wife. I will never sleep with you again. I will not live as a woman with you. Can I make myself clearer? Can you not have the guts to face these facts? There is to be no other chance for you in this respect. I am not your woman. I have no love for you, only a vague fondness and respect for your sensitivity and loyalty as a friend and parent. I will not live with you. You have no right to ignore this. You have had a fair go. Don't try me too far. If you come to London I will beg my fare from Sun and leave England before you arrive.

I have done everything in my power to behave in your favour but it is not possible for me to extend any further generosity towards you, who continually demands a relationship you have not earned. Even in London you behaved in a simply impossible way. If your interest in Jane were genuine you would not provoke me any further. I am not an ugly old woman. You are not the only man to have seen me or cared. You treated your property too badly and it's too late to speak of changing. No word you write sounds much like a change to me. The only thing is that you cannot face your bad luck or whatever you call it. I have spent my life facing bad luck and have never seen any sense or gain in whinging, and things are as they are and don't change.

You are spoilt like an only child. You cannot believe you are not wanted. To me you are spineless and cowardly. If you had any guts you would have accepted fate years ago. If you really loved me your words would be vastly different. You know little of love. Jane is your only love as she is part of you and very beautiful. If you didn't behave so badly she would be with you now. Do you know how far you could drive me with all this talk! There are ways and means of escaping forever your pernicious, selfish, egotistical, self-pitying love for me. You have no character and so we continue to hate and battle thousands of miles apart. Jane is very happy with just me.

If you were a man of dignity and control and love of other people we would be functioning as a unit of loyalty at Rose Cottage, an intelligent way of life with energy being used creatively not destructively. Loads of intelligent people live in groups of loyalty without emotional ownership. You could never do this as you are as always unable to function without tragedy. Jane is an absolute miracle child. I have never seen her happier. We function together better than ever and she shows absolutely no neurotic symptoms of any sort. She is blooming and I love her greatly. As for school, God knows. If I had my way, I wouldn't send her anywhere. There is a little private school down the road that Jane's next-door neighbour Sarah attends. It costs 19 pounds a term. Highgate is a bit rough so I am not keen on a state school. Other than that who knows. I shall have to think.

I would love to be coming straight home for Xmas but I am too confused to think of it now. As I have decided to keep this garden flat on at five pounds a week, I see no point in considering "Summerhill". Why are you such a pig-headed stubborn stupid

idiot that you make human relationships into terrifying agonies.
Life is so simple if you stop raging and demanding. One other
complication is that this private school has a uniform. On the other
hand, Jane has no bloody clothes. You expect miracles from me.
You rave on and on about money. I do not know, your calculations
sound much more frightening than do mine. The total amount up
to date in my bank book is in all 222.00 pounds. 82.00 pounds paid
to Summerhill. Leaves 140 pounds. 140 pounds over the period
since you left is certainly only 7 pounds a week at the most and that
has covered everything, new shoes for Jane, new slippers for Jane,
bathing suit which she promptly lost, new jeans, new socks, fares to
Leiston, stamps, rent, living, concerts, Christ almighty, how do you
think I cope? Jane has been fed like a prize cow so that she copes
with London. You are heartless and impossible to tell me I am
extravagant. I would like to see you manage.

We have had our weekend holiday by the sea. There was a fog
over the whole of East England the whole weekend. We enjoyed
it as best one could in a fog. It was a bitter disappointment for us
both. We were around the coast from Dover. A place called Deal
which is where Caesar landed on English soil. It was charming in
one sense but only pebbles and buildings and fog. We stayed with
my friend's family and Jane was a model child and everybody
adored her. Rail fares are so bloody expensive we have little hope of
doing it again. I miss the sea so very much. I cannot live inland for
long. In fact I cannot live in London. Sometimes I get so depressed I
do not want to live at all.

Jane is my great joy. The Blackmans live upstairs but their
child is a monster. The small one is sweet. I do not like Barbara
Blackman at all. She is also a monster. I try to keep Jane away.
We have nice neighbours next door. Jane plays with their child.
Sometimes I feel like an ill-fated bitch to have ever met you. Your
existence chokes me. What right have you got to be such a person?
If it weren't for you I would be home by now. You know, ever since
I went to France I haven't been able to stomach London. You

write about your nightmare. Ever since I met you I have had bad
nightmares. I too am alive. I am tired and old and tempted to give
in to anything that will protect me from you. London is grey today
and it will get greyer steadily now. I think of my little beach and my
darling Rose Cottage.

I think often of Sun and am very sorry she is so troubled. I do
not understand what you think is wrong but to me it is purely and
simply a matter of breeding mixed with lack of discipline. Another
child may have blossomed in Sun's care. Sweeney is half Joy and
half Bert, both very talented but doubtful personalities in many
ways. I hated Bert. I liked Joy but from what I've heard she was a
strange girl. How do we know what sort of an adolescent she was.
From what Bert said to me she was a terrifying young girl and
any man who can talk so about his wife, strikes me as being pretty
nasty. He said some vile things. Also he said vile things about my
best friend Sun. Sweeney, genetically, has a bad start. Anyhow,
I love Sun and feel deeply for her. Please be very kind to her and
forgive her her faith. Personally I begin to dislike human beings.

⤜∾

It is strange that my mother seemed to blame genetics almost entirely for Sweeney's behavioural problems. In some of my father's
earlier letters he indicated that he had many discussions with my
mother about problems that might arise due to the Reeds inconsistent parenting. My mother's simple explanation came as a surprise to
my father. He must have also wondered why she referred to Sweeney
as being half Bert and half Joy when she knew that was seriously in
doubt. It was then known by quite a few people that Bert Tucker was
probably not Sweeney's biological father. One person who didn't yet
know was Sweeney.

My mother's letter continued:

Jane, by the way, has developed a new nose. It is now the same
as mine. She looks more like me than ever these days. She is very
beautifully formed and her little head sits on her neck like Nefertiti.
She is a regal little being. I do not mean that is how she is like me

171

*but you know what I mean. I'm sorry I'm being so nasty. I hate
all this terrible talk but I cannot see how to deal with things. I am
sorry, you had nightmares, I am sorry you are lonely and sad, yet
I know so well it is your own doing. You risk even further. I do not
know what to say. You counteract my nicest thoughts.*

*Do not think of coming to England. It is ridiculous. Out of
proportion. After all, my fare home is cheaper than that. I would be
furious if you come. I would whisk Jane away. For Christ's sake be
sensible. What have you offered me in the way of freedom? Simply
nothing. I can't bear it. Do you want me to give up living? For God's
sake.*

Jean

⌘

This last angry letter affected my father rather badly, but by the time
he sent off his confused and pleading response, my mother had
recovered some equilibrium and this relatively friendly letter was on
its way. The explanation for her mood swing appears to be the arrival
of my father's fortnightly payment. Although he had expressed his
money worries in a couple of previous letters, there was no suggestion that he would cease these payments.

13th September

Dear John,

*A note from the bank this morning to say 20 pounds had arrived
was, needless to say, my lifesaver. Things are hard with me and
your tone of previous letters made me feel I was not going to get
any more help from you. I was so depressed. The struggle for
money is just about my whole existence these days. I hardly have
my fare to London to spare. As from this week my rent is down to
five guineas but I have my mad landlady to put up with instead.
However at least it will be a bit easier. So thank you for the money.
Goodness I know it isn't easy for you, but I cannot starve. Jane
began school yesterday. She is a marvel. She waltzed into a large
Middlesex state school like a hero. She loves it and so far it is
excellent. It will cost no money.*

Replying to my mother's angry letter of 4 September:

Friday. Sept. 15

Dear Jeannie,

Your last long terrible letter came exactly a week
ago and I spent most of that marvellous spring day
answering it. But then I did not post it because I
wanted to have a second look, to be quite sure that
I meant what I said and that I said what I meant.
And I did and this letter is substantially the
same, no better, but perhaps a little clearer.

When I first read your letter I walked around the
garden so bewildered and shattered that I would
have liked to have rushed in to ask Bob for his
advice and help. I just did not understand. You
can't believe that, I suppose. And now, with the
saga of your life and mine, and your letter running
through my head every minute of the day and night,
I feel as though I have been badly beaten up. And
at first I truly did not understand at all because
while I might have written you some silly sandy
stone letters, I have not written one hostile word,
made one demand or implied one threat since I left
London, and if you re-read my letters you will
see that that is true. And now all I can really
understand is that you took my talk of returning to
London as a threat to come back and try again. It
was never meant to be that.

He then points out that he has offered my mother complete
freedom and any sort of living arrangement that would make the
thought of coming home peaceful for her. He agrees to a divorce if
that is what she wants. He goes on:

I might say I was a little surprised at the
superficiality of your comments on Sweeney but
the good thing about that is that it will make it
easier for you to write to Sun, and your sympathy
for her feeling for Sweeney is likely to mean a
lot to her. And God knows we are sad, everyone is
sad, but by Christ, the outlook at Heide is sad.
The night before your letter arrived I had spent at

Heide in response to an urgent call from Sun. They
live, and not without some reason, almost in fear
of their lives. Sweeney has beaten up John once and
is now in complete control of Heide. John and Sun
have seen my cousin who held out no hope for their
relationship with Sweeney and in fact advised them
to get out quick. There has been talk, very serious
talk, of closing Heide down and there is not more
than a 50-50 chance of it being lived in when you
arrive home. They are simply waiting for Sweeney
to go to jail and waiting for what he does to them
before that. He has five summonses including one
for theft and I think it is quite certain he will
be in jail long before Xmas. So when you speak of
asking someone to help you I would cut Sun out of
it. She needs your help more than you need hers and
you mean a lot to her. Next to the phone at Heide
these days in large letters is the police emergency
number. I am sorry to have to tell you all this but
you can write to Sun and say I have given you the
complete picture.

But I am worn out and must finish this. Yet I
cannot do so without wondering sadly about what
kind of man I am and what kind of man you think I
am. This last letter of yours was motivated by a
reaction to a statement of mine which was stupid
in that it was likely to be misunderstood. But
before that you had often accused me of hatred and
hostility - quite unjustly because that was not in
either my heart or my letters. I have not loved you
enough and for that we have all suffered terribly,
but I have often loved you and been gentle, very
often in London and Europe, when you never knew
because your vision was clouded by the past. One
night in London after I had helped nurse you for
about the third time you said that never before had
I looked after you so nicely and uncomplainingly.
The following night you bashed my face.

But all this is silly and hopeless. I sometimes
find myself thinking that perhaps some magician
could teach us not to love each other but simply to

really and truly understand and the rest would be
easy. But that is fantasy.

The letter ends with:

The weather is more like summer than spring and so
blue and quiet yesterday that at Rose Cottage you
could hear if a man clapped his hands at Beaumaris.
But I'm sorry I'm tired and must finish.

Good luck Jeannie.

John

꧁꧂

Twelve days later my father wrote again.

28 September 1961

Dear Jeannie,

I was sitting at home last Wed. desolate, when your
last letter arrived. Thank you. Thank you. It meant
at least as much to me as the letter from the bank
meant to you. Why? It changed nothing. You are
still in London with Jane, a lover and a terrible
image of your husband. Well, there was lots of
information and not one hostile word and you will
never know how glad I was for that. Your previous
letter had buggered me more than I realised and
when this last one came, it felt as though a great
load had been taken from my shoulders.

All the news of Jane was good. I am sorry, very
sorry that you are sick and of course very worried
about you in every possible way and afraid that
you will do things which in the long run will only
add to your unhappiness. But I wanted to say a
hundred things about your letter and will try to
do so later. At the moment I have not a minute
to spare for myself (that does sound like a boy
scout). But I had an urgent call from John last
Saturday. Sweeney had just beaten them both up and
shot through with the car. Sun called the police
and they came in a small car and Sweeney just drove
past the gate and invited them to catch him. By the
time the patrol arrived he had gone. John felt he
had no alternative but to report the car as stolen,

which he did and it was then up to the police to find S. They didn't, and of course nobody slept much at Heide.

Today I drove Sun across to where S has worked (very rare) for the past week and there was the car in a side street. I immobilised the engine and then did the only unpleasant thing possible, told them [the police] to go there at 4.45 and pick him up, which they did. He is now in jail and will remain there unless bailed out (and this is to be discussed tonight) until Wednesday Sept 4 when he comes up for trial. John has a black eye and a badly bruised rib but I do not need to tell you how they both look at present and it is only now that the really hard part begins. Nobody is confident that he will come out of jail better than he went in and indeed the danger is that he might be much more aggressive. Sun is terrified and I don't blame her.

Well, now it will be hours and days of talk and worry about a problem to which there is no satisfactory or happy answer. As for that bastard Tucker, your opinion is favourable compared with mine. Would you believe it that apparently his role since he returned has been to take S aside and tell him "the truth", and you might imagine what that means.* I shudder to think about it. This is not the kind of story to make you homesick or anxious to return and I tell it to you firstly because as Sun's friend you should know, and secondly because you should also know that I am absolutely unable to think about the serious problems of my own life, or at least to think consecutively about them, and at the very moment when they seem to me to be critically important.

---

* The truth was that Bert may not have been Sweeney's father. It is more likely his biological father was Billy Hyde, a well-known jazz drummer at the time with whom Joy was having an affair. Despite my mother's earlier contention that Sweeney's problems lay in the genetic mix of Joy and Bert, my father presumes she will understand. And I believe she did, but was too absorbed in her own problems to give it further thought.

But I must fly now back to Heide and to hours of
exhausting and round and round in circles talk.
I will write to Jane tomorrow and you too if I
can. You ask if I have forgotten Oct. 5. COULD I
HAVE FORGOTTEN. On this Wednesday I will send you
another 20 pounds, that is a week ahead of time
and then every fortnight. But that means an extra
10 pounds. Buy her ballet shoes if you can. Hug
her for me and for Christ's sake, occasionally
think how much I miss her. And can I quickly plead
with you, to say that your notion of yourself as a
cat frightened to return home is false and self-
engendered, and I think you are mad to consider
another winter in London. I am not the same man
I was before I went to Europe or even as I was in
London and if, as you say, I thrive on tragedy,
it is only that the avalanche of it this year has
left me burnt up perhaps, but with some real and
absolute faith in my own human dignity.

But there is no time. I am sorry I must rush.
Please try not to be too depressed about the Heide
story. Perhaps we will find a constructive answer,
and if my last long letter to you was depressed
and depressing, please try to forgive me for that
and to remember that it sprang out of a terribly
depressing and hurtful letter from you. Off now.
None of your friends in Australia have forgotten
you.

John XXX

Three quick kisses for Jane

꧁꧂

Sunday Oct. 1. 61

Dear Jeannie, this is the quickest note ever.
Tomorrow morning I will post this plus a parcel
addressed to Jane. It contains two records, one
for her and one for you. Her record, this time, is
really disappointing. It could have been good but
I had to rush out to Glen Iris to make it after a
hectic morning, and after spending nearly an hour
with John R on the telephone and my head was full
of everything except Jane.

After spending five nights at Heide I got back
here and had a shocker of a dream that left me
like a wet rag for the next two days. It was not a
nightmare, it was just the truth only it was silent
and horrible. Anyway, these things are not new to
you. The position with Sweeney is that he has been
at Tarana (the junior Pentridge) since last Monday
and will stay there until the case comes up, I
think next Wednesday. Apart from the charges about
illegal use of the car, there are about a dozen
others of petty theft of parts from cars in the
Heidelberg area. After a solid week of talking the
plan now is, assuming that he will be released on
probation, to put him in a boy's hostel at Kew and
see what the probation officers and the doctors can
do to help.

I must say I have found the week both very
depressing and terribly exhausting, mostly because
it has often been so difficult to be honest. I
think that in my last letter I probably gave you
an exaggerated idea of Bert's part in the saga, but
while it was over-stressed, it was not basically
untrue. He has been fooling round with Sweeney,
aided by that great psychiatrist John Gooday.*
They are bosom pals. Nobody is optimistic about
the future for Sweeney, and both John and Sun are
very tired and depressed. But they have a nice
psychiatrist now on the job, Bill Bloomfield, and
perhaps by the end of the week things will brighten
a little.

If you know what you are doing, it is probably all
right for you to stay in London. But do you know?
And is it possible that your fear of returning
(your fear of me) is partly a rationalisation
because you are torn between two worlds? But three
people at least are affected by your decision, and
so far as you yourself are concerned I am sure that
the longer you remain in London, the more you will

---

* My father was being sarcastic. John Gooday had an interest in psychology
but no formal training.

suffer a feeling of being "removed", and I know
what a torment that kind of feeling is.
But I must go and have no hope of making myself
clear. Please try to relax and be well.
John

⌘

If her letters are anything to go by, my mother already felt too removed from life in Melbourne to fully grasp the awful situation at
Heide. Sun and John were her dearest friends and John had just been
beaten up by their teenage son, yet my mother barely mentioned it.

Sweeney was nine years older than me. When I last saw him he
was no longer a teenager and had turned into a suave, good-looking
man who drove a sports car. My strongest memories of Sun and
John are from their later years. They had weathered many emotional
storms by then, yet their wrinkled, weathered faces were redolent
with a deep sense of serenity and gentle love for each other, and
the world around them. Both had fine silver hair and a consistently
modulated way of speaking. I never saw Sunday in a dress, nor do
I remember her wearing any jewellery. Both Sun and John usually
dressed in such things as baggy corduroy trousers, fine linen or silk
shirts and cashmere jumpers. Tall and thin, they looked elegant
whatever they wore, despite Sun developing quite a stoop as the years
rolled on. Everything about them seemed clean, soft and fragrant,
with an understated suggestion of wealth and exquisite taste. In 1961
John Reed was almost 60 and Sun was just four years younger; it is
heart-breaking to think of such violence being inflicted on them. It
is also heart-breaking to imagine Sweeney's disturbed state of mind
at the time.

⌘

4th October

*Dear John, Thank you for your friendly letter. I haven't had a
second to reply. I am looking after the Blackman kids for two weeks
and they have a house like a pigsty so my work has been cut out.*

Jane is very good but I will be glad to get back into our pretty little flat.

Yvonne arrived this morning with a cheque for 10 pounds to start paying back your money, as the Insurance Co. repaired the car after someone crashed into them when they were parked. She had made it out to me, so I will put it into my account here. With that and the money I am earning with the Blackmans, I will pay a deposit on a berth to Australia. I hope that will please you. I do not know when I will come home nor do I know that I am sure I want to. But I will feel a lot happier with a booking so that I have at least that security.

This is a very hurried letter and without any real thought. Just to say the party is on and I received the money all right. Autumn is here now. London is pretty but it gets a bit colder. Seven years is a long time isn't it? Sorry you are to miss another party.

In haste, Jean

I'm sure my father would have been pleased and relieved to receive another gentle letter from my mother but her confusion over what it meant to have a passage back to Australia booked would have left him perplexed. Once a deposit is paid, you either pay the rest of the fare then travel on the date the ship sails, or you lose your deposit. Her words suggest she intends to book before deciding when she wanted to return, which was not possible.

⤛⤜

My father wrote a letter on the day of my birthday. He hadn't yet received my mother's letter about booking a passage home.

Thursday October 5. 61

Dear Jeannie, it is nearly midnight, that is, nearly 2 o'clock in the afternoon of Jane's birthday, and needless to say I have thought about England all day. As I left for the concert, I imagine Jane would have been going to school because that was 7 o'clock here and 9 am in England. Anyway, I hope it goes well. I am sorry that my birthday record was so bad, or do such

180

self-criticisms drive you mad? Well, it could and should have been good.

The weather continues to be marvellous. We are probably in for the best summer in history, but also, I fear, for a terrible drought. Forgive this scatter note and my present haste. I am of course very sad tonight and you can scarcely blame me for that. The thought of Xmas is awful. Well, so what ... the only thing I do want to say, and it is a thought from several days ago rather than tonight, is that if you are sure about what you are doing, then do it and to hell with me. I mean that. But be sure and for God's sake be quick. You, like me, have only one life.

Anyway, Sweeney appeared at Heidelberg court yesterday. The police did not lay the theft charges so it was only driving without a license and illegal use of a car. He was put on probation. He is now living at a hostel in Kew and will continue with his job, his girl (a hard bitch) and be under the guidance and control of the probation officer. It is not a hell of a marvellous arrangement but something good might come of it. Anyway, we will see.

Forgive my haste. My main concern was to tell you about Sweeney because I thought you might be worried and imagine much worse things than have happened.

John

⟨∞⟩

12th October

Dear John, Have just received your latest letter dated Oct. 5. Now it is the 9th. The party is over, the birthday is over. All was good, as always I did everything in my power. Jane was more than delighted and bewildered to find herself the owner of a new dressed doll as an extra present. The party was gay and full of goodies. Thirteen children and Jane's latest crush girlfriend Caitilin O'Shaughnessy (Peter's child) [was there].

I am still in charge of the Blackman family and the mother of three. It is surely hard work as the youngest is just over two. Getting everybody dressed and ready for school etc. just about kills me. I am now home with the youngest and having a cup of coffee before I sort out dirty socks and wet sheets (not Jane's). I am getting paid (not handsomely but I'm making a bit of profit). Charles is a nice bloke but Barbara is a terrible power girl, second only to Margret Langley but even more self-centred. I can't tolerate her.

However Jane is splendid and very happy, her only complaint about life is the tinned peas in the school lunches.

I was a fussy eater as a child, who wasn't forced to eat anything I really didn't like. That was until I went to a normal London primary school and discovered the potential horror of the English school lunch. It has long been a requirement that every school-age child in the UK receives at least one hot meal every day they attend school. It's a truly wonderful idea. But for all the fussy little eaters like myself who sometimes sat in front of a plate of something awful with fork poised and tears welling, knowing it had to be eaten, it was hard to appreciate how lucky we were. I had the idea that my mother wrote to the school excusing me from having to eat liver or tinned peas, but I think I might have invented that memory. There was usually a choice of at least a couple of different meals so I could easily have avoided the liver. Presumably there would have been times when tinned peas were part of all the meals, but whether schools allowed parents to decide what their child didn't have to eat, I'm not so sure.

The letter continued:

The record was too adult to make much contact with Jane. I do not know what she thinks of it. Maybe when we are free of other children, she will concentrate. At the moment she doesn't really listen but chatters on herself. It is a very nice recording but a bit slow and drawn out for a child. She likes the announcing part very much. I loved the bird recording. Particularly the Plover and the wattle bird and the mopoke.

I do not know what you are raving about all the time about making decisions. Do what quickly? I do what I want to. I do whatever I believe in, don't you know that? Do what quickly? I have a boyfriend or lover, whatever you like, I have told you that, what else do you expect me to do? There is nothing new in that. This is my third love affair since I left you – what is it that you talk of me doing quickly? I am bored with men mentally. I am sick to death of sex really yet I seem to still be a full-blooded female. I do not see all this drama.

I have told you, I can never sleep with you again because you illtreat me mentally and physically. Apart from that, you are Jane's father and I like you. The trouble with you is you will never give me emotional freedom. As far as YOU are concerned my body is me, as far as I am concerned at thirty-five, my body, my heart and my soul are three different things with different appetites. My body belongs to my bloke, my heart belongs to my true love for ever and my soul belongs to ME. These days my soul is the important life. It is my soul that is homesick. You think you know me but you are mistaken. I am too tired to trust you. I am sick of human beings. I want to be alone. Unfortunately I am not well equipped for being alone. I become frightened and I have no money to live on. I am a strong being somewhere in my heart, this you know.

Autumn is very beautiful here now but soon will come the grey grey grey that I hate so much. I plan to come home. I do not know how to do this or when. I do not know what to do as yet. My bloke is very young and gentle and worships me. I do not know what to do about him as, although I do not worship him, I am happy with him. He is very like my brothers and I would not wilfully hurt him. He plans to follow me to Australia. I do not know what to think of this as I feel very responsible.

It is impossible for me to settle down to a suburban conception of life. For me, life must be true. My first responsibility is still Jane. Nobody can tell my heart what to feel or my body who to respond to. Am I then to stay outcast in England because I cannot be your

wife? My conscience is clear as I feel I have given you and others
lots of love and tenderness – if the flow is stopped it is your fault.
Leave me the peace of my own temperament. I am sick of talk.
You talk, talk, talk. If I come home it would not be to live as your
wife. I couldn't do it because I don't want to. I would like to see
you, to talk to you, to laugh with you. THAT IS ALL. If my bloke
comes, you would have to swallow your pride and if he doesn't, I
would give myself back to my true love who I love so well, I can
live without as long as he exists. You cannot change all that. It is as
strong as the universe.

Enough of this talk. I want to live my free way and fully. You
have a beautiful child of great courage and wit and I love her
dearly. For God's, sake get to grips with reality. Jane is so well and
so happy.

Sorry this letter will infuriate you and you will write back and
say I am cruel. No, it is not me who is cruel. It is you. You want
back what you never bothered about when you had it. IS THERE
NO END TO WORDS. For God's sake, What do you Mean?

In haste, tired and sick of kids.

Jean

I imagine my father's relaxed attitude while reading what at first appeared to be a relatively friendly, chatty letter about our life in London, before finding himself blind-sided by my mother's sudden change of tone. In her mind she had turned his fairly straightforward words into a confusing maze of potential entrapment. Adding to his confusion would have been her previous letter in which she told him she intended to put down a deposit for berths on a ship back to Australia.

❦

Six days later my mother wrote again. Luckily for my father, her mood, as well as her life, had quietened somewhat.

18th October

Dear John,

At last my life has quietened a little. The Blackmans are back from Paris. I am back in my own little flat. We have Peter O'Shaughnessy's little girl staying with us but this is a great treat for Jane as they are girl friends in a most loving way. Jane is so mad about her friends, I realise she is going to be a woman very like me. I think already she feels she would die for her friends. She is a very open-hearted little girl and of course in the same way, as with me, people are always a bit frightened of such (all yours) type of feeling. Anyhow Jane is very happy loving people and with any luck, will deal with things more peacefully than I. This is where Lucinda Boyd was a soul mate for Jane as she too, had that burning human passion for love of the chosen.

Today winter has come to London. The weather has been for weeks like a dream. Glorious hot sunshine and golden autumn leaves. Now it is wet and cold. In fact today is rather like a Melbourne winter day. I am so relieved to have my job over. It was a great strain and how strangely that living in this three-storeyed house and spending my life running up and down stairs brought back my muscle trouble, and so it seems to me that it is most obvious. Anyhow, this flat is on the ground floor and, apart from going to the bathroom down a flight of stairs, I can stay on ground level from now on.

I am babysitting for the Blackmans now for money. I seem to be able to manage drawing out five or six pounds each week with earning extra. I haven't had time to count my finances yet but I spent a lot on Jane's birthday but I hope that I will have enough money soon with Yvonne's cheque for ten pounds, to pay my deposit on a passage home. I haven't had time to do a thing as yet.

Jane (cross fingers) keeps remarkably fit and looks in splendid shape. I haven't been to a concert for months but on Saturday I hope to go to a Bach Cantata in the St. Bartholomew's church.

There is no news except that a shocking little upstart called Brett
Whiteley won an important art prize in Paris. There is a beautiful
Nolan exhibition on (American Sketch Book). Also on show
are some pages of his writings and I was most moved. Charles
Blackman has his show in about two weeks. He is most depressed in
an anxious sort of way. I like Charles but I dislike Barbara. I would
like to spend some time doing London museums etc. while Jane is
at school so I hope I don't get caught up again.

I haven't heard from you so I guess my last letter was too strong
for you. You men really are unreal emotionally. When you say my
friends still love me, whom do you refer to? Have I any friends, save
Sunday and Hermia and John Yule?

I have come to the age of demand. At last I know myself. I must
have certain things. I will not come home to Poverty and Suburbia.
I will need more now. Time to paint. Means to get into the bush
as my soul requires care also. I cannot dream of being imprisoned
by working or struggling for my living. I am not young and not a
prostitute. The answer is not in my mind but the question is, what
if I do come home? What do I live on? Where do I live? Who really
cares? Owning me is one thing. Loving is another.

Sorry.

Jean

My mother was right to suggest that I was like her in my willing-
ness to offer up my open and vulnerable heart to the special person
in my life, whether it was an adored childhood friend or, later in life,
any man with whom I was romantically involved. But sometimes
that tendency is a little close to the edge of being neurotic and needy.

Compared with the simplicity of a childhood love, an adult's
emotional needs naturally become darker and more complex. As
with my mother, the intensity of my feelings for the man in my life
often resulted in destructive behaviour. I used to jokingly say that
I was such a considerate girlfriend that during arguments with my
boyfriend I would bang my own head against the wall to save him

the bother. It's shocking, and I know it's not funny, but it is unfortunately close to the truth.

Like my mother, I had little control over my extreme and irrational emotions. But unlike my mother, I turned the violence on myself rather than inflict it on the other. I'm glad I also inherited enough of my father's rationality to be able look at my behaviour somewhat objectively, and accept my weaknesses.

But all that is behind me now. It was a long and painful road that thankfully ended before I had a child of my own. There was no family violence or screaming arguments during my daughter's childhood – my heart avoided having to bear that dark smudge of guilt.

⬱

Wednesday Oct. 25

Dear Jeannie, now I'm two letters behind and you, as usual, will be wondering why. For the past week I have been very, very busy and still am. Had to go to Albury over the week end to judge a singing competition. It was my first view of the Australian country and it looked marvellous, better than anything we saw in France.

Anyway I must not digress because I write in haste and indeed today I nearly sent you a cheer-up cable just so you would not misinterpret my silence. Because you are all out of touch about time. In your second letter you note that I had not replied to your last one - WHICH WAS WRITTEN SIX DAYS BEFORE. Work it out. Anyway, for your first letter, why do you write to me like that? What had I said to provoke that kind of outburst? Are you so tormented within yourself that you, without the slightest provocation, unleash that hostile barrage of self-justification? When, in all my letters since I left England, have I suggested that coming home meant coming home to me? True, I was not exactly jubilant about you having a lover, but did I complain? I did not, and I accepted it as a fact and that was that. How all that letter was provoked by the phrase of mine "do what you like but do it

quickly" I just don't know. The phrase came from
my own torments and loneliness but it had not the
slightest hostile intention, nor did it mean that
I assumed, expected and least of all demanded
anything.

Anyway, I must go. Will write again as soon as I
can. Thanks for the drawings and you must learn to
try to think sometimes how much I miss Jane. Seven
years as you said is a long time, and just guess
how I felt when I got a letter from Summerhill,
the outside all covered with kisses. But give her a
kiss from me.

Off now, sorry for the haste.

John

Letter from Jane, as dictated to her house mother at Summerhill.

Article about Summerhill, with headline: Should Bobby Have A Knife? Jane (middle), is sucking her thumb. Bobby, Jane's school friend, was mentioned in one of Jean's letters. He and Jane were six at the time.

Chapter 12

No Happy Ending

It was more than a month before my father wrote again and my mother's reaction to this lack of communication was almost inevitable. She presumed he was cross with her without considering any other possibilities.

5th of December

Dear John,

Not a word from you. Weeks and weeks have passed so I conclude that I have offended with something I have said or done. God knows and I can't be bothered. O.K. but I have sent on several drawings which Jane has done for you and with you close to her thoughts. Never a word for her. I don't care if you don't write to me, but do you think you could not just want her for yourself but think of what she might like from you? She misses you a normal amount. Is very happy, well and good and is getting on very well indeed at school. It is fortunately an excellent school.

The reason for this somewhat hurried note is that I want to notify you of my plans for the twenty days or so before Xmas day. I plan to go to Wales very soon. I will not be home (Aust.) for Xmas which is disappointing in one sense, but London is winter now and Xmas festivities are cheerful and I love it all. I plan to go full pelt into everything I can get out of a London Xmas. Tonight a Bach B Minor Mass and lots of carols coming off all over the place. I want

*to go to Kings College. Have had two trips to Stratford on Avon
with Peter O'Shaughnessy to see Richard 111 and Othello. Loved it.*

*I have broken my relationship with my English bloke so he will
not be coming to Australia. For this reason I want to get out of
London to breathe some fresh air, to adjust myself to the future and
think calmly. Daphne is in North Wales in a cottage with the twins,
way up in the snow and mountains with wilderness and waterfalls.
I plan to take Jane up on about the 13th Dec for a week, regardless
of cost. I may never have another chance and that will only cost me
my fare which will be bad enough.*

*I am having Xmas with the Boyds and Blackmans so Jane will
be very happy. Should be back in London by the 20th Dec. Jane
lost her birthday doll in the woods last week. She was so broken-
hearted I bought her another one but it cost two quid so I have told
her, her Xmas present will not be very grand this year. I have got
lots of junk and bits and pieces I have picked up at jumble sales
that she will love. Also lots of clothes for Jane. She is so tall she has
outgrown everything she had last year.*

*Anyhow if you have any thoughts you had better write with the
first mail for it to get here before the 13th.*

In haste, Jean

There is nothing in my father's letters, or from what I knew of
his life, to suggest he ever used silence to express his displeasure. So
there is little reason for my mother to assume hostility lay behind
his lack of communication over the previous month. It was far more
likely to be the result of depression, as indeed it turned out to be. On
the other hand, my mother often resorted to sulking, as she called it,
although I think it too benign a word to describe the internal fury
that prompted her bouts of tight-lipped silence.

In fact, my father had written to her on 3 December and sent
it Express Delivery, so a letter with apologies was on its way. He
explained that lately he had been woken in the early hours by nightmares and had been very sad since posting my birthday presents.
In the long letter, he suggested several possibilities for the future,

including my parents divorcing and my mother's next husband buying Rose Cottage. Another idea was to divide Rose Cottage to allow my parents to live completely separate lives on the one property. He asked my mother to buy the new Madeline book as a Christmas present for me out of the 50 pounds he had just sent. He also told my mother that he had a new little cocker spaniel pup for me if I was coming home, and if she approved. He ended the letter saying he would just like to send her some gentle thoughts.

❧

The next letter was started before my mother received my father's Express Delivery letter but the money had already arrived at her bank.

December 6

Dear John,

Yesterday I wrote you a hurried note rather crossly because I think you should write to Jane or do some such thing occasionally. This morning I received a note from the bank about 50 pounds. What on earth does this mean?

Could you tell me briefly what is on your mind? I could get to Greece by train on that and be halfway home. You give me no clue. I have been very careful with money but I do not know how long I can manage on so careful a budget. I told you yesterday I have broken with my English bloke, mainly because of my much deeper attachment, which I'm afraid, may well last with me all my days. I tell you this in case you conclude that my heart is vacant. Any relationship I can ever have with any one will have to be a pure and civilised one. Anyhow, what I meant to say is that I will not have you thinking you can patch up my broken love for you with sticking plaster. I just want to be at peace with my own heart. I have just had an attempt at make believe with love and hope. Also I have learnt that my dedication brings me far greater happiness than all the slaves under the sun paying court to me.

Enough of that subject. Our Xmas should be jolly enough and

our trip to Wales will I hope come off. Charles Blackman is trying
to push some drawings for me so I may be in London a day or two
longer to see how things work out. Jane is very well and happy.
Please do send her a postcard or something. She is of course well
settled here and happy. We are good friends with Peter and Shirley
O'Shaughnessy who have a girl to whom Jane has lost her heart.
They play together nearly every afternoon after school and most
weekends. She is a good child for Jane as she comes from a similar
type of home and has great imagination also.

Since I put this down to finish later, your special delivery letter
arrived. Goodness knows you do sound depressed. Needless to
say, I felt very sorry and sad about you. You always sound such a
nice person in letters. After all, I too have my memories. I suppose
I cannot go past the law courts without feeling your hand upon
mine. No, it is unfair to dig into my feelings. We are not compatible
emotionally and there we leave things alone. I am too old to be
battered or tormented any more. My heart is given for all times
to the only person who has given it peace and love in return,
regardless of hardship and loneliness that must accompany love
such as ours. But there it is, together or apart, our hearts are united
for as long as we survive this jungle of human emotions.

I am sorry, my conscience is easy. I am a good person! I owe
you nothing more than friendship and loyalty. You nearly killed me
once. What right have you to talk of love to me. I am very homesick
and sad. I'm sorry.

I will write a letter very soon.

Jeannie

My mother was sometimes quite unpredictable. At the start of
this letter she seemed cross that my father had sent her 50 pounds
without an immediate explanation. Yet the depressed, express-post
letter he thought might infuriate her, instead produced some sympathy and a sentimental memory of holding each other's hands during
their registry office wedding.

Given the numerous references to the need for my mother to

have the deposit for our fares home in so many letters, her confusion about the 50 pounds is strange.

⁓

Wednesday Dec. 6. 61

Dear Jeannie,

I wish this letter could fly fast enough to overtake my last which I fear was very gloomy. I hope it was not as gloomy as I imagine and hope that it did not add to your worries. Even as I posted it I wondered and was of half a mind to tear it up and start again, and now I don't know whether I should have done that or not. Now, having started this, I feel just too tired to write and will cut this short, post it and get home to bed. All I want to do is send you a warm friendly greeting without the slightest tension of any kind. Yet I am of course worried about you and Jane. During the last two days I have become increasingly convinced that you have found it impossible to get a berth and that you are probably now thinking of remaining another six months or so - or roughly something along those lines. At the same time, I have wondered and feared if you are well. What if you are terribly sick and if London's winter is dark cold and unbearable? I don't know any of these things and I worry for you and for you both. God knows I would gladly pay your air fare home. I would do anything, and gladly. But silly that I am, I am too tired to write and tend to get gloomy again. I will post this useless note and try to write a little longer and better tomorrow.

John

⁓

Saturday Dec. 9

My darling Jane, was there ever a daddy in the world who got a more beautiful letter than the one you just sent to me? I don't think so. It was waiting for me when I got home last night. I was feeling tired and perhaps even a bit grumpy and

then I opened your letter and it made me feel happy
and warm like sunshine. And of course you wrote
those words as well as doing those lovely drawings
and that was VERY clever. I will stick it on the
wall next to my bed so that I can see it every
morning and night. And it was specially nice of you
to write and draw for me because I had been very
naughty in not writing and thanking you for the
lovely letter you sent me after your birthday with
the drawings of people dancing. So now I must thank
you for both of them and say that what I would like
to do more than anything else in the world is to
put my arms around you, give you a big hug and a
hundred kisses. You are a darling and my special
sweetheart.

Do you like your new school? I hope so. And I hope
that you will keep learning and then very soon you
will be able to read daddy's letters yourself - and
also write (and draw) long ones to me. Christmas
will soon be here and I suppose you will get some
lovely presents and have a lovely Xmas tree made by
mummy and have lots of fun. Perhaps there will be
some snow. I hope so because you would like that.
Please tell mummy that no matter how difficult it
is she MUST go to Cambridge to hear the carols -
but I don't think you should go because you would
not like waiting in a queue FOR HOURS as mummy
would have to do.

Well now I must say goodbye to the most beautiful
girl in the world (that's you) and get this posted.
I will put some extra stamps on it and a special
red sticker which means that the postman must take
it to you as fast as he possibly can. I will write
to you again before Christmas and perhaps even
send you a present like perhaps an old potato or a
carrot. We shall see.

Meanwhile here are lots of kisses xxxxxxxxxx from
Daddy

The next letter was undated:

Dear Jeannie, Oh to be in England ... Well this is
a note rather than a letter and I am too tired to
feel much about anything tonight and in a way that
is an advantage. But thank you for your last letter
which was I thought basically gentle and kind. I am
sorry for that silence and did not mind at all your
long rebuke which was just and fair. But this note
tonight must involve my head more than my heart as
I must clarify some odd details. The 50 pounds was,
as I probably said in my long letter, so that you
would have ready money. I will send you another 20
pounds as early as possible in January. Two days
ago I sent Jane a large book of Australiana and
the packet also included a calendar for Arthur and
Yvonne. I have not sent you anything but could you
shout yourself a few bottles and think of them as
coming from me.

Did you get my cable before leaving for Wales?
Please answer this. I assume that you are not short
of money at present because I am sure that Sun sent
you some for Xmas. If you are, of course write
hastily.

∝≫∽

December 27

Dear Jeannie, it is Dec. 27 and I write at the
point of tears. I have no wish to appear pathetic
but the truth is that I am terribly sad, bewildered
and confused. Why, please Jeannie, why not one
word, one letter or card for Xmas from either you
or my darling girl? That torments me night and day.
Surely something must have gone wrong with the mail
and your letters have gone astray. On Xmas eve when
the postie had nothing I hoped that you had just
been naughty and missed the mail. I hope that my
packet and my envelope full of cards reached you in
time. They should have. But when there was nothing
yesterday or today I could scarcely believe it.
And do I have to? Surely you do not think of me so
badly that you could not send me, or see that Jane

sent me, one small greeting. But then if that is
the truth, then I am tormented by not knowing why.
What on earth is happening to you to make you sad
enough to do this to me? And then, please God, if
this is true, what might I expect to find in the
first letter after Xmas?

I am not bitter or resentful, but simply sad
confused and fearful for you. I don't understand
and can only guess and wonder in torment. In the
last letter you wrote and posted on Nov 9 you said
that I sounded such a nice person in my letters
and that you were sad and sorry for me. Those
were much nicer and kinder words than I had ever
expected, especially as I was worried about the
depressed letter I had written you. I was grateful
and immediately sent you a cheer up cable for good
wishes for Wales, believing that you would be
happy to get it. Even before this I had written
apologising for my silence and my depressed letter
and I HAD ALSO SENT the most loving letter I could
write the day I got Jane's beautiful letter.

But since then you have been absolutely silent.
Why? A week ago Vera showed me a lovely, lovely
photo of Jane.* Oh Jeannie, is it possible you
could send one to Vera and not to me? Vera offered
it to me which was very nice of her but I refused
because I was sure there would be one the next day
for me. And that photo was taken in Sept.

A few days before Xmas I enquired about a phone
call but found the line was booked out until Jan.
3. Perhaps that was just as well. I do not know. So
I spent Xmas alone at Rose Cottage until evening
when I went to Sun's new house (excellent) at
Aspendale for dinner. Our Christmas dinner never
happened. 20 people came uninvited. The Percevals
(fair enough, perhaps), David and Hermia plus some
unknown young bloke, Peter Burns and even Bert
Tucker and with him Barbara Russell. Led by David,
they had their party and seldom even spoke to John

---

* Vera was my maternal grandmother.

or Sun. After an hour of this disgusting orgy I left. Soon after, I gather, Sun went back to Heide.

When I arrived home it was 11 p.m. It was then 1 o'clock mid-day in England and Xmas dinner was probably about to begin. It was so silent that I could hear the ticking of my watch and I went to bed to sleep, to dream and to wake up in a cold sweat. Whether or not this letter sounds pathetic or self-pitying I do not care. It is the truth. I am a very sad man and have reason to be. Next Mon. I begin my holidays. I will probably not leave Melbourne for more than a few days and will certainly not leave until I hear from you. I feel I cannot chide Jane for not sending me a Xmas greeting because that would hurt her. Yet I feel I should do so very gently and I might do that. You can be the judge and censor. Did you buy her the Madeline book? Whether or not you gave her the photo of the puppy I left, without saying so, to you for obvious reasons. What on earth did you do with my Xmas greetings and presents such as they were? But all this is about me.

There are two possibilities. Firstly my loneliness over Xmas might have been the fault of the post office. But then supposing that your silence was deliberate, then what please God is happening to you and the thought torments and frightens me. But I cannot write any more. I'm sorry for all this but please, please write ...

John

⁂

Friday December 29.

Dear Jeannie,

I wrote to you last night a rather distraught and sad letter. I'm sorry, and sorry too that this one is not much different. Since then I have slept heavily but even this morning it is a struggle to keep going against the exhaustion which is the result of sadness. But even as I say this, I know that I do not want to pass my sadness on to you.

and in truth I would not do so but for the terrible
hurt of Christmas. Could you believe that THE LAST
THING I WANT TO DO IS DISTRESS YOU or add to your
burdens. If you believe that, then that may help,
it should help to stop the infectious process.
But somehow this morning before I put my head out
of the door I must write, I'm sorry but I have no
alternative.

You have often spoken of wanting peace between us
and I think I want it just as ardently. And what
have I done ever since I left England to disturb
that peace? I know I have done nothing unloving and
many times you accused me falsely. But all this
is assuming that your silence over Christmas was
deliberate. It may not have been and even if it
was deliberate, it might have been that you simply
could not bring yourself to send me a greeting and
I could forgive you for that. But all I would beg
you to do is to treat my last letter and this one
with just a little respect. Please do not hit out
and say that I protest too much. That would be
both cruel and very unfair. I am, I know, given to
depression and self-pity to an unhealthy extent.
But I also know that tendency is not so bad as
you suppose. It is hard to judge oneself but I
ask you if it is not fair enough that a man with
some imagination and some capacity to love in his
heart should find it hard to bear a Xmas separated
from his love by the whole world and silence. So
I beg you to be gentle with me, not really for my
sake, but for the good of your own heart. Can you
understand what I mean because I have not put it
very clearly? BUT I DO NOT WRITE TO ASK FOR YOUR
SYMPATHY and I am not so stupid as to think for a
moment that such letters as these two would ever
revive your love. Writing is the only way I know
to fight off depression and I try as best I can.
But as I said months ago, I think I know, vaguely,
something of the movement of your heart these
days and I try to follow that with some warmth and
affection. But are not my thoughts to you quite

unreal and untrue? I do not really know but I feel
sure that if you had the slightest idea of what
kind of man I am, you could never have allowed me
to go without one word of greeting through this
past week. With real peace between us it couldn't
have happened.

But this letter is not a plea for either sympathy
or affection, just for peace and as much gentleness
as goes with some human respect. But all this
is surely all wrong and a nightmare. And please,
I do not judge you, I do not complain really,
Jeannie, but I do not understand, and that failure
to understand brings in its train this unending
cycle of sadness, worry and a kind of gnawing fear.
Perhaps now a letter from you is on the way and you
will know then how much of this to disregard. In
any case, would you believe that despite this self-
centred letter, many, many of my thoughts are for
you ... no matter what happens between us ... can
you believe that? Try to because it is so.

John

Chapter 13

Not Just Another Boyfriend

In late December 1961 the hills surrounding the small Welsh village of Betws-y-Coed was a land of heavy frosts, ice and thick fog. To a six-year-old Australian girl it was magical to see breath turn white as it hit crisp, cold air. Or the strange glow of pale sunlight, diffused through heavy morning fog, and the sparkle it made on the ice encasing every blade of green grass as far as one could see, before the landscape blurred gently into fog. I remember small puddles of solid ice, and cracking the icy surface of larger puddles, in a muddy track heavily pockmarked from the hooves of the cows herded back and forth daily to the milking shed. Just fragments of memories, nothing more.

One icy, moonlit night during our brief stay in Wales, my mother decided to climb a mountain with a virtual stranger. This was to change our lives forever. We were staying with Daphne, who had recently moved to Wales with her two children and her new love, Dennison. When they met and fell in love, Dennison was already married, so the rented cottage in the Welsh hills was to be a fresh start for them and the beginning of a long life together.

John Hull was a friend of Dennison's who had driven up from London with his truck full of furniture for them. He also was married at the time but the fate of that marriage was sealed by the time he stood on a mountainside in the moonlight with my mother.

Yet this nascent romance wasn't enough to keep my mother

in good spirits after receiving my father's unhappy letter of 27 December. In her last letter before leaving for Wales, she had told him we would be back in London by the 20th. He didn't know then that we hadn't returned until Christmas Eve. On Christmas Day my mother and I had joined the Blackman family at the Boyd's house for a big Christmas lunch.

❧

1st January 1962

Dear John,

Happy New Year. Your hysterical letter has just arrived. It is New Year's Day. Your brain doesn't carry you very far. Is it possible, I would send Vera a photo without sending you one? It was a school photo which was ordered in Oct. but only printed and delivered just some three or four weeks ago. The very day it arrived back from school it was posted to you from the city with a sweet message from Jane. Some five or six days later I sent one to Vera who has asked me for six years for a photo of Jane. I bought four copies. If yours doesn't turn up you can have another. Also were sent several drawings from Jane over that week before we went to Wales. In Wales we were five miles from any shop of any sort. It was a world of ice and mountains.

When I got back into London on Xmas Eve all shops were closed, then came the snow. Have you not read the papers? London is in a big freeze. I cannot even get to the bank. Life has been cold and exciting but difficult in the extreme. To cope has been my main concern. The children cry with the cold. If it is of any news to you.

Last night I did the washing (New Year's Eve). How ridiculous to think I would behave resentfully at Xmas time. God knows if you will ever get this. London is at a standstill. It is the heaviest snow since before the war for London. The whole world is white and frozen.

Wales was wonderful. Your letter makes me cross. How can you indulge yourself in such self-pity? Everyone has been very nice

to you. Particularly me. Jane sent you some most beautiful Xmas
drawings. I far overspent my quota on Xmas cards etc. this year.
Thought I had done well by everybody. I imagined you would be
overjoyed by Jane's photo. It was very sweet, I thought.

You are not the only lonely soul. I decorated the Xmas tree with
tears. Perhaps you will check for me. The postal business is not
good. I haven't had a letter from Sun for over a year. I was very
hurt. Some photos of Wishnu arrived after Xmas and a note from
the bank from John R. We all suffer. Happy New Year.

On the record my father sent me from Zurich, mentioned in an
earlier letter, there was a song about a little girl who told lies. It starts
with these lines:

> Matilda told such awful lies,
> it made one gasp and shut one's eyes.
> Her aunt who from her earliest youth,
> had kept a strict regard for truth,
> attempted to believe Matilda,
> the effort very nearly killed her.

It is not a subtle cautionary tale, as her aunt's house burns down
with Matilda inside. The Firemen didn't believe her when she
shouted "Fire!" and simply answered, "Little liar."

My mother also kept a strict regard for truth, yet what she failed
to disclose sometimes came very close to what might be called a lie.
No doubt it was true that my mother did the washing on New Year's
Eve, but the implication that she didn't do much else is decidedly
untrue. What she neglects to tell my father is that she also went to
a party at the home of the owner of Thames and Hudson, a well-
known publishing house, and was later escorted home by Arthur.

⸎

The following day, 1 January, John Hull arrived on her doorstep
declaring his love for her and informing her that he had left his wife.
My mother was right when she told my father he was not the only
lonely soul – John Hull's wife was probably feeling very sad and

lonely as well. We all suffer, but some suffer more than others when a marriage breaks apart.

My father's plea for a little understanding and gentleness in his letter of 29 December went unheeded in her response to his sadness and confusion.

My Dear John,

Your second letter arrived this morning. The affect is not altogether good. I suppose on the whole it just makes me feel that I can never share Rose Cottage with you. You expose too frail a personality to me. This death agony you call your life strikes me as too painful to witness and too desperate to expose to Jane. After all, I know that you were just as frail and just as full of anxiety when I worshipped the ground you walked upon, and that very same desperate agonized nothingness is something that has weighed down my heart for some fifteen years. You found it just as agonizing to have a wife as to lose one.

I just feel so depressed myself and your despair and lack of understanding are like salt in my great wounds. I took careful aim before Xmas in my letters to you. I told you exactly that I would be away until Xmas was in full swing. I had planned to send a post card from Wales to you and to Betty and Jack but it was not possible, it was unbelievably remote for the land of Britain which had previously felt overcrowded. As for your Xmas card, if only you knew the thoughts and joy that went into my great plan of the photo planned three months before Xmas.

Then came Xmas Eve. On the way home from Wales at Highgate we stopped after being on the train all day. It was seven thirty. Icy cold and dark and all London was with its Xmas Eve. Jane and I went and had a photo taken in a 2 Shilling machine for Daddy. We both tried to smile into the box, a Xmas Eve photo for Daddy. It wasn't a great success but I post it now. I look too good and Jane looks not good enough for the truth of us both.

However the whole of England has been in an icy grip ever

since. Bloody icy. Couldn't get to the bank. Scratchy mad existence of trying to keep warm. Then came the snow. Londoners don't remember it so heavy. You have never seen anything like it. It is still here and transport and everything is at a standstill. It may sound very gay and it is for a tourist but it buggers everything.

This morning I aim to battle to Piccadilly and get some money. All being well, I will post this and a drawing from Jane. In fact I've had a bloody awful Xmas. Too mean to use the radiators because I'm stupid. I've had my poor rejected man driving me mad because I dumped him and he has been unable to cope. Bloody men. I couldn't tell you how irritable it all makes me. You wouldn't have known how depressed I am had you not written such a bellyache of a letter. O.K. it's shocking bad luck about Jane's photo not arriving. It was posted ages ago. Also before I left on the 16th Dec for Wales I was in a state of tremendous panic. I had to buy everything for Xmas, I was not well, I couldn't get rid of the London man, I had to deal with extreme cold and bad rheumatism and worry about money.

Your story about the ill-bred Melbournians on Xmas day makes me feel like staying in England. I am truly sorry for Sun and John but I know with a terrible instinct that Bert Tucker will wreck the Reeds because he hates too violently. He is as evil as a fiend. Beware of him. He hates everybody but particularly John and Sunday, and will make them pay. Anyhow I do not know, you complain even though you know that every ounce of my Xmas energy would have gone giving your daughter the best available Xmas. The prettiest Xmas tree, the sweetest presents available with my limited money. She is never neglected and I exhaust myself trying to cope with her and provide her with a suitable environment. Every other Aussie child in London is ill. Jane is as fit as a fiddle. Take it or leave it. I work hard at being a mum. But you complain.

I haven't had a word from Sun since Joy died. Over a year. This is hard to swallow. I have sent endless letters and wishes. I do not utter one word but sit and go through my Xmas mail like an idiot, not believing it possible. Nothing but a word from the bank manager saying John Reed had sent money. Jolly nice. God, I need money. Wales at Xmas cost me twenty quid. But what of love, I need love too. That money sticks in my heart like one of the icicles hanging on my kitchen window. Not a word for Xmas. Not a word for a whole year. Three or four days after Xmas came, a familiar envelope but only love from Wishnu. Bitter Xmas for Jean.

I climbed a mountain in the moonlight and I was truly happy. No, my good husband, you are spared the heartache of others, how about keeping your own despair for a change. Today I hate everybody. You have plunged me into a black pit just as I was trying to hold my proud head up against bitter odds. It is a cold world, yet I loved the mountains of Wales. I will try to get back there and find peace in a solitary heart.

Everybody here is sick, the Boyds are all in bed, the Blackmans too. Life is not easy. The one nice thing is Jane, and when I feel at odds with humanity it is hard on Jane. She said to me this morning after I had read your second letter, "Mummy, you look and sound like the ugly sister this morning." Do you think I could tell her I had two wretched hopeless letters from Rose Cottage which cut my heart off from humanity? No. All I ever say is, " Look, this lovely book from your Darling Daddy." A photo, a drawing for your Darling Daddy. Little does she know that her Daddy hasn't the guts to live life out with his head held up.

Sorry, I am wrecked by your letters. Nothing was meant to be like that. Under great strain and against great odds I coped with Xmas. 1962 has brought so far a terrible nothingness. I hate everybody now.

I have met a man who tries to teach me the ways of contemplation and peace amongst men but I fail, as I am nought but a wild little animal fighting to rear my child. Even Arthur cannot teach me to be gentle with my sadness. The snow depresses me now just as it excited me at first. It has a hemming in affect.

206

It is mad and quiet and heavy all around. I must go back to the
mountains where I am at one with life.

I enclose the poor photos of Jane. You should not complain. You
get fair consideration.

Love Jean

With so much going on over the Christmas New Year period it is
hard to understand the source of my mother's bitterness in these last
two letters. In the right mood, she was quite capable of listening to
the pain of others with a great deal of compassion, but it seems that
when she could be accused of being responsible for it, her reaction
was defensive anger. In the wrong mood, she could see no one else's
pain but her own.

My father had warned her that Sun might be too distressed to
put pen to paper, yet my mother reacts to her own sense of neglect
without due consideration, and as if she didn't understand that love
sent from Sunday's cat Vishnu was in fact love sent from Sun.

⤌∾

By 5 January my father still had not received any of my mother's
letters.

> Dear Jeannie, it is Friday Jan 5 and 12 days since
> Xmas Eve. Never before have I waited for a letter
> so anxiously and I hope never to do so again. Not
> an hour of the day goes without me thinking of you
> and Jane and for the most part I am frantically
> worried. Whatever could have caused you not to
> write for all this time, not only to me but so far
> as I can discover to anyone here? The papers have
> had stories and pictures about the great cold in
> London and I wonder if you are in fact terribly
> sick and miserable. Each day I think of sending you
> a reply paid cable but I put it off ... but I must
> know. Are you sick or caught up in some terrible
> personal crisis - or both? I wonder and wonder and
> wonder. If you are frozen, then for God's sake buy
> whatever you need and to hell with the cost. I
> experienced sub-zero temperatures in New York but
> then I had American central heating and I would

207

not have liked it otherwise. But please write to
me quickly and be gentle. I think I deserve that at
this stage after the saddest Christmas and New Year
of my life.

But whatever happens, please do not regard my
present anxiety as neurotic or unreasonable, that
would be both cruel and unworthy of you. All I can
do to allay my worries is to send you my love.
I'm sorry. Let's all cheer up. I enclose a letter
to Jane which it was terribly hard to write, hard
because I could not be honest in my feelings about
her, darling that she is.

Yours, John

⟨⁂⟩

My father's birthday is 9 January and my mother's is on the 11th. My
father sent her an early birthday cable as soon as he received one of
her missing letters.

HAPPY 1962 BIRTHDAY KEEP WARM STOP CURSE POST
OFFICE – JOHN

⟨⁂⟩

Monday Jan 8th, 62

Dear John,

*Tomorrow is your birthday. Thursday is mine. This morning I
received yet one more hurt letter from you. Goodness knows you
have been struck by an innocent arm that didn't even raise itself. I
have sent you off four letters over the last ten days. You sound as if
you haven't received anything. Yet your cable that arrived last night
suggests that you have had some communications.*

*London has been in chaos. Even now dustbins haven't been
emptied since the snowfall. Apart from the big unexpected freeze,
the postal workers are having a dispute, go slow, complex something
that I know nothing about. So now I wonder what has happened
to even your Birthday envelope which should arrive by the ninth.
Also could you check postal since the New Year. Two airmail letters,
just drawings from Jane. One letter with Xmas Eve photos arriving*

from Wales at station, One airmail cheap letter from me and then Birthday letter with three lots of photos.

Anyhow Jane was terribly upset that her photo didn't get to you. I wasn't going to tell her but you talked about it. She couldn't comprehend the situation. She chose the one for you herself. They were the same but colour varied a bit. Could you but have witnessed the delight and planning with which we organized the photos, and the anxiety in case the school didn't get them done in time for Xmas sending. So that was one great surprise cooked up by Jane and I that fell flat in a big way. We deliberately waited a week before posting Nana's. So your photo should have arrived quite early. Anyhow I got four copies. One for you, one for Nana, one for Jane and one for me. Jane says you can have her copy, so I will post it. If the other turns up then you can keep Jane's copy for her.

It has been cold, bloody cold. My metabolism has changed completely. I don't feel it much. I am always too hot and airless in London as if my veins are bursting to pump life into my lungs. My nose is still sore from the cold and my hands don't like contact with the world of ice but I am always hot inside. Jane felt it rather badly and cried in the snow with cold. It was very exciting in one sense and very difficult in another.

My worst worry was getting money as I couldn't get into the bank. Anyhow the snow has gone now completely. Jane goes back to school tomorrow. I have been madly patching up clothes to begin the new term. We had a lovely but icy holiday in Wales with Daphne and the twins. I cannot wait to get back there. I loved it most passionately. It is very beautiful, like Australia, and remote and full of Nolan and Boyd landscapes. Dreamy soft mountain textures and colours and atmospheres. I adored it. I walked miles every day. My poor tired London veins that cause me so much trouble, love to walk. My legs never hurt when I walk. I climbed a mountain. It was marvellous. I want to go back.

I do not know now what to do with life. I am homesick and yet very frightened of your heavy heart. If it were not for Jane I would retire to Wales. For the moment I think Jane should stay in this excellent school until she can read and write. This is coming rapidly now and it should not be long. Also I have to think about the seasons. Soon it will be Aust. winter again unless we leave immediately. Jane is very happy but I am a bit tired of struggling and battling with finance and humanity. I am exhausted by the thought of dealing with you in the future. Yet my heart would dearly love to set foot on Australian soil for evermore.

I have had a lovely letter from Sun. Thank God, as my heart was heavy on that score. I am not quiet in my heart yet so I will think about the future a little later. It will sort itself out. For my birthday I am shouting myself a trip to Covent Garden to the Magic Flute under Klemperer. My seats are the cheapest so God help me but I am looking forward to it. I dare say you know that I would like you to be going. The first night they had Joan Sutherland singing the Queen of the night but I will not hear her. My friend Shirley O'Shaughnessy went and said J.S. was too gentle and motherly. Also she said the costumes and décor were dreadful and vulgar. We shall see.

The last twenty pounds has not arrived as yet but it should soon. My bank account has thirty pounds in it but I will try to keep that there constantly as I regard it as the deposit on my fare and I will not touch it. So you see, as soon as Jane goes back to school I will haunt the shipping world and try to make some decision. There is a vague possibility of a ride to Scotland which I would dearly love. I do not know. Wales was more than rewarding for me. I have not even seen Cornwall. Also I would love to be here to see the English spring which we missed last year. I do not know. I am torn betwixt and between.

Thank you for the present of two quid. That eases my conscience as I bought myself a funny black velvet dress to wear to the opera on Thurs. It cost two quid exactly which is very cheap. It is mad and too big for me but I weave a magic spell on it and cross my fingers. Jane is delighted and regards it as a great treasure. Also I

got at these London sales of last Friday a pair of blue suede party
shoes like Cinderella. Jane is so happy about this, every time
anyone comes she insists on them being displayed. She pets them
and kisses them and has a quids worth of dreams out of them even
before I have worn them.

My mother then told my father that she looked unsuccessfully
for the Madeline book he suggested she buy before Christmas. She
explained that books didn't usually interest me, but because of my
love of animals, the book of Australian animals he sent was a great
success. She wrote that she had seen a lovely dress in Harrods she
would like to buy for me, telling him that clothes were my passion
and it is one she understood very well.

You must remember that I have been a little girl and am secretly
not much removed myself even now. I love pretty clothes and it is
funny to hear little Jane in the other room explaining to Caitilin
that her mummy loves pretty dresses but is too poor to buy them.
This is half a truth. Jane and her friends discuss in detail their
mother's wardrobes from nightgowns to ballgowns. Jane and I
cannot agree about colours etc. but somewhere I will have to
fill a role for her. Then, as from now she will have to have some
improvement in her own wardrobe. She is exactly four feet tall now
and nothing of the past really fits her. Next summer, here or there,
must see for Jane some improvement in clothes. She has never ever,
ever been bought a garment by either you or I. She has been dressed
entirely by cast-off clothes. So you see, I feel this is where her heart
is most involved. Forgive me for making decisions but I feel sure
you will be only too ready to do what is to make Jane the happier.

Jane has just done a nice drawing for you, I will post it with this
so you should get them together. This postal business began in New
Zealand. Do you remember? The first postcard we ever sent, first
stop out and you never received it.

I always feel that your inner unhappiness wills outer
unhappiness. But enough of enough. This is not a contest of
sadness. Spare me please any further knowledge of your heartache

as I spare the world mine these days. God, I hate London so don't
imprison me by your melancholy. Thank you for the Cable. Both
Cables.

   Love Jean

⤙⤚

Friday. Jan 12.

Dear Jeannie,

What a mess. I am terribly sorry and ask you to try
to understand and forgive me. You will forgive if
you truly understand. Jesus, after all, was kind
to doubting Thomas and I ask for the same attitude
towards my own lack of faith because that was
my only sin. True, those Christmas letters (all
three worse luck) were shockingly hysterical and
I regret them intensely. But you must be fair to
me and THINK not only of what you wrote and sent
but of what I received - and I received nothing
after the two airmail letters you sent before
going to Wales ... no photo of Jane, no Christmas
drawings, nothing. Then came the weeks to Christmas
and the long sequence of days over Christmas and
New Year and I think it is cruel, unimaginative
and absolutely unjust to wipe off all the sadness
of those days as self-pity. There were to be sure
elements of self-pity in those letters and for that
I feel ashamed. But there was also a lot of genuine
and thoroughly understandable sadness and you
should not confuse the two things. After all, was
it unreasonable of me to be so very, very sad?

But I cannot find words to thank you for that
photograph. You are my two bob Madonna. But
seriously, Jeannie, do you know anything about
yourself or photographs about yourself? Did you
know that this photograph (apart from my sweetie
in front) would tear my heart out at first glance?
Surely there are tears under your eyes, you poor
sad and lonely girl. My heart went out to you
completely and those photos, along with the old
one of Jane, are now in my wallet and closer to my
heart than any photograph has been before. Many of

212

the words in your letter distressed me. But that
is fair enough. I do not complain but I do ask you
to try to be gentle with yourself, and for your
sake stop cursing me as illogically and unjustly as
you do in that letter. Even in this letter, while
saying how careful you were to advise me of your
plans before Christmas, you are thinking of what
you did and not what I received, and you almost
ignore the reality my end. Because I knew you
would be out of London until Christmas I assumed
you would write from Wales because there was no
Christmas greeting in your pre-Wales letters, and
is it not asking a bit much of me to foresee what I
now know - that postage from Wales was impossible?
O.K., I should have had more faith but do not be
too hard on me.

Indeed do you not yourself show some lack of faith
in Sun, whose feelings you have absolutely no
reason to doubt. Remember that I told you a long
time ago that I could not see Sun writing while
the Sweeney situation lasted. Then remember there
was Joy's horrible death, then Doody's spread over
months and at the same time Sweeney was becoming
ever more frightening. You are a long way from all
this but you must realise that the Reeds live with
it every day and they still do in a sense. Sweeney
did not come near them over Christmas, nor did he
send one word of greeting. The fact is (whether
the Reeds face it or not) that he has wiped them
for good. So far as they are concerned he may as
well be dead, but the more painful reality (for
them) is that he is alive. It is a terrible story,
an unanswerable problem and the story has not
finished. Where it will end, God knows. Sun did
not let Christmas go by and I do hope that by now
you have her letter. The house at Aspendale is a
joy to live in. They can watch the sea in bed,
as one can over dinner in the living room, and it
seems to come right inside the house. The beach
is surprisingly empty on most days and so far the
house has been a joy. It is only 10 minutes away

and so I go over for dinner every other night.
The summer has been wonderful but seriously dry
and without good rain we will be in real trouble
before March. The garden is hand watered every day
and looks marvellous. A year's methodical work has
produce the best ever crop of (nearly) disease-free
apricots, apples, peaches, pears and nectarines.

Give Jane a big kiss for me and on your part
please, Jeannie, for your own sake, try not to
think of me so badly so quickly and not so much
as a man who has not the guts to live but more
as a man who, with all his personality failings,
suffered needlessly because of the diabolical
incompetence of the post office. With the photo of
Jane I still have hopes because before you sent
something sea mail by mistake. Please let me know
if you got my three cables - one before Wales
and two within the last week. Because I intend
protesting (for what good it will do) to the post
office. Too many letters have gone astray - at
least two it seems, possibly more. Perhaps by now
the weather has improved and the mail strike is
over. I hope so.

Don't think of me as a man who is concerned only
with his own feelings. I pray in my own kind of way
for you and Jane daily and my heart is with you.
Keep warm. Cheer up.

Yours, John

&

Monday Jan. 15. 62.

Oh, Dear Jeannie, thank you, thank you many times.
I have been showered with letters since the new
year and I am very grateful, very happy and very
penitent about being so naughty with my thoughts.
There were too many words in my last letter ...
all I want to say is that I am very sorry, without
any qualifications. And you have been so nice
about it since the new year and especially in your
last letter which came this morning and which was
written after you got the third and last of my

gloomy epistles. And of course, you had been so
nice about it before ... and I did not know. Now I
do and I am overjoyed.

Later in this letter he thanks my mother for the little Christmas
Eve photos, saying:

... and what marvellous photos of you and Jane.
So dazzlingly glamorous of you that if I were a
drinking man all I would have to do would be to
produce this photo in a pub, say that it was my
wife who left me, and I would never have to buy
another drink

He agrees with her reason for not buying the Madeline book and
suggests she buy me the dress in Harrods. While sympathising with
my mother's shortage of money, he explains that it isn't easy for him
either, telling her he had to borrow 50 pounds from the bank to
replace the hot water service at Rose Cottage. He ends with:

The enclosed photo of Sun's new house gives no
real idea of what it is like. It's much nicer.
That bookcase thing, on the other side is a sink,
workbench and cooking affair, the cupboards behind
contain a complete laundry with washer and dryer,
electric stove, fridge, pantry and the whole works.
But I will write again soon. Keep warm somehow,
cheer up and realise that your letters and photos
and Jane's drawings have made your morbid old
husband into a schoolboy,

love John

In another letter twelve days later, he wrote about the devastating
bushfires that had burnt miles of country around The Basin, and
between Warrandyte and Eltham. He described the sky at Mentone
as being thickly overcast with smoke creating an eerie orange light
as if looking through stained glass. There were burnt gum-leaves on
the lawn at Rose Cottage and Bob had told of being out in his boat
on a calm sea littered with burnt leaves and twigs.

Explaining the importance of rent from Rose Cottage to help

support my mother if she stays in the U.K., he told her he really needed to know whether she planned to be back by the Australian spring, and whether she would be prepared to share Rose Cottage with him. The Kirks were planning to move out in the next two or three months so he wanted to know whether to look for new tenants or wait for our return.*

He wrote that he didn't ask her to return as his wife, "only as a companion on occasion, and always as Jane's mother." He reminded her that he was missing me dreadfully and asked again if I had seen a dentist.

⁂

A month later my mother hadn't replied, and in the meantime my father heard from Sun that my mother had changed her address. The news created in him the same old questions. Was it the fault of the postal service, the state of my mother's life, or had he perhaps annoyed her with his request for a decision? He needn't have worried.

She wasn't cross, she was just busy having a good time in her new relationship. Before long, he received this reassuringly friendly letter. She told him I was doing well at school and how pleased and proud I was to be allowed to bring home the class pet, a white mouse, for the weekend, and my first library book. And at the top of the letter was our new address.

> There is little news. Life goes on rather much the same as ever.
> The sun has now been covered with more snow clouds, dark and
> depressing that they are. I haven't done anything exciting except
> Wales. Wales I adore. It is a great pity you never saw it at all. The
> North is so lovely and so very like home. I can hardly wait to get
> back to it. Jane gets more holidays soon, end of term. We saw lots of
> marvellous things last time, a circle of stones (like Stonehenge), very
> strange. A manmade mountain which we climbed which no one
> has ever found a reason or understood. We saw a burial chamber
> of prehistoric men all weird and hidden in the Welsh mountains.

---

* Sometime in the previous six months the Kirks had returned to Rose Cottage.

Nearer to our time, lots of Roman bridges, Roman roads etc. Jane is a bit young to understand it all. When we were exploring a field on the moors of Wiltshire that the National Trust owns which has a long barrow in it, a warder drove up and talked to us.* He gave Jane a flint he had just found. Jane looked at the treasure which looks very insignificant and thought it was a joke, however I took control of it and one day she can be glad of it.

I am sorry to say, when I say we, I mean Jane and I and my new man in my life. I am afraid to say I am very much keen on this new bloke which causes me great conflict as I do not want to leave him and cannot for the life of me think of how to work the rest of my life out. I am not thinking of my life really but of Jane's and my life. When I split up with John Folkard just before Xmas and fled to Wales to be quiet, the last thing in the world I wanted to do was to meet another Englishman. Yet in the space of scarcely three months of knowing this new man, I am sure that I do not know how to leave England since he is here. However I have not the time to elaborate now but I do not know about the future.

Jane is very happy even though she says she misses her Daddy. This is true I think but she is still very happy, well and developing marvellously. I do not know. I want to live in Wales with my man on one hand and go home to Mentone with Jane on the other. How very homesick I am, how I would adore to be there basking on Mentone beach. It's so cold here, so very miserable, yet I have found spiritual peace and have been taught harmony and some sort of fulfilment. I now am as two people, the Jean that was and the Jean that is. Yet in all this new stargazing I haven't found a cure for homesickness that belts me in the pit of my stomach out of the blue. We shall see. I do not know what to do but somehow it will work itself out . Yet it is serious, this time it is not just a boyfriend in my life but somebody I just love by the very nature of things.

---

* The moors of Wiltshire are down in the south-west of England, a long way from North Wales. It is likely my mother is conflating our pre-Christmas trip with another weekend away with John Hull.

Forgive all this talk. One wants to do what is best for everybody concerned. In haste, I didn't mean to deal with serious things. Forgive me. I am gentle now so do not be too hasty.

Love Jean

Tuesday March 20

Dear Jeannie,

I was on the point of replying to one letter of
yours three days ago when another arrived, to
my great surprise. It was not registered, thank
goodness, because I was rather frightened about a
letter so important that it had to be registered.
In fact it was probably the gentlest letter you
have written to me since I returned and I wonder if
you know me well enough these days to even guess
at how much that gentleness means to me. True,
for me, much of your last letter very saddening,
but it was gentle and that means an awful lot. You
concluded by asking that I should not be too hasty.
You need have no fear of that ... you don't quite
understand, (I think) ... you still half expect me
to hit out, to hurt, but unless I misunderstand
myself completely, I think that is just about
impossible. Sure I am sad and disturbed and even
fearful but in no way hostile and I beg you to
believe that I write and think of you and Jane
these days with a kind of quietness that is the
product of very real loneliness and suffering. But
this is not the night for a serious letter.

He then promised to try to think only of what was best for my mother and me, adding that to separate father and daughter was a big price to pay, so she needed to be very sure of what she was doing. He expresses doubt about that, pointing out that her recent letters suggested "more torment than certainty".

The weather continues to be marvellous. It is a
pity you missed this summer. The peaches at Rose
Cottage are huge and now deep golden yellow and so
beautiful that I don't want to pick them. Living on
wholemeal peach pie. Tell Jane I will write her a

real letter within the next day or so. And I will
write you a real one too.
Love John

His next letter contained the sad news that the little cocker spaniel
pup he bought for me was killed by a car on Beach Road. I had
already been sent a photo of "Cinderella" and had taken her into
my heart. According to my mother, as soon as I was old enough to
stretch out my arms from the pram I would reach out to every dog
I saw.

My mother and I sent my father a postcard of a crinoline dress of
blue-striped taffeta from the London Museum. It had no stamp and
must have been sent in an envelope with some photos.

Highgate Ave. Monday 9th

*Happy Easter from Jane and Jean. Jane chose this card (I think to
please me as she talks of Mummie loves Blue best). We went to the
London Museum last Sunday. This is just a hurried note. I will
write tomorrow. We cannot go to Wales as there is no money left
after London life these days. May get a ride up for the Easter days.
This is the second collection of photos I have sent. Did you get the
others?*

Love Jean and Jane

I presume what my mother wrote would have confused my father
as to whether or not we were going to Wales for Easter but he took
the hint and sent extra money. The possibility of a lift to Wales was
with John Hull, the new man in her life.

10th April

*Dear John, Just a brief note for now. Have sent another collection
of photos, did you get them? According to other Aussies in London,
there is a lot of mail not arriving in Australia. This is very poor.
Have you still not got Jane's Xmas photo? This is why I talked of
Reg. letters, no other reason.*

Prices in London are frightful at the moment. It is very hard

to shop as Highgate is even higher than other places. I am having
a constant struggle to cope financially. Don't scold me, London is
twice as dear as last year. Unless one lives on bread and jam as
English people do, one just has to pay. Jane demands a great social
life and tea parties after school are constant. I feel she deserves
this as she is so good. I do everything to make her happy. She is
happy and well and, if I may say so, a credit to me. She is a little
lady by nature and intelligent and loving and at all times creative.
I have had a great jumble sale time lately and have bought enough
school coats for her until she is fifteen, you will laugh, 6 Pence each,
beautiful English raincoats of twill as all the girls wear. Viyella
shirts, 6 Pence, beautiful summer dresses. You can't complain
about this, seems there are certain seasons for jumble sales. Got a
marvellous trunk for 2 Shillings. Five beautiful woollen vests for
Jane at 1 Shilling each. I've done very well, concentrating on Jane.
She is so tall and needless to say needs constantly a supply of clothes.

Sorry about the untidiness of this note. I'm in a hurry to get this
posted off. You seemed rather anxious. I was terribly upset about
the puppy. I am sorry. I haven't told Jane yet. I do not know how
or when to, as she has built up a real feeling about HER puppy, she
tells strange people in shops and it has a great place in her heart.
She is just the sort of child to love a puppy. I will deal with it as I
can when I think a good moment has come. I am sorry.

Spring hasn't even begun yet. How homesick I am. Very
homesick indeed. Yet I must tell you also that London holds me
these days as I have found a saint, an incredible person, a person of
such goodness and quality and wisdom that I know you too would
be impressed. I know this and I know how rare such folk are. So do
you.

Will write a big letter soon.

Love Jean

❧

John Hull had probably been living with us since leaving his wife.
My mother was not one to take things slowly, and the speed with

which Hull left his wife indicates he was just as impulsive as she, if not more so. Passion throws caution to the wind. My father may have wondered whether my mother was already living with her "saint", but he never asked and she didn't tell.

Monday April 16

Dear Jeannie, oh thank you, thank you for the letter, the photos, the drawings and the Easter greeting. You make me feel terribly ashamed because I had, over recent weeks, quite forgotten about Easter as a time for greetings. But in the month since your last letter I have become even more sad and worried ... and now tonight my heart is bursting with gladness ... and that is just a little bit different from, and better than happiness, I think. But thank you.

This is in extreme haste, and of course by return mail. Tomorrow I will send you a greeting cable and also cable you 30 pounds. I am sending Jane a handkerchief which I bought in haste but with love (more love than taste) last week. Life is not easy for either of us but God bless you and do have a happy easter. Will write tomorrow.

Love John

⤜⤏

2nd. May. '62

Dear John, I have just had a letter from Vera and she says you are not very well. I am sorry to hear this, are you all right now? Thank you so much for your generous Easter present. We had a simply marvellous four days of beautiful mountain air and sunshine. Spring is very late this year but nevertheless all is very lovely. Jane is very well and she and the twins had a wonderful time together. It was rather funny, your cable made me rush to the bank and allowed us to go to Wales. I didn't know but the money didn't arrive in London until yesterday 1st. May. I had an embarrassing time as I therefore was overdrawn rather heavily and I had to explain about the cable, so it seems the cable service didn't function very well. Anyhow the bank manager was very nice about it all.

The same thing happened to Barry Humphries who left for Aust. last week. The money that was supposed to be cabled just didn't arrive in time! I dare say you will see him in Melb soon. He has a bad arm and apart from their world being topsy-turvy, they seem recovered enough for the tour ahead.

There is no other news here. London is hateful to me nowadays. I feel completely choked and frustrated. I cannot manage to spend money enjoying myself and the cheap concerts are unbearable. The B.B.C. is depressing beyond measure. I haven't got a pick up these days so I feel culturally starved.

Jane went back to school yesterday. She is, as always, very fit. She sends her love. The handkerchief was a tremendous success. It was adored. It has ended up draped around dolly. She has the most marvellous collection of dressing-up clothes, all sequins and lace and the works. On Monday she went to the dentist. He didn't do anything and seems quite pleased with her teeth. She has those same old holes but he says they are about to come out. She has five loose teeth. Her new big front ones are Sinclair and very good. Her bottom new front ones are small and don't seem to have enough room. He said it will be all right in time. He said her tender gums which bleed sometimes with the toothbrush action were a secondary product of catarrh which he thought would disappear in time. He said London was a bad place for such children. He took an X-ray, much to my horror.

After the dentist her treat was a trip to a West End cinema to a grown-up film about the Empress Elizabeth of Austria (a shocking Hollywood idea of history) Jane adored it as it was full of beautiful gowns, waltzes, weddings, chandeliers and women with long hair. She really is a most romantic child. She just adored it, I was bored stiff but it was worth it.

Have you seen Sun? Did she get my parcel? How is she? I only hear terrible stories of Melbourne life and the hostilities of the different camps. It all sounds so very horrible from here. I gather

Bert Tucker is upsetting everybody's apple cart. He really is a bastard. It all sounds terrible. I am most terribly homesick. It is like one's heart leaking to even think of the beach and my darling Rose Cottage and garden and all my treasures. Please protect it all. I cannot bear to realise I am so far away.

This is such a horrible flat, now the sun shines occasionally and there is some spring but it is so depressing where we live. Having taken it on, I cannot leave until Peter O'Shaughnessy comes back, that was the bargain, so I have another six weeks to fill in here. My friend who is a picture framer is teaching me gilding and we are doing all the gilding for Arthur's show. Forty or fifty large paintings to be framed and gilded. It is a beautiful old craft and I enjoy it but it is a hell of a lot of work and we shan't make much profit, as Arthur is broke and worried.

London has become a prison, so you must forgive me but I have decided to go to Wales for a while when I can leave this flat. I love it very much and I have found a beautiful, very ancient cottage overlooking the mountains, near Daphne. I dare say this is sad for you but I can't return home under the circumstances and the next best thing is Wales for a while. I intend to come home when it seems possible. You see, I like my new relationship very, very much and feel as if it has all worked out, except for you. I do not know what to think. I want to live in Australia. I am an Aussie and I hate Europe but I can't have two husbands. It is very hard on you and also in a way hard on me because my home is Australia and I yearn for it and I get very sad and worried in case I never get back. Jane is very happy and developing beautifully. She is O.K. As for me. I'm sorry I ever left my beach.

Love from Jean

Although not clearly stated, it doesn't take much reading between the lines to realise my mother wasn't leaving her new relationship behind in London. John Hull, the picture framer, was coming with us to the Welsh hills. At least that was the plan.

John Hull.

Jean and Jane, 1962, in front of a fishing boat on the beach
(photo taken by John Hull).

Chapter 14

The Best-laid Plans

6A Highgate Avenue N.6

P.S. This letter becomes too sad. I am sorry. London has got me down at last. How I hate it. Forgive me.

Dear John, I can't remember what I wrote to you last week so thought I'd better drop you another short note. Poor Jane has to go to the dentist again after all. She doesn't know yet. They phoned this morning and said the X-ray showed up some hole they thought they should fix up, so that means she will have to have the dreaded drill. However, she doesn't have many troubles to deal with. She is very happy. She had a special weekend last weekend as when she was at Lucy Boyd's birthday party. I went to a jumble sale and found a magnificent dolls' pram, a very grand one, worth six or seven quid. I had to pay a pound for it but it was worth it just to see her face. I put it in Arthur's studio and took her in, she literally leapt around with joy and couldn't believe it was for her. What a pleasure it is to give Jane a present. The funds went to the ban the bomb boys, so I felt all around, although I couldn't afford it, it was a great day. She is a continual doll girl. Plays with them by the hour. Never gets bored with them. Funny little thing. They are terribly real to her. Also I am well pleased as Middie has a posh doll's pram and a great collection of dolls etc.

Did I tell you I am fleeing to Wales in five weeks' time. I cannot

bear this flat. I will go mad if I don't clear out into the open spaces.
We are just three houses from the great North Road here, and all
day and night the sound of the traffic drives me mad. Also the
terrible fumes of the great trucks as they prepare for the last lap of
the steady climb uphill from Archway. It is poky and horrid and
I am depressed. Wales is so wonderful, so fresh and so beautiful.
I have found a dear little ancient stone house near Daphne. I can
hardly wait.

Life seems so problematic. I am very homesick, seriously so but,
it is best that I go to Wales now. I am sad when I think of you and
Rose Cottage and all that is my true self and my home. After all,
you haven't said anything other than that you are sad. What would
happen when I do face coming home? I feel a bit self-exiled but sad
because I know that if I was coming home, I would be very afraid
about the future and your inconsistent personality. I am very fond
of John the picture framer. I am at peace with everything except
you and England. I am sorry I ever left Australia. Sorry I ever
married you. What a waste of human energy.

Love Jean

❦

The bathroom at 13 Hampstead Lane where the Boyd family lived
was on the third floor. From its window I could peer down to the
street far below. In front of the house grew a huge plane tree, the size
of which I hadn't seen before. But as high as the bathroom was, when
I looked out the window I looked out through the branches of this
tree. It was as close to being in the sky as I could imagine.

In 1960s Mentone, all the houses squatted firmly in the middle
of their own plot of land. That was the only world I knew until we
arrived in London, with its streets of many-storeyed terrace houses
and their long, thin gardens stretching out behind them like back-
yard shadows.

On the ground floor of 13 Hampstead Lane was Arthur's studio, a
large room that smelt strongly of linseed oil and paint. Paintings that
would dwarf a man leaned against every wall, paintings that, in my

mind, dwarfed the very concept of a painting. I was used to ones that hung on walls above fireplaces or bookshelves. There was no room in any domestic setting for these works, either in size or in content.

As a child I had little interest in art, and my response to standing in Arthur's studio was purely visceral. I was overwhelmed by the sheer size of the slightly nightmarish images and nervously hypnotised by the strange, twisted, floating figures coming out at me through dark, thickly textured paint. But when taken in there to see my mother's surprise present, I saw nothing but the beautiful doll's pram that, I was delighted to be told, was for me. I only hope Lucy Ellen had received birthday presents that brought her much joy, because to a small child it would seem confusingly unfair for one of her birthday party guests to receive such a wonderful present for no apparent reason.

Wednesday May 16

Dear homesick Jeannie,

I sent you a cable for mother's day and to cheer you as much as I could and I hope it worked, just even a little. For myself I am sorry for my silence of these past weeks. Every day I have wanted to write but over the last fortnight especially, something has always turned up to deny me either the time or the peace of mind. I cannot remember such a music season as this has been since Feb. with the LPO, the opera, the Hungarian String Quartet and the locals gone mad with activity. Of course I do not worry these days as I used to, but even so it means being out seven nights a week at present.

Yes, I have been sick for a week or so with flu and its aftermath but I am quite better now, and the only thing I am sad about is that I could not answer your last two letters when my heart was filled with them.

I was also very glad to hear that the handkerchief was such a success and that it is now draped around dolly. As you say, it is a joy in itself to give

Jane a present. And it seemed excellent news about
the pram which is just what she would adore. It was
bad luck about her tooth and I can only hope that
the hole was not too big. I was of course worried
by the reference to catarrh and X-ray. I take it
you questioned the dentist on this to see if he had
any suggestions. Would there be any point in seeing
a really first-rate specialist? I will talk to Alan
about it but it is difficult at this distance.
Perhaps the dentist could say whether he thought
a specialist opinion would be worthwhile. But I
am sure I don't have to ask you to leave no stone
unturned because you know as well as I do that this
could be a big factor in her whole life.

Ah, she is a darling, and have you any idea of what
it feels like not to have seen her for more than
a year? It is a long time for me and perhaps a
much longer time in the mind of a little girl, and
many, many times over that year I have repressed an
almost irrepressible desire to beg you to bring her
home immediately.

But enough of that. I am not writing well tonight
and will leave most of the things I wanted to say
until tomorrow when I will write again. I saw Sun
during the weekend and she said your parcel arrived
last week, that she loved it and that she would
try and write this week. The news of Sweeney is of
course not good, he tried an overdose of sleeping
tablets, got himself into Larundel mental hospital
for a fortnight or so. He is now out of there, as
large as life, installed in a flat in town and
working at Cheshire's bookshop but for how long
God knows. More about this later, but don't be too
optimistic.

I am too remote from the Melbourne art world to
hear anything of the enmities you refer to but I
don't doubt they go on as they have always here,
and I suspect everywhere else. Bob, as perhaps
you know, is back with Mag, solely for financial
reasons. I don't know just how happy or unhappy
they are at the moment but will try to find out,

and to help what little I can, and will also on
this one write more later. But of course, the big
issue is what you intend to do and how this affects
Jane and me.

Going to Wales seems to be fine and I envy you.
But for how long do you intend to stay? I take it
you mean for the summer holidays because otherwise
it would mean disrupting Jane's schooling and you
would be as reluctant to do that as I would be.

I'm sure my father was aware that our intended move to Wales
might not be just a holiday, but the confusion and conflicting desires
expressed in my mother's letters allowed room for hope. I suspect
his mention of disrupting my schooling was an attempt to tug at
her conscience, as he would have guessed she was not likely to have
given it much thought.

My father's brief mention of Sweeney's suicide attempt is surprisingly lacking in compassion. Sweeney was seventeen at the time but
there had been much in his childhood to cause him anxiety and confusion. In a way, he had lost his mother twice. From the perspective
of a young child, she deserted him before he was three years of age,
and now she was dead. Then his identity as Bert's son was dragged
from under his feet. It is little wonder if he felt he was falling, unsure
of who he was or where he belonged.

⬥

Friday. May 18

Dear Jeannie, I wrote to you on Wednesday, not
very well, I fear, as I somehow felt unable to
get myself working properly. Today I hope to do
better. I've been out every night for weeks past,
very often to the opera which has been a modest but
real joy ... Ariadne, Traviata, Don Giovanni and
Verdi's Falstaff which was a masterpiece. Thank God
they are doing another season next year. They talk
vaguely about an opera house but I am not really
optimistic. However the new cultural centre at
Wirth's Park is under way and has provision for one
or two new concert halls. Dorian's Sinfonietta is

one of the works included in an hour-long telecast made by the ABC for world release and it is being shown in New York this week.

Enough of such fragments, I will add more when I think of them. The real problem is what we are to do with ourselves and I will just have to jump into that and do my best to make myself clear. I know very well that for you the problem of whether to come home or not is complex and painful.

Finally we are both concerned with Jane, just Jane herself and not what she means to either of us. True, many times when her absence has been almost unbearable to me I have, as I have said in my last letter, almost come around to pleading with you. That of course is egocentric. It's real enough but it comes under the heading of what I feel and not what is best for Jane. Yet for Jane herself I often feel very sad and I would be a funny man if I didn't. Is she to grow up in England or Australia? In one way I would like her to remain in England with Mark and Elizabeth because they have become her friends and she should be making and keeping friends right now. But that would mean losing her daddy and so it is not ideal either way. One objection to her living in London is her catarrh ... At least I was very concerned by the dentist's comments and I think we should take that very seriously. This is all very roughly stated and the guts of the matter is that of course I am biased as hell in the issue, of course I want her to come home and quickly, but at the same time I try hard as I cannot to be blind to all that is involved. And I try just as hard on your behalf. You have someone you love in London and that is something. But you are obviously very homesick and, especially if you agree that Australia would be better than England for Jane, the pressure to come home is likely to become increasingly great. I wish you were not so fearful about coming home but I do not know how best to reassure you.

My father went on once again to offer my mother as much

freedom as she wanted should she return, and explained that if she didn't intend to return by the Australian spring he would need to find new tenants for Rose Cottage, as the Kirks were planning to move out within the next two or three months. He emphasised the necessity for rent money if he was to continue to support us in the UK. He ended with:

```
I'm as biased as hell in the matter of your
homecoming, and with the clearest of ulterior
motives I dare you to think of Rose Cottage in the
spring, with the trees laden with four varieties of
apples, pears, peaches, nectarines and then the tea
tree and the beach. Sorry about all this, but I'm
optimistic enough to hope to write better tomorrow.
A quick note for Jane is enclosed.
Love John
```

The fruit trees of Rose Cottage were indeed beautiful in full bloom, but the house itself was very old and so was the electrical wiring. This was something that had concerned my father for a while, so he wasn't surprised when the lights fused and the whole house had to be re-wired. He wrote and told my mother about it, and in the same letter told her that Bob had been unwell with high blood-pressure and sinus trouble. He told her that he had tried to have a reassuring talk with Bob in an attempt to help him relax but added that, unlike my mother's sister Margaret, he was under no illusions about his skills in healing the sick. Bob was my mother's favourite sibling, and to say Margaret was her least would be quite an understatement. My father wasn't to know that by merely putting those two in the same sentence would cause my mother a few moments of panic.

25th of May 6A Highgate Avenue. Friday

Dear John,

Just a hurried note in answer to your letter which has just arrived with some news of Robbie. I am due to leave any moment to take Jane to the dentist for a final filling before Wales. All is well but

231

I'm not so sure that your dentist is as good as you say, as a year ago I took her and he ignored the very holes that he is filling today. Anyhow, he is also giving me news of the North Wales dental world.

We are off in two weeks. This is not an answer to your three letters which I think have been very pleasant and agreeable, this is just a note as I shan't get another moment to myself until Monday when I shall write a real letter with some ideas, etc. We are terribly busy day and night with Arthur's frames. I am a real gilder now. It is a beautiful old craft and I enjoy it. My main concern is Bob. I do not care for the sound of it at all. I beg of you to be most kind and approving of him. Please, I beg of you, keep Margaret Langley away from him. She is a most evil woman, of this I am sure, quite positive in fact. Do not trust her with anyone, least of all Rob. Believe me, it is a long story, but I am sure she would wreck him if she could. I do not think she is just mad and egotistical, I think she is sick, so sick that she is quite evil.

I nearly got blood pressure myself when I read your letter. How ill is he? Is his life so heavy these days? Is he at Rose Cottage? My God, would that I could be there, just so that he could giggle at my jokes. What a bloody mess.

As for me, I would get on the next boat if it were possible. I am quite seriously homesick now and sometimes fear that I will crack. You don't seem to realise that I am penniless and tired and despondent of living and I do not think I have any idea how to cope with things at the moment. I will never make an Englishwoman, I loathe England, I loathe Europe. I have been so lonely and depressed that I have let my life lead me. I wish I was at home, I wish I had never left home. I am now in a great depression as life seems to be wrapping me up in a parcel and my soul doesn't really want this. I do not know, what or how to cope, I can only go on day by day.

I have the love of the nicest kindest man I have ever known who has left his wife and is ready to devote his heart to me. I am so depressed I don't want anyone. I don't want to be a woman, I just want to lie on a beach until it is all over. If I come home I have your emotions to contend with. It all seems too much for me. I hope to God I feel more cheerful when I get to Wales. I have been somewhat ill these last weeks and more depressed than ever. I fear I am somewhat either a bit insane or a bit too sane. I am not sure which but I really care only for Jane, other than that I would be content to chuck my life in as it's already been too long and too full, also it is possible that I am pregnant, which just makes me feel as if I will go mad.

So you see, you say come home, what can I think, what can I feel, I adore Jane, I adore Rose Cottage, you have given me a hell of a marriage and so I don't want to live with you, my new bloke is as kind as a lamb but I want to run home. I am wretched and care little. I am sorry to say all these things, I do my duty and give Jane a marvellous life. I am kind to everyone in my life and have no conscience but I am very heavy in my heart and soul. Forgive me, I don't care how cross you get with me, you have brought about the wrecking of our lives, so how it finishes up is partly your fault.

Do not fear, I will never do anything silly, not before June is safely in your hands anyhow. I am not a coward. I will write again to let you know how things are with me. I thought such a thing would have made me radiant with happiness but no, the reality is too great. Surely I am too old. Time will tell but I have felt very ill. My heart will break as it has a true home.

Forgive me,

Jean

There was one small sentence placed quietly between my mother's overwrought rambling that would have leapt off the page and hit my father in the chest. He knew a pregnancy would change everything.

Wednesday May 30

Dear Jeannie, your letter came this morning and need I say that I am distraught? But I will try to stop the torrent of thoughts in my head and

try to write calmly because that, and only that
will help. Try to be patient with me for my sake,
for your sake and most of all for Jane's because
every vibration of resentment you feel towards me
rebounds on her. But please God, where to start????
Months ago I said that I was concerned by an
element of irrationality in your letters. Sun said
the same thing to me at the time and it came from
her spontaneously, of course, because I never talk
to her about you. She sometimes says little things
to me, kind and loving things always, as you should
know, but I do not encourage the discussion because
we have violently different viewpoints.

But your letter today is quite another story and I
am not concerned but terrified. Are you going out
of your mind? And I ask the question not unkindly
but earnestly, with love and in fear and trembling.
You must calm down somehow and quickly. As I think
I said in one of my recent letters, I have not
written one word to hurt you since I left England
and have done all in my power to understand and
help. But you don't really understand that even
now, because in this letter, in addition to a dozen
other things, you say that you do not care how
cross you make me. Are you so out of touch that you
do not realise that a heart that is quite filled by
sadness has no room left for anger? No, your letter
tore my heart and guts out but it never aroused a
flicker of anger or even bitterness. Except for one
point as I read for the third time tonight and this
is not relevant really to what I mean.

Yes, tonight as I read about the dentist I was
burning with anger. You say, "When I took her a
year ago he ignored the very holes he is filling
today." Of course he did. Do you really mean that
Jane has not been for a year or thereabouts? I have
asked you a dozen times but you have never replied,
except for the last time when, on first glance,
he said there was nothing. But have I got you
all wrong because you have put it all wrong? Yet
I wonder, because when I arrived in England Jane

had toothache and holes you could put a match in.
Now if this makes you in turn angry then stop and
ask yourself in your heart whether you are being
fair about it. This is the only point on which I
am directly and strongly critical. But please, for
God's sake, don't harbour hostility to me for it
because that will finally do more harm to Jane than
all the bad teeth. I write honestly and in good
faith. But I write against a terrible feeling of
hopelessness.

I think what will happen is that you will take what
you want and reject the rest, not deliberately but
naturally and even unconsciously. But in any case I
must admit that I am much too distressed to write
lucidly, and I can talk of you much more lucidly
and exactly than I can about myself. Only too well
do I know that I am what I am, not only what I
think I am. Yet I am Jane's daddy and you are her
mother and please God it is from there that we
start in all this terrible mess.

If you had written to me and said you had found
a man that you loved and that henceforth your
life would be spent in England with him and I
suppose Jane, then that would have been something
to put against the terrible price of tearing our
little girl in half. But you don't say that or
anything like it, you are absolutely convulsed by
conflicting feelings, to come home, to stay despite
your hatred of England. Then you say that I don't
seem to realise that you are penniless and tired
and despondent of living. Jeannie darling, I have
sent you every penny I could, and gladly, and I
have offered you everything I could should you
come home. Yet you say that you are frightened of
me even though at every turn I have offered and
never had an answer. I offered my love, either as
a husband or a friend. I offered to respect your
relationship with Arthur which you said was life
long and irreplaceable. And all I can offer you
today is a man so radiantly happy to see you that
you would think me a little boy, and so willing

to help and comfort you that coming home to Rose
Cottage would be something like a dream come true.
Too simple and bright, perhaps, but it is much
nearer the truth than you know or could know.

And then you say you think you may be pregnant. Do
you wonder that I am alarmed? For you and for my
poor darling daughter who is in the centre of this
maelstrom. And is it any wonder that you yourself
say, and you probably express yourself very well,
that you just want to lie on a beach until it is
all over. How well I understand. But you don't need
me to tell you that such a wish is impossible of
fulfilment. What you must do is to make a decision
and at present you are trying to say yes and no at
the same time.

O.K. you are soon flying to Wales, and then to
where ... and that is a terribly real question.
But meanwhile you may be pregnant and this may
well take some decisions out of your hands. And
have you really considered the realities of this,
not for next year but for the rest of time? You
seem to have to some degree, at least enough to
make you feel your heart will break, poor girl.
Jeannie, it is not a question of whose fault. Who
am I, or you, to judge. But it may be a tragedy.
Your responsibility to Jane should have meant that
you became pregnant only deliberately and after
considering what it would mean not only to you but
to her and even to me.

But my heart is with you and do not forget it.
Yet what do you expect from me? You are poor even
though you and your bloke are working and I am
sending you 10 pounds weekly. What happens then if
you are pregnant and decide to go ahead with it,
do you still expect me to send as much money and
for how long? And please do not interpret this as
a threat, or even a vaguely hinted threat, that I
will stop sending money. Only what is possible, and
what is fair to either Jane or me. I am confused
now and writing very badly. But you have to make
decisions not only on the feeling of your own heart

236

but with complete responsibility and an awareness
of the consequences for you, Jane and me.

You must write quickly, work or no work. I want to
know the exact date of your departure for Wales and
whether she will be attending a good school there.
When does Jane think she will see her daddy again?
Oh Jeannie, I am just too tired to write and have
said nothing. But for me this is a time of crisis
upon which the rest of my life depends and I will
act accordingly. That, again, is not a threat but a
fact, and no action of mine is likely to be meant
to hurt you.

Terribly sorry this is so bad and pointless, be
calm and cheer up.

Love John

P.S. Bob is much brighter and I will help if I
can, but who am I at present to help Bob? While
rejecting me as a husband do you not expect me
to be a miracle man? Of course he doesn't see
Margaret* and is not likely to.

On the day my father wrote his distraught letter, my mother was
writing this next, strangely jaunty one. I doubt it's relatively gentle
tone would have done much to reassure him about the state of her
mental health.

May 30

Dear Daddy John,

*Just some beautiful photos of Jane in the woods. Sorry about my
depressing letters of last week. There is no change and I am in a
great depression and not at all well. Jane is excellent, as you can
see, she is very sweet and very happy and I am sure you will believe
me when you see these photos, that Jane and I are, as always a very
happy team, and at no point does Jane suffer through any of my
feelings, sad or happy. We are very happy together. Today I had to*

---

* Margaret Langley, Jeannie's older sister

buy Jane new shoes once again. I suppose it's OK as each time she requires a new size, but it is only four months ago that I bought the last pair.

Forgive me for the things that will make you sad and worried too. If you like, I will write again a big letter soon but life seems a gamble at the moment and maybe you would rather I didn't write for a while. There is no change as yet but it is all terribly early to say. I have been feeling simply wretched these last few weeks.

I hope Robbie is feeling better. I am so homesick that, in all seriousness, I feel as if I will faint, or fade away, when I think of home. Odd sorts of places haunt me, like the ti-tree area of Warrigal Rd where we used to collect firewood and mad areas of my childhood where I used to ride bicycles etc.

Do not do anything about new tenants until we see what is to become of me. The weather here continues bitterly cold, drizzling rain and grey skies. There has been no spring. This flat drives me closer every day to insanity. I hate it. The sooner I get to Wales the better. The irony is that Arthur's show has been put ahead two weeks and I shall miss it after all, as once I get to Wales for Jane's winter* holidays, I shall not be able to afford to come back for the show. I really only stayed for that. However.

Sorry my world is so cheerless.

Love Jeannie

In my mother's desperate and sometimes irrational letter prior to this one, there had been a clue as to what could entice her back to Australia. It didn't go unnoticed by my father.

---

* She meant the summer holidays.

Lucy-Ellen Boyd and
Jane in the Boyd's
garden, taken days before
Jean and Jane left for
Australia.

Jean and Jane, Highgate Woods, 1962.

John Hull, Jean (pregnant at the time) and Jane in Arthur Boyd's garden (with Boyd's sculpture in the background) only days before we left England for home. John Hull sent this photo to Jean after their daughter was born. On the back he wrote 'Love from John Hull and London to 1 + 1 + 1 = 3, Jean, Jane and Kate'.

Chapter 15

The Offer

Telegram, June 1:

> BEACH HERE FOR YOU AND DADDY FOR ALL
> CHILDREN RELAX LOVE JOHN

❧

Friday June 1

Dear Jeannie, this will not be a long letter, just
a note to try to help and cheer you a little. I
tried very hard the other night to write my heart
out but I was at the point of exhaustion and it did
not come off very well. Today I sent you a cable.
You will surely realise that it was sent two days
after the letter was written and it is the result
of my thoughts over that time.

What I meant by the cable was that if you are
pregnant and wish to remain so and also wish to
return to Rose Cottage, then that would be all
right by me, for now and always, and I meant it.
That is one of the decisions I made with myself
today. When I awoke and found it was the first
of June I was terribly depressed at the rapid
passage of yet another lonely year. But as the day
proceeded it was as though the cares and troubles
of years were finally precipitated, leaving me
calm, clear and resolute. I have my fears right
enough for both you and Jane but at least I have
lost the terrible feeling of hopelessness.

What I fear, of course, and knowing something of
your state of mind and the problems you have to
face - and I fear it very intensely - is that you
will allow a situation to develop that will make
it extremely difficult, if not impossible for you
to come home. I am optimistic enough to hope that
that will not happen but I wish I could say that
it COULD NOT happen. It could, and all too bloody
easily. So far as this possible pregnancy itself
goes, I think it is vital that you should see a
doctor and at once get a decision. If you decide to
proceed then what I said in my cable stands without
the slightest doubt, even though I have violent
opinions on unwanted pregnancies and regard them as
inexcusable and the broad road to disaster.

I write hastily and not very precisely, but I think
you know what I mean and I think you know the great
problems in everyday life, not only for you but
for the child. If however you decide to terminate
it then I would not be terribly happy about that
either in thinking of you as you or thinking of you
as Jane's mother. Either way it is pretty sad. But
it is time for urgent decisions and all I can say
is that my heart is with you, completely.

But would you be mad enough to go to Wales in
uncertainty? Well enough if you wish to remain
pregnant, but you would need to be very, very sure
and your letter sounded the reverse of that. I
cannot write much more on serious things tonight
because it is just too late and I must get some
sleep.

Bob, as I said in my last letter, seems a little
better, a good deal better in fact. He sold 12
pounds worth of stuff to Miss Macmillan last Friday
and this did more for his blood pressure than all
the doctor's pills. I will help when I can, and
probably can a bit. The re-wiring of Rose Cottage
is finished after a hell of a week. It looks nice
with new switches and power points in every room,
and no chance of getting electrocuted.

I was listening to the BBC last night, in interview

with Nolan, when he said that his stuff for
Covent Garden was based on a motive (Moon Boy)
which originated as a portrait of a friend of his
... J.S. Should you see him, tell him that I was
touched and gladdened to be so described, because
after all the years and all the nonsense, that's
how I feel about it.*

Perhaps if there are ever happier days than these I
will teach you all about Verdi's Falstaff which to
me is what whisky is to some people. No matter how
murderously depressed I am, if I put the record on
this marvellous laughter with which Verdi said good
bye to the world it gets right inside my veins. And
it is so exquisitely beautiful ... As Tovey said,
"the almost Chinese refinement of Falstaff".

But I must go. Forgive this ramble. All I would
like to say before I finish is that it is high time
that you began to think of me or about me as I am
and not as I was years ago, or even as I was in
London. I don't suggest you do this for my sake but
simply for the truth of things...

Love John

The following day my father wrote a brief note to tell my mother
that he had sent 30 pounds in case my mother was broke. He hadn't
had a letter from her yet and told her he was worried.

On the front of this next aerogramme from my mother, my father
wrote, "Received morning Tuesday June 5." It was written before she
received his telegram or his 1st June letter.

6A Highgate Ave.

Dear John,

In great haste to catch tonight's post, I say something that has not

---

* Sunday Reed never got over her love for Nolan, and in 1947 John Reed sent
my father to Sydney to ask him to return to Heide. By then Nolan was living
with Cynthia, John Reed's sister. He was furious and accused my father of
coming to spy on him. Nolan was not a forgiving person so it was the end of
their friendship much to my father's regret.

243

been thought in great haste, but has had a haunting birth in my somewhat lame brain over the last saddened weeks. The reality about my life seems to be this. I must either leave London for home NOW or NEVER.

Once I set foot in a new life in Wales, I must stay in England forever as it seems that I am pregnant. I haven't seen a doctor but it is six weeks since I had a period and I have been very ill and too many symptoms fit the complaint. You see, I don't mind really as I am fast approaching change in life, and was told by my London doctor that I had really begun rather early as some women do and that I was probably already too old to become pregnant. This saddened my heart as, both for Jane and myself, I thought it tragic. In some way I personally don't care about the pedigree and nothing would make me have an abortion. I don't care about being pregnant although I feel very ill and old and tired I have very little else to live for but motherhood really, as I seem to have made a mess of my emotions over the last year.

The thing is that my sad adoring young man thinks the sun shines from me and is delirious with happiness. Although somewhat carried away, I realise that I do not care to either spend my life with him or in England. It is all rather cruel of me but if I am going to run away, then I must do it now. I vaguely planned to leave for home immediately.

Arthur will forward necessary cash but he is in financial trouble himself and it would have to be a very short-term loan as he couldn't manage to float much for long as he has spent a fortune getting sculpture etc. to England for the show. He has only sold his first painting for the year and is beginning to feel frightened about his own livelihood, in spite of his fame.

The rest is up to you, either to borrow dough or tell me to stay here forever. This is a very tragic moment for me. I am very depressed and only Arthur knows of my panic. You must write immediately or wire as I must make this decision. I am tired of being away and know, by the nature of things it is NOW or

244

NEVER. Please take me seriously. I am deadly serious. I am homeless in ten days and very depressed. I am too old for this to happen.

Love Jean

⌘

On the front of this next letter he wrote, "Received Tuesday afternoon June 5." She would have received the telegram but the long letter she referred to must have been my father's previous one of the 30th of May. Once again, she wasn't taking into account that letters between England and Australia took at least three days to arrive, sometimes more.

6A Highgate Avenue Saturday 2nd June

Dear John,

Your telegram arrived with long letter this morning. I have wired back to you. By the time you get this you will have to have an answer to my question of money. The ship, a Norwegian freighter carrying 12 passengers sails from Rotterdam on the 19th June. I have booked a cancellation that I got through Aust. House. This is my only chance of getting home at all as it is very complex and I am far from well and bloke is begging to either come with me to Aust. or me stay in England. I reject either but I am tired and it becomes very difficult to continue to hurt someone so nice and good. One of the great fears that has kept me from returning ever since you left, is the thought of enduring Hell on an Italian ship in an eight birth cabin full of Italian migrants. Also now it is deadly serious as Italian cooking and noise would kill me. For the same price, I have a two berth cabin with shower and peace and apparently great comfort. It is this or nothing for me, as I am frail indeed and in spite of your bone pointing at my mental weaknesses I have had over the last year good reason for being somewhat irrational.

At no point has Jane suffered and if you look well into the coloured photos you should have by now, you will see a lovely child,

245

of great poise and grace and character. My warm motherhood strangely is the point that causes me to be so much adored, I have never failed Jane.

This ship will arrive in Melbourne on the 27th July. I cannot stay in London any longer. What can I say but repeat, now or never. I would either have to go to Wales (which would have to be for good under these new circumstances) or come home immediately. Whatever method is used for payment, I repeat, I am penniless. Either my fare is offered or I cannot come home. Don't you see it costs nearly 300 pounds, WHERE do I get it FROM? It will cost that however or when, Hellship or peace. Therefore if you could borrow it and get it to Arthur within the month of June I can go ahead with his money. I must pay by Tuesday 5th June. Could you wire me yes or no by Tuesday morning.

There is one point I feel I must make clear, I want no emotional life, I do not want to be anybody's wife. I am not coming home to any such demands as I am tired beyond measure and require only peace. I will live with Betty Langley or on my own if you prefer it. Rose Cottage is yours and I have no right to demand any of it. My heart is as always bound up in it. I am very homesick and sorry I ever left home. My inconsistencies have come about in my search to find something to live for that I had a right to live for. However, I fall down badly and yet my conscience is still clean.

Could the money be borrowed from the Bank or the Reeds or Dorian? Have I any right to ask this? I cannot come home without it, I will fret badly if I can't as having for the first time allowed myself to consider home, I will find it hard to forget. I cannot ask Arthur to lend it indefinitely as he is in queer street and has no income and has to leave his house in July. You must believe this and I can only use his money if it will be replaced from another source. You ask why I say I am penniless, not only am I penniless but a beggar into the bargain. You know my pride surely. When are the tenants leaving Rose Cottage? Should I write to Betty, she has offered before.

I go around and around in my head, I didn't sleep a wink
last night with anxiety. Your telegram was cheering but how
was I to know how you would react to such a delicate situation?
Yesterday before I went to Aust. House, I fell down the stairs in the
underground, I would have crashed to the concrete bottom had
not a man saved me. It gave me a terrible fright and made me
realise things are a bit much for me. I then went to see Nolan's early
works in London and I was nearly in tears with the sheer beauty
of his paintings of that period. Dimboola, St Kilda, Kelly, Gum
trees, light horizons, sea and Australia. What a painter he was. No
reproductions do them justice. I was moved to tears.

Until I hear yes or no to money, I cannot really know what is to
be my future. My telephone No. is Mountview 9516 (MOU9516).
I haven't told Jane anything as yet for fear of disappointing her. If I
can't go in two weeks' time what would I do with myself? London is
getting me down. It is worth a frantic effort. I cross my fingers I can
do no more.

Love Jean

❦

My father rang London on 8 June, presumably to agree to my
mother's plan. Around the same time he sent a telegram telling her
he had taken out a mortgage on Rose Cottage and would send 100
pounds immediately so she could secure our passage home.

When my father sent his next telegram he presumed only a deposit had been paid but my mother had borrowed the money from
Arthur and paid the full 300 pounds.

Telegram, 11 June:

CANCEL PASSAGE REGARDLESS LOSS. WONT
PAY. REMAIN LONDON TEMPORARY. DIVORCE
INEVITABLE. LOVE NOT ANGER. LETTER POSTED.
JOHN

I have known about these two telegrams for most of my adult life.
My mother often told of how my father offered what she most needed
and desired at the time, then cruelly and inexplicably changed his

247

mind. That was how she saw it and I didn't care enough to seek my father's explanation of his "treacherous" change of heart. Now I see that my mother missed the implied happy family concept behind his offer to be a daddy to her unborn child.

My father's response to her clear rejection of any such idea was slow, but perhaps not surprising.

Sunday June 10

Dear Jeannie,

Before this letter arrives you will have received my cable. If I say I write with the sound of your voice and Jane's soft, warm and gentle "Hello Daddy" in my ears, that should give you enough insight into my present feelings. There is not a vibration of anger, resentment or the like in this letter or my last cable and please, please Jeannie, no matter what you feel at first, please try to think and consider and to reply without bitterness. Because bitterness or anger at this stage would be untruths.

We are all in a tragic situation and I have made my decisions, and I write this letter with the desperation of a man trying to save three people from a whirlpool. Believe me, if only because it should be obvious that by taking my present stand I am very likely to get badly hurt and not likely to gain a thing. In the most immediate sense it means that I will not be able to embrace Jane on July 27, and who knows when after that? What do you think that feels like for me? O.K., I have changed my mind after six days of torment, considering one painful alternative after another. It is little comfort to me to realise how slow I have been, to realise that if I had taken my present attitude six days ago that would have been far better for you and Jane and that if I had acted three months ago you would have been spared your present suffering. I don't need to be told how much of the present situation is my fault but I am also quite clear that any further hesitation on my part could only add to the tragedy.

When I wrote and cabled inviting you home and
offering to be daddy to your new baby, that was a
decision made partly out of affection and sympathy
for you and partly in the belief that it would be
the best thing for Jane. It was completely unwise.
It presupposed that we would resume some kind of
life together, but in your very last letter you
made it quite clear that you had no intention of
doing anything of the sort. How then could I be
a daddy? It could not possibly work out and this
unpleasant truth became clearer as the days went
by.

So what then are the alternatives? There are two
as I see it. One. That you remain in England, have
the baby, and live there for the immediate future
at least with Jane, the Baby, and John, I think
his name is. With me paying for Jane's upkeep and
education. Two. That you return to Australia with
or followed by John, and live here with him and
Jane and the baby, with me keeping Jane of course.
This seems to be preferable and even a fairly happy
solution but there is so much that I do not know
that I cannot judge.

But the terms upon which you propose to return
seemed to me at first to be pretty sad and worrying
and they now seem to me to be so impossible that
I cannot see how you begin to justify them. Since
I left London you have acted as a completely free
agent and it seems with terribly sad results. You
did not consult me when you agreed to your first
bloke following you to Australia. Then you decided
to live in Wales with John and Jane, presumably for
some years, without considering my feelings beyond
feeling sorry that I would be sad. I do not mention
these things in a spirit of recrimination, Jeannie,
but simply to outline the situation.

But now, when, for some reason which I do not
understand, you decide not to go to Wales, not to
live with John but to come home and have his baby,
and you immediately ask me to do several things. To
borrow a lot of money to bring you home, to have no

say at all in whether or not Jane has a brother or
sister, to accept the fact that you are no longer
in any real sense my wife ... And then, I suspect,
you would look to me to maintain all three of you
indefinitely. You may of course say that you had
no intention of expecting me to maintain you all,
but let's face it. You have no income, and nowhere
to live, and you certainly could not live with
Betty these days as she now has a tiny flat. So I
would either have to see you homeless and starving
or move out of Rose Cottage for you and pay your
bills.

Is that not quite certain? Yet if you think about
it, does that not mean that while I have not a wife
and family in the real sense, I have a financial
burden that would make the rest of my life pretty
much of a wipe off. To that degree I have some
self-interest in this. But my attitude is not
really one of self-interest and it is certainly
not one of sticking up for my rights, because when
a marriage breaks up there is no real justice for
anyone, and certainly you may rightly feel that an
awful lot of this is pretty sad and cruel for you.
Yet so much of this proposition is so fantastically
unfair to me that I feel it is up to you, not to
justify it, because that is impossible, but to
realise that this proposition is unjustifiable. Yet
what stops me accepting all this is not that it is
unjust, that is for me a secondary consideration,
and the only reason I say that is because it is
true.

What stops me really is that I am convinced that
it would result in certain disaster. The fact
is, Jeannie, that you are in a terrible spot and
I can't get you out of it. You can't see that at
present but it is absolutely true. You have to
choose one course of action with all it involves,
and not simply take the most pleasant elements from
two courses of action which is just what you are
doing. I suspect that you do so for two closely
associated reasons. Firstly you are pregnant and

your whole being rebels against abortion, and
whether you know it or not, my heart is with you.
Secondly another child would be a companion for
Jane. It would up to a point, and especially at
first, be a good thing, even if she is too old
to be anything else but an only child at heart.
That is a truth that haunts my conscience. For her
another child would be an advantage, but one bought
at great risk and probably at very great cost.

Just the simplest point. Imagine Jane at Mentone
Grammar with her mother the talk of the town ... or
do you think that the women of suburbia have become
mild and gentle? Right enough for you and I to
brave their hostility, but it might be very tough
on Jane sticking up for principles which after
all are ours and not hers. As I have said before
the question of abortion is your decision and not
mine. But it is a decision that must be made not in
isolation but in relation to all that is involved.
In any unwanted pregnancy, someone must get hurt.
But I ask you, is it not more moral and much nobler
for a woman to suffer the personal tragedy of an
abortion, rather than give birth to a child which
she cannot rear with normal amounts of comfort
and happiness? And what in this case would be the
consequences for Jane if you decided to bring up
this child, regardless of any and all difficulties?

It is all very well for John to be radiantly happy,
but his place is with you in relation to this
child. What does he intend to do about the child's
upkeep, and if he does want to come to Australia,
has he shown you his wife's permission in writing?
I'm sorry to sound mean and sceptical but you must
remember that I know nothing about him. But I know
enough about you to want to see that permission
before I would be completely convinced, and that is
not an unkind remark at all.

But what I cannot understand is why you want to
undertake the very difficult, complex and even
dangerous venture of having his child while
rejecting him as a husband. I cannot of course do

anything to stop you doing exactly what you wish but it is too much to expect me to come in and help you make possible a course of action which I believe would finally be disastrously sad for both you and Jane.

This is a terribly sad and hurtful letter for you and it will I know be read through tears. But it is also written pretty much that way. All I would ask you is to try to think clearly and to accept if you can my good faith. Don't simply say that the guts of the matter is that I am a bastard, that I did not love you and Jane enough to accept another man's child, or after saying that I wanted you both home I have finally made it impossible. Such accusations would be quite untrue as you know very well, and it would be unworthy of you to make them.

You may well ask why I had to leave it until this last minute to come to such decisions, and of course the answer to this is not that I do not love you and Jane but that it was only when the writing was on the wall in big and terrible letters that I could bring myself to take a course of action which is not only painful to you but which might well mean that I do not see my daughter for a long time to come. And please, Jeannie, for God's sake, what do you think I feel when I think of what she must feel in all this? Your real complaint against me should be that I should have acted months ago and for that I cannot forgive myself. But now I think that a divorce represents for both you and I and Jane the wisest, of most painful, first step.

I would suggest that you took as good a room as possible in London and I will maintain you there on 12 pounds English weekly until we reach a decision and, if you still wish to return, until we get another boat.

It is 4 am and I am too tired to write another word and even though this letter is incomplete, it is a start and it must be posted.

Love John.

There will be a heavy loss on the boat fares but
I accept that. The things involved at present are
worth much more than a hundred quid or so.

⚬⚭⚬

Monday, June 11

Dear Jeannie, late this afternoon, which is early
morning in London, there was probably little
difference between what went on in your room at
Highgate and in my room at Rose Cottage, except
that with you was our darling Jane, hurt perhaps
terribly badly by a message from Daddy which she
could not possibly understand. Your tears and hers
were no more real than mine. And now I write in
despair.

What I most fear is that you will simply regard
my cancelling cable as a diabolical betrayal and
with blind hatred swear to make me pay for it for
the rest of my life. Such a reaction would be a
lie. I know that and so do you. Hatred is always
a lie and a cover up and there are no exceptions
to that eternal truth. None of us can side-step it
by saying all hatreds except mine ... But Jeannie,
in this awful crisis we have no alternative but to
speak to each other and act towards each other with
absolute truth. To encourage us we have a little
girl whom our lies could tear to shreds and we
have as a discipline the knowledge that in any real
human struggle, nothing can disguise truth. Nothing
can disguise my guilt for my part in the breakdown
of our marriage and our lives. Now, whether you
act selfishly and basically for your own sake or
unselfishly for the sake of Jane and as many people
as are involved, nothing can prevent your motives
and actions (and mine) from being recognised for
what they are. It is useless and in fact terribly
destructive for either of us to pretend, even to
ourselves.

React to me any way you wish at present as a
safety valve, that I would completely understand.
But Jeannie, I hope and pray that finally you

253

will be peaceful enough to reject anything that
springs from anger, bitterness, resentment or,
what is probably the greatest danger in your case,
pride. Do you think that I do not know that the
present situation for you is laden with anguish
and suffering, and that you now have to make
decisions in accordance with terms which must seem
to be mercilessly cruel and unjust. You will, I
know, think that I am responsible for deciding
those terms, but it is not so. True, I could have
suspended them for a time by paying your fare home
and so on but, and it is the one realisation that
at present strengthens me, that would be asking me
to help us all on the broad and certain road to
disaster.

Try, Jeannie, I beg you to get beyond the view that
I am a bastard who has deserted you in your hour
of greatest need. That view is deceptively easy
to take, but it is quite false. Think about the
following facts, not with sympathy for me but as
a possible guide to my motives. For months past,
every time I hear a little girl cry Daddy a knife
goes through my guts. Last Friday I heard my own
little girl call me daddy in a voice I will never
forget. Yet this morning I sent you a cable which
means that I will not see her next month, that I
might not see her for a long time and perhaps ever
again. Now is it possible that I am such a monster,
and so mentally disordered that I sent a cable with
even the slightest trace of anger or self-interest?
You may find it terribly hard to understand my
present attitude but at least, Jeannie, I beg you
not to misunderstand.

God knows the present facts seem hard enough to
me and how much harder must they seem to you. If
I could change them I would, and God knows what
I would give to be able to do so. But I can't and
you must realise that. The problems of your life at
present centre on London and it breaks my heart to
admit that they must be solved there. If indeed you
are still pregnant then that is something between

254

you and John because without him, without a husband
or income, it is fantastic for you to imagine for
a moment that you could rear his child. Don't see
that as a threat from me Jeannie. If you do, think
again. Yet if you are to have his child, then his
presence either in London or Australia might well
be the key to a reasonably happy solution for all
of us. And what pleasure do you think it gives me
to thus drive you into his arms? Yet I cannot do
otherwise because my responsibilities to Jane are
alone enough to make me now realise that there may
be no alternative.

I am quite sure at this stage that a divorce for us
is the only possible solution but I have not yet
seen a solicitor ... And why not, Jeannie, do you
think? Yet do not misinterpret my hesitance. It
is in one way the final betrayal for Jane but in
another it is no worse and much better than a lot
of other things. But I must finish. All I can say
briefly is that never before and I hope never again
will you be asked to pay so high a price for being
Jane's mother. If you think that I see myself in
all this as a poor wronged and unloved husband then
forget it, and quickly. All I see is three people
in a hell of a sad mess.

Yours, John

P.S. Could you in the best words you can find tell
Jane I love her truly and send her a kiss.

⬚

Telegram, 14 June:

DIVORCE BEGUN PLEASE CABLE YOUR PLANS + JOHN

Chapter 16

A Difficult Voyage Home

My mother's plan was well in action before she informed my father. She was so angry writing this letter she dispensed with the usual, "Dear John".

15 June

By the time you get this note I will be on the sea. You can shove your filthy money up your jumper. I would rather go on the streets than live with any man for a meal ticket. You talk of pride, my pride has grown out of all proportion over this last week and if you think I feel any shame you are greatly mistaken. I have asked many times for a divorce and it seems now that it suits you to be rid of me, I am granted this pleasure. I take it this is my reward for my seven and a half years of little else but sheer bloody, good bloody constant devotion to our child. I have worked very hard at being a mother and have spent tremendous energy and time to make some human being free of spirit and full of love. A magnificent child is the result.

It seems it is more important to you that I suffer my body to be cut and tortured by a filthy abortion, than to face the world of stupid women whose values I personally despise. You own Rose Cottage. O.K. But it is my personality that created it, my scraping and saving and doing without, almost to the point of malnutrition, that paid for it. All you really own is your conscience and God help you deal with that, as because you have made it impossible for the woman who married you in good faith to be able to live with you, you intend to hound her into poverty at a time where it is desperate that she has some security. You always kick me when I am down.

I am a good woman who has paid a big price for marrying a man incapable of anything else but demand. You were welcomed in London with warmth but because I say I will not sleep with you any longer, I am to be cast into a tragic life. I will sleep with no man anymore, I am through with men. If I do not love my London John, then what right have I to drag him twelve thousand miles because he loves me. So that I have a meal ticket and you are not faced with any social embarrassment. I have to spend my life somewhere by myself with two children. I work hard for one and it is the only thing in my life that has been worthwhile, so why should I not work hard for two children.

Five years ago, I asked you to give me emotional freedom. Had you been big enough to grant me that, we would still all be under the same roof. Because my body is the only part of me you love, you couldn't bear to help me now by giving me a home because I made it clear I wouldn't sleep with you. You freeze my guts until I despise life. All this would not be so bitter in my uddled brain, had you simply been clear of your reaction from the start. But to wait until I told Jane and bought a ticket and packed my trunks. I have no flat now. I am living with the O'Shaughnessys. I have no money. All I have in the world is a beautiful daughter and a ticket to Australia. If I stay here I will kill myself as I am very cheesed off with life. My courage is strained. Your masculine pride which is immense and stupid, I am sure, is responsible for dealing me such a blow.

I am sure, had I suggested that as your housekeeper and Jane's Mother I adopted a child, you would have been only too willing. You, who have denied me the right of motherhood, as I intended always to have a large family, you have the audacity to tell me not to come home unless I have an abortion. I despise the stinking corrupt society, I despise suburbia, why should I allow it to rule my life. I cannot live away from Australia any longer. How strange,

I would not have credited you with letting me down in quite this sort of way. You, who have always known how embarrassing I find money. However it seems you have justified your behaviour in your own eyes. Good luck to you. I wish I could do the same.

Thank God I have many good friends and they don't treat me like a shopgirl. However I am at peace with myself even though I am extremely worried about practicalities. After all, you and I both know that you made life Hell for me when I was pregnant with Jane, your own child. What have you ever done but ill-treat me? You have kept me for some time now but after all, I have worked 12 hours a days at being a mother, or do you think I have been having a high life? After I have paid rent for nearly all the time in London I have had to keep house and clothe Jane on four pounds a week. If you think this is easy in a freezing London winter, you must try it sometime. I assure you I have had a hell of a bloody time. Lonely, poor and sad with my only little treasure kept blissfully unaware of the strain.

My attempts to gain some happiness have been unsatisfactory, but nothing would make me continue them once I have got to grips with reality. It is a pity my trip home will be no more fun than staring at the blank sea wondering what would become of me and mine. I am not a young woman and my body has been through too much to find it easy to cope with the strain it is under now. I advise you to be very careful with Jane as she loves me very dearly, and seeing me cry my heart out when we had both innocently been waiting for your telephone call with excitement for days, has made her very protective towards me. I will not say anymore. I care little what the world does to me now. I am tired of life. I have had enough. Do not delude yourself too much. It is evident to me that you are quite happy in your new role. It is a new tragedy for you to thrive on. You have never had any desire at all to be happy. You have paid me back for what your mother and father did to you. Enough is enough.

Sometime just before or after leaving London I contracted rubella. In this next letter my mother wrote as if my father knew of my illness, so there may be a letter of hers missing. It's one of life's little ironies that my mother, with her tendency to catastrophise about her health, was unaware of the very real and serious danger this posed to her unborn child.

Dear John,

I am not making overtures to you by writing a second letter so soon, I am writing only as Jane's mother as there is, I feel, a certain need. Things are not too good with us on board and I feel it's all very hard for a child to cope with. Jane is to be two more days in bed as the doctor seems to think her pulse is a bit fast and she doesn't look herself at all. Her spots have practically vanished but she is bored to tears. It is very hot now and we are about to enter the Mediterranean Sea. In fact she's having a terrible time so far. She is tremendously good and so I feel she should be rewarded. I want so much to buy her something very special but have only enough to buy rubbish in Spain tomorrow. The only thing I could do was tell her I'd write to you suggesting you bought her a special present for her when we reached Melbourne.

Sorry to bully you but I didn't think you would mind. Yesterday was a tragedy. We arrived at Magic Lisbon which looks so beautiful I was delighted from the port. The stewardess and Jane insisted I go ashore. I promised to find Jane a treasure. The Queensland couple and young doctor insisted I go with them in a taxi. How I hated it because all this woman talked about was how dirty everything was and the clothes in the shops. The doctor is terribly youthful and a Scot from Aberdeen, and although he is a good lad he is no companion for me.

I hated the taxi ride and was planning my escape to wander on my own, when the woman developed an attack of asthma. She was bad so the doctor got a taxi and back we all went to the ship at some speed as they were a bit concerned at her difficulty. Half way back she suddenly died. Christ, it was terrible. We ordered the taxi to turn back to a hospital and the doctor tried to resuscitate breath to breath from the front seat. The taxi then with his hand on the horn went at a tremendous speed in and out of the traffic like a maniac. Mostly the traffic parted for us like magic but we went at such a speed I thought none of us would get there alive, the streets are mad and very narrow and winding.

Lisbon is built on seven small hills and is very old and tightly built. A nightmare ride if ever I had one with the poor doctor nearly bursting himself to get a breath from the woman. The hospital was unbelievable, terrible, as no one in Portugal speaks a word of English. The police are the big bosses and poverty is rife. The hospital was the most sordid place I have ever seen. The woman was dead, it was all over, they couldn't save her, she was dead when we got there. She died in the taxi, her heart gave out, according to the doctor, and she was a little over fifty. The poor old husband, a self-made rich sugar farmer from Tully was taken from us by the horrid Portuguese police. They were impossible and no one spoke a word of English. It was like a nut house, not a hospital.

I felt as if I would die with shock myself, it was all so mad, so quick and so very horrible. The natives crowded around us, as if we were all monkeys. The doctor and I were both half crying half shaking and the taxi driver was crying. It was awful. Finally the doctor and I went back to the ship. The police wouldn't let the old boy go with us. We got the Captain and the British Consul who took over. The sugar farmer left the ship to fly home, we left him trying to make up his mind what to do with the body. It was horrible for him.

The hardest part for me was to tell Jane what had happened to the woman who Jane thought was marvellous. I didn't beat around the bush but it was hard for her to comprehend the reality. She could only think of the woman in the posh hat that had said goodbye cheerfully a couple of hours beforehand. It was a terrible ship last night. The Captain, the doctor and I sat down to a miserable dinner. Now there are only two and a half passengers.

All this has added to my concern for Jane. This woman had a sixteen-year-old daughter at boarding school and Jane knew all about her. Jane was very concerned about the daughter, the practicalities of the body, and very much worried about, could that ever happen to me, her mummy? I told her I was a very strong mummy and that she was a very strong child and that you were a strong man and that we were lucky and didn't have to worry.

All told, it's put a great heaviness on us, and the only thing I could think of was to promise her you would buy her something very special, when the doctor said two more days in bed. She is so bored and yet so very good-natured. It's all terribly depressing. She had set her heart on seeing Spain. She has a great romantic notion about Spanish ladies. Tomorrow is our only day in Spain in Malaga, and I couldn't possibly risk taking Jane ashore as she doesn't look well. She cried deeply and sadly, like an adult, about the Spanish port. Poor little pet, I would do anything for her. She is so romantic, yesterday when she was in bed, she asked me to hang her party dress where she could gaze at it. So you see, I beg of you, do what you like to me, but don't hurt Jane, pay me back separately, spare Jane.

She is worried about me, that is bad, she is worried about Rose Cottage, she is too young to have these problems. She is very affected by life's happenings. Death is hard to understand. She was terribly upset about her puppy being run over as she talked about it all the time to her friends and ladies in shops etc. When I told her he was dead, it was like telling her fairies weren't true. A great dream shattered. I would think another puppy an ideal present but as we don't know where we will be living it would be foolish.

Even though you will hate me for saying so, she will love a baby. She doesn't know yet in case I lose it at three months which is a bad time for older women. If the tragedy of yesterday didn't make me miscarry, well who knows. But until I am past this time I see no point in Jane being informed. Yet she has been asking me for years *to have a baby. Her girlfriend at school had one and Jane asked me every day after school, could we get one somehow. She will find it better than a puppy.*

I do not know what to suggest, not a book, she is not a book child. She has a doll, she loved the doll's dress by the way, I brought the doll's pram home. She has it in the cabin with her. She has a new swimming costume and new sandals. Prettiness is her great love. I would suggest a dress but she is already 4ft 2 and a half inches, and it will be winter in Melb. I beg of you find her a treasure as she deserves it. Ballet shoes would be good. She takes Size 1. She has seen a ballet, and wants to be a ballet dancer. Maybe a book of ballet dancers if there are lots of beautiful pictures. Won't be able to afford to write again.

Please love Jane.

Jean

I try to imagine how my father felt when he read those three words, "Please love Jane". Even reading them so many decades later makes me want to scream with frustration. How could she write those words after all the anguish he had expressed? Did she not feel the pain of him missing me that he describes in so many letters? Maybe his anger was rapidly crushed under the weight of a bone-wearying feeling of defeat, futility and despair. Or did her crude attempt at manipulation elicit nothing more than a long, slow sigh of resignation.

❧

Posted in Aden and included was a drawing of mine with "FROM Jane to DADDY" written by me at the top:

Somewhere in the Red Sea.

Dear John,

It seems now a reality that Jane and I are on our way to Melbourne. It's unbearably hot. Seems this is the worst time to travel the Red Sea. Poor little Jane is perspiring and red and finding it rather hard to cope. We have a swimming pool made of plastic which saves us from suffering heat all day long. The nights are fearful and we expect to get out of this heat zone in about four days' time when we hit the Indian Ocean.

Jane has recovered from the measles. At last she looks all right. Life is very tedious for us both. Strangely, in this heat all red and puffy she looks just like Patricia. She is thin after her little illness. As for me, it will be another week before I am clear of the measles. The more I think of it, the more certain I am that I have had them.

My reason for writing again, is Jane. She is undergoing tremendous anxiety about our return. She cries about Rose Cottage and about you and I not loving each other, every other night we have a session now. The measles and boredom have weakened her cheerfulness about life. I still haven't told her you are divorcing me but she has a thousand questions that I find impossible to answer. Then hot impossible nights without sleep, I toss and turn physically and mentally, as to what I am to do with life.

Strangely with both of us, as we get further and further away from England our memories are returning to life in Australia. In England Jane's memory of life before was scarcely existing. Everyone except Nana seemed to be gone from her mind. Now she is brimming with memories of everyone and everything that ever happened. Rose Cottage is for both of us home and it is hard enough for me to bear the thought but I cannot make Jane understand why we cannot return to it. She is violent about it all and begs me to write to you. Her last question was, "Will Daddy meet us?"

It made me cry as crying comes easily to me at the moment. What is so hard for her is that I never mentioned returning to Australia until your first telegram arrived, and when I told her what was happening, we hugged each other and danced with joy, and of course all we could talk about was Rose Cottage and the beach and the cats and home. How is she to understand why it is suddenly closed down? She asked me yesterday, "Who owns the cats? Daddy or us?"

I beg of you to meet us. I beg of you, for Jane's sake, to behave
with chivalry towards me, even if it costs you much supressed
anger. Personally I think it is all very out of proportion; do you
think I am the first woman to have had a child in this manner? I
always thought of a divorce being something calmly planned by
two parties as the best thing. Not like a door slammed in the face
of a woman suddenly in a precarious position. Especially amazing
after your telegram of approval of my return pregnant or otherwise.
However I grant you the right to divorce me. Fair enough under the
circumstances but it is a very bad time to do it to me, after all, you
have approved of my confessed infidelity for two years, you have
had plenty of time to get upstage. Why now? Is it because I am in a
most helpless position???

I have only one alternative to survive. Unless I marry English
John, I must become somebody's housekeeper. It is the only way
I can approve of earning a living and keeping a home for my
children. What a boring and tedious life to keep house for a strange
man and probably his children for the sake of existence. Do you
want to destroy me that badly. You do me great injustice when
you say I always do what I want. You judge from outside of my
character. I always do what I believe is right to do for Jane and
myself. I am not a selfish person and have never indulged myself.
Until quite recently I have carried a tremendous frustration as a
female being. Do you remember?

You know as many things about our marriage as I do. How
many children do you think I would have liked, had you been a
kind husband to me instead of a sadistic tormentor? My one big
frustration over the years was the size of my family. Only the reality
of it being too late has made me decide to keep this child alive as
my last chance. The strange thing about the female is that it is
possible, now the mechanics are in motion, to even have another
child very soon after this one. No, you cannot tell me I am wrong
to keep it, just because of Mentone old women, that is your only
objection, or perhaps your own pride, or perhaps the memory of

my attempts and miscarriage, which I am certain about now, in that last Rose Cottage reconciliation.

There must be much in your knowledge of me and our marriage to know that you have let me down very badly. You always admitted you never loved me but I still cannot see why that was any reason to be so openly cruel to me. None of this would have happened had you been a good husband. You know all these things, so do I. You know bloody well that I would have stuck to you through thick and thin had it been humanly possible. You know as much about the history as I do.

Well, it's so hot tonight it's hard to believe. The sky has been yellow all day with sand blown across from Arabia. There is sand all over the deck and one feels its fine grains in one's mouth if one looks to sea. It was 98 in the shade and the water in the swimming pool was hot. Really, it's stinking. Jane is bearing up but she can't get to sleep. Tomorrow night we will be in Aden, after that the Indian Ocean. My feelings are mixed and muddled and although I can't wait to get home, I completely dread it in another way. Much against my better judgement and against my pride, I suggest you hold your peace for a short while. I do not ask you not to divorce me but I do ask you to help me. It is not possible for me to earn my own living at the moment. I cannot live on charity. If you want your divorce immediately then one must be very careful not to allow the guilty party to sleep under the same roof. I tell you this in all fairness. If you do continue with the divorce, I beg you not to tell Jane but allow me to do so when I see fit as I do not think she should undergo too much emotional strain on her return. It is asking too much.

I personally think the divorce should wait. After all, there is always the evidence you require of any sort, every sort. It is not hard for you to divorce me. I would like to take Jane back to Rose Cottage to give her time to settle herself. Would it not be possible for me to be your housekeeper? When is the flat vacant? Could I not be your housekeeper even if you divorced me? After all there are three flats at Rose Cottage. Could you not live in the Cottage if you continue with the divorce and I could earn my keep doing your domestic work, or if you will wait a while for the divorce, could I not have my bedroom and my own sitting room and keep house for both you and Jane having the rest of the house, leaving Rob in the Cottage, or let Jane and I live in the Cottage with you and Bob in the house.

What I would like for myself is my little sleepout that I made and the yellow sitting room which I love passionately, Jane could have her old bedroom with the roses and you could have the big room as music room and the sleepout in front, making kitchen community, with me as chief cook and bottlewasher. Maybe I dream, maybe I am mad, I love Rose Cottage, it is more than a roof, I love it dearly and I adore my little Jane. I am tired of battle and quite willing to work. It should be Jane's home, the whole idea of Mentone and Rose Cottage was a home for Jane long before she was conceived.

I feel sick with worry and the heat. I beg of you not be so hasty as to turn against me so ungenerously when I am in such a state. You will force me to behave foolishly as I am indeed tired. Many times your beggings have been answered by me. Many times before I went to England did I give you another chance, each time to my own heartbreak. Heartbreak that is in me still and heavy as lead. Ah well, I suppose I am behaving foolishly, God knows, I care not. To me, life everywhere I see is foolish and dishonest, mine may be foolish but at least it is constantly honest. You owe me some helping hand now as you really cast me adrift with your cruel behaviour. I find myself crying as people are so horrid to each other and life is passing us by.

I am thirty six and feel as if life has suddenly become a terrible barrier. You have tricked me into coming home whether you know it or not. 300 pounds was paid in good faith and would have been wasted had I not caught this boat. I wonder what love letters and

promises you would be writing to me now had I never suggested
coming home to have this child.

I am not young, John, to be having a baby so long after the first,
also it is true, that I had begun to have symptoms of the beginning
of the change in life, very early, maybe because my heart has
been so tired, maybe just naturally. So I write this begging letter,
swallowing my pride, for Jane, my little sleeping lamb, whom I love
more day by day, who is so fine, so sensitive and yet so practical,
to her, you and I are not practical, she is a force now and is highly
critical of all this war and hatred and when she says Rose Cottage
is very big she believes us to be fools. If you have any kindness of
any sort to offer me, would you write as I am suffering for Jane and
can tell her nothing.

Yours, Jean

⌘

My mother also wrote to her brother Robert. In this letter, the distortion of my father's words suggested she read my father's explanation of his change of heart, not just through tears, but also through the blinding anger my father feared. My mother believed in her own emotional truth and, unfortunately for my father, it was sometimes very far from reality.

My Dear Rob,

I don't know whether you have been informed of my recent
activities or not but here we are on our way to Freemantle. On
Sunday we shall be there and after two days in Perth we shall be
heading for home. Two weeks after that we shall see you, I trust.

God knows what I'm doing. It's a bit of a riddle, muddle, fiddle
diddle, anything you like to call it. All I know is, I suddenly had to
come home, the old pigeon, there was nothing for it but to flee as
things became somewhat complicated. It would have been quite
simple had the original plan been stuck to but somehow John
Sinclair did the dirty on me at the last moment and so I owe my
voyage, rescue, whatever you like to call it, to my old friend Arthur.

267

However it's a long and complicated story and as Arthur says, it's all for the best. My English John wants to follow but as yet nothing has been decided. All I know is, I had to come home.

We are a bit battered but Jane is tremendously excited. So far it's been an awful journey. We have had no end of sheer bad luck. One passenger out of four died, sandstorms in the Red Sea, too much heat all together after England and then a bloody monsoon in the Arabian Sea that caused our poor little boat a great battle with the mountainous waves. Everyone was ill, even Jane. It went on for days as we had to go off course, what a nightmare, all the time the temperature was killing, it was still ninety on deck at midnight with the monsoon blowing like a wild hot madness.

For the rest of the two weeks we have had wild trade winds and heavy seas. God, what misery. I've never understood before why it is hell, but it is. I could have cheerfully allowed myself to finish life there and then. Today we have had a little sunshine and the sea has calmed down to a heavy swell which is not so bad. The temperature has dropped and although I feel as if I've been through a nightmare, the thought of Australian soil in two days cheers me up considerably, and after that the Australian Bight which has a bad reputation. So far the Captain says the weather has been just sheer bad luck so I'm crossing my fingers for the rest of the journey.

Jane has proved herself a mighty adult little human being and I must say I'm most proud of her. One of the reasons why I came home is because I believe she must be educated in Australia and must have the beach and sunshine and what is more, her own father accessible and a musical and creative education of the Australian type. I see too many people who have stayed in England too long. All this is by the way and I shall have a lot to say on the score later as the whole thing interests me. Arthur agrees with me, they are literary people, nothing else and that doesn't suit a Langley or a Sinclair for that matter.

Well, I don't know yet where I'll be living or how or why. Anyhow I'm on the way, so it'll work itself out somehow. It's a bit complicated but I had to make a smart decision. The reason for my sudden change of plans etc. is because I'm pregnant. Well, I didn't tell you or the family as I thought I'd give John Sinclair time to digest the news privately. It has always been my policy to tell him anything and everything first. It was very obvious to me I had to decide whether to stay in England for ever or come home to have the baby. I just couldn't bear the thought of being trapped in England for either my sake or Jane's, so at John Sinclair's suggestion of me coming home to have the baby at Rose Cottage under his protection etc. I bought the first available passage to Australia as I had no flat to live in as the O'Shaughnessys were back.

My poor English John was terribly broken by this but I just couldn't live in England forever, not for anyone. As soon as I had paid for the ticket John suddenly demanded I have an abortion, AT MY AGE, Christ! So after all those promises of protection, I am to be divorced. The worst thing is the money angle as he agreed that Arthur should pay the fare and John S. would pay him back a bit later. John wired to say he had taken out a mortgage and sent the first hundred quid, so naturally I went ahead and bought the ticket for 300 pounds, I paid Arthur the first 100 pounds but then John sprung this dirty trick, leaving me a week before the boat sailed with no flat to live in and all my trunks packed with Jane as excited as a kitten. He knew I had no alternative but to come home as the ticket was bought but he says I can go to buggery as far as money or a home goes. Nice way to protect me.

However I am absolutely delighted and warm in my heart as Arthur's reactions to everything have been incredibly loving and kind. John has written and told me I must stay in England and that the money must be wasted, my bad luck. Me dying with homesickness, to let three hundred quid go down the drain. Christ, I was wild. He had his chance earlier to tell me to stay. Now I had Jane to contend with who dotes on her father. It's an awful mess really.

Anyhow, I see his point, it's an awful blow to the male pride, *but hell, our lives aren't bound by anything other than Jane. I have written him several letters as calmly as I could, pointing out that I consider his actions will do more harm to Jane than I see fit to allow. She is so mad about her Daddy and Rose Cottage.*

I haven't heard at all from John as I didn't let him know what I was doing until I was on the boat so I expect some communications at Perth. The only person I feel badly about is English John who adores me and cannot wait until he is a father. Poor Darling is madly in love with the whole idea but I have begged him to wait until I see how the Sinclair thing works out. Jane is to me tremendously important and at a most delicate age as far as human relationships work out. I want to try, if I can, to manipulate the whole situation to a peaceful relationship between all parties. As far as I can see, John is only cutting off his nose to spite his face as his first reaction to my pregnancy was one of the utmost boy scoutish good fellow stuff.

The one important thing to me is the fact that I am very close to the change in life and one London doctor told me it was too late for me to have another baby, so I am a little pleased as it is sad to become barren and one child is not much even though I adore that one. I have suggested many things to John S. I do not know what will happen. John told me the Quirks, or whatever their name is, would be leaving and that I could live with him or by myself in one flat or however I liked. I do not know what, or who lives where. Have the Quirks gone? I wonder. If so, why can't I live in a little of Rose Cottage? The trouble is I love Rose Cottage terribly much, I love Mentone terribly much. Ah Well, we'll see.

John's objection to me coming home pregnant was what would the local people think. It's all rather silly as I'm only three months and look quite normal and hell, so what? What do I think about the local people? I'm afraid my trip around the big world has convinced me that life must be lived according to one's own values. Odd babies have been coming into this world for so long, who really cares? John has the right to care but no one else. Anyhow we shall see what happens. I have been asking for a divorce for a long time but I think from Jane's point of view it will be an awful blow to her. As far as I can see, the legal aspect doesn't mean a thing. Being legally married hasn't protected me from John or John from me. I don't want to get married again, I have no faith.

My English John is a terribly sweet person and full of love and faith, but I am too old and full of cynical thoughts about human beings. I see no point in shattering Jane unless John wants to get married again. Anyhow, I'll be there on the battle ground soon. I haven't got a battle in me I'm afraid as I was very ill and depressed before I decided to come home, and now this lousy sea voyage has nearly wrecked my poor little tummy. I must say it's not a good time for a girl to be travelling.

Well, it looks as if I'll be for the poor house or the work house or whatever you call it. Keep your old baby clothes for naughty Auntie Jean, you can tell the family whatever you like, I don't care much. There aren't many people I care about and those few are right behind me. If I was rich I'd go and live all by myself. I suppose I stick my neck out but I can't really say I'm sorry. Anyhow I would have gone mad in England sooner or later, sweet John or no. English John is still working for Arthur. They get along very well but God knows what he would do if he follows me to Australia as he's a real Londoner and has a shocking accent of the worst sort. All the folks in England, the O'Shaughnessys, the Blackmans, the Boyds, etc. think it's all marvellous and have been very sweet to me. A female is a female even when she's a mad irresponsible Langley with no STICKABILITY.

Cross your fingers for me. Maybe it'll all be O.K. Homesickness is very real, so is morning sickness.

See you soon,

Love Jean

<hr/>

In her last letter to my father, my mother had pleaded with him to allow us to return to Rose Cottage for my sake, but he was not persuaded. The alternative was for us to stay for a while with her sister, Betty, who had recently moved from a small flat to a large house. He would have known that the thought of spending time with my cousins would make me leap with joy.

My mother, on the other hand, knew that the noise of that household alone would be more than she could bear. But her dreams of Rose Cottage didn't take into account the fact that none of the three living areas were vacant. The Kirks were back in one side of the house, and Mag and baby Charlotte were living in The Cottage, with or without Bob.

There was no room for my mother and me now that divorce was being considered.

Chapter 17

All's Well that Ends Well

Mrs. J. Sinclair, Passenger MS Themis, c/o R. G.
Lynn. Pty. Ltd., 7 High Street, Freemantle W. A.
Wednesday, July 18

Dear Jeannie, all day I have thought of you so
that I have found it impossible to work. At the
same time the inescapable obligation to get my
day's work done has prevented me writing to you
with any freedom. And do you wonder that this kind
of dilemma has persisted with me since I phoned
you in London? Yet poor girl, you do not really
understand. Even in your last sad letters you talk
of returning to aggression and hostility. That is
not even remotely possible. You return to find me
worried and tired with a sadness that I now feel
will be with me for the rest of my life, but not
angry. I was not angry when I rang you in London
and I am not now. I was, to be sure, extremely
anxious because I felt then as I do now that you
were embarking on a course which could finally lead
only to sadness for me, for you and most of all for
Jane.

And do you know me so little that you really think
that I talk hastily of divorce? It was a decision
made slowly, painfully and with the greatest
reluctance. Or do you think that buried somewhere
was just one little grain of vindictive pleasure?
If you think so, then our life together has been a
joke. But you ask me to help you and that is a plea

which I could never in my life ever wholly reject.
But now, for the first time, I am in a situation -
we are all in a situation - where I can no longer
act at the dictates of my feelings or yours but
must act as best I can, considering everything
involved.

That is a brief and poor summary of my present
attitude. But you, poor girl, want to know to what
and where you return, and I fear that the realities
that follow from the decisions you have made are
becoming clear to you only slowly. I could not ask
you to return to Rose Cottage without abandoning
once and for all divorce proceedings, and that at
present I am not prepared to do. Nor could I give
Margaret a fortnight's notice from the Cottage (Bob
has once again tossed in his job and leaves Mag yet
once again this week). And with your fare yet to
be paid, with God knows what expenses ahead, and
with the state of our lives as it is, I could not
ask the Kirks to leave and so reduce my income by 4
pounds a week.

Betty expects you and I suppose that is the best
immediate solution though it makes me shudder. She
has written to you and will be at the boat, as will
the Reeds and, solicitors or no solicitors, so will
I unless you change your mind and ask me not to.

In an earlier registered letter to the agents
I sent you 12 pounds and one for Jane. Don't
bother about cigarettes for me but buy yourself a
bottle of whisky. If you would send me the name
and address of Arthur's bank I will pay him the
outstanding 250 pounds (E. 200).

Forgive me, my heart is not as poor as this letter.

Yours, John

Two telegrams also awaited my mother at Freemantle. One just said, "MUCH LOVE, VISHNU" the other, "HAPPY LANDING LOVE TO YOU THREE, MONDAY (sic) AND JOHN".

The welcoming party that greeted us at Station Pier Port

Melbourne on 27 July would have been much warmer than the weather. No doubt my father clowned around in an embarrassing way as we came down the gangplank until we reached the wharf and I could leap into his open arms. Auntie Betty would have hugged us both enthusiastically while I exchanged shy smiles with my cousins Glynis and Russell. Owen, the youngest, was probably ignored. He was too young to know me and I knew little of him. Meanwhile, the Reeds would have stood back waiting for the excitement to die down so that Sunday could greet my mother with a gentle smile, searching eyes and much warm hand-holding. My father wouldn't have expected any warmth in my mother's greeting. The cool resolve he had shown in his last letter would have infuriated her because it left her no choice but to take up Betty's kind offer.

At least, that was how I imagined our homecoming, until I found a letter my mother wrote on 22 July as we crossed the Nullarbor by train. Apparently we jumped ship at Freemantle to avoid the rough seas of the Great Australian Bight. The letter was to John Hull c/o Arthur Boyd. In it she wrote:

> Have been thinking such a lot about you and worrying and looking at your photo. I wonder what you are doing and fear you have every right to hate me with passion as I walked out on you so horribly, not only leaving you lonely but leaving you in a muddle with nowhere to live and our beautiful cottage on your hands.
> There is no point in trying to tell you why.

London was the only place Hull could make a living. A cottage in the Welsh hills was of little use to him, so he spent many nights sleeping in his van until friends took pity on him and invited him to stay with them for a while.

My mother also told him of her plans:

> I am going straight to my friend Sunday's place and then to stay with my sister, after that God knows. I have told John Sinclair that I will not even meet him.
> I have no real sense of excitement about arriving tomorrow as I

am just worn out. My family are very pleased about the baby and
my sister Betty says John is as mad as a snake lately, so I'll cast him
out of my mind, he deserves nothing as far as I can see. I haven't
the vaguest idea how to cope with telling Jane about things. Poor
kid, but she will be happy about the baby well enough, I will have
to find some little flat or cottage somewhere, somehow.

Be patient, I will send you an address in the next couple of days.
Love to you for now.
Jean and Jane

The letter was never posted.

❧

I had underestimated the longevity of my mother's anger towards my father. It seems the closer she got to Melbourne, the more she resented not being able to return to Rose Cottage. With a better understanding of my mother's state of mind, I now imagine that the only people at Spencer Street Station to welcome us home would have been the Reeds. My mother was craving the sort of peace and pampering that only Sunday and Heide could provide. She would have been in no mood to tolerate her relatives just yet. As she explained to John Hull, "I would like to sleep for a week before I even think."

Betty's house was a stone throw from the beach, much closer than Rose Cottage, but it would be many months before there would be any lying around in the sun, and by then my mother and I were back living with my father at Rose Cottage. I don't know how long we stayed with Betty. It may have been months but I suspect it was only weeks. Nor do I know how or why my parents reconciled, but reconcile they did.

The Kirks moved to a house nearby and apparently my father's car was later seen on several occasions parked outside. My new little cousin Charlotte spent the first few years of her life living in The Cottage with her mother, and sometimes her father.

Now we had the house to ourselves, my parents tried to play happy families, but neither cared to follow the rules of the game. Still, they persevered for many years. My father was happy to re-embrace the "daddy for all children" idea and greeted the birth of my sister with absolute delight. She was born on 8 January 1963.

My mother had her time to relax on Mentone beach.

As for me, I received the welcome home present of a pair of ballet shoes my mother had suggested. There was no further talk of a puppy but all that was forgotten in the excitement and joy of having a beautiful baby sister at last.

And so it was John Hull who was left out in the cold. He wrote many letters, sometimes referring to himself in the third person, and with a very idiosyncratic use of language:

> John Edward Hull has been waiting for you to say you would like him to come, as with all his heart he would like to, and to be by your side. But thought Jean Langley do not want him at all.

Not long before the birth he wrote:

> All my life I have wanted to have a family and be part of one. But now I feel like a man who was told of a beautiful picture and as he finds the room where the picture is in, before he goes in he is made blind.

As an only child, John Hull's early life had been a lonely one. During the bombing of London in the Second World War, along with most of London's children, he was sent to the countryside to stay with strangers until it was safe to return. Being only five years of age, he felt frightened and alone. He was too young to understand and it created in him a deep sense of abandonment.

⋙⋘

In January 1963 there would have been no leaves on the trees in the woodlands of Hampstead Heath. The leaves of autumn had long fallen to the ground and were either a wet, decomposing mess hidden beneath a layer of pristine white snow, or brittle with frost and ice which crackled underfoot. At night in the middle of winter it would have been a very lonely place. That is why John Edward Hull chose to go there when he heard that his baby had been born on the other side of the world.

> *And I had to go on the Heath to be by myself to cry to the moon. I cry so much and so loud that I came faint and had to rest.*

Jane, Kate and Jean in the garden of Rose Cottage.

Jane with baby Kate in the front garden of Rose Cottage.

A rare moment of Jane's parents clowning around, as John laughs at Jean's antics, holding baby Kate. (The other man is probably Geoffrey Golding.)